Return to Sender

Return to Sender

The Moral Economy of Peru's Migrant Remittances

Karsten Paerregaard

Woodrow Wilson Center Press
Washington, D.C.

University of California Press

EDITORIAL OFFICES

Woodrow Wilson Center Press
Woodrow Wilson International Center for Scholars
One Woodrow Wilson Plaza
1300 Pennsylvania Avenue NW
Washington, DC 20004-3027
www.wilsoncenter.org

ORDER FROM

University of California Press
155 Grand Avenue
Suite 400
Oakland, CA 94612–3758
Telephone (510) 883-8232
www.ucpress.edu

© 2014 by Karsten Paerregaard
All rights reserved
Printed in the United States of America

2 4 6 8 9 7 5 3 1

Library of Congress Cataloging-in-Publication Data

Paerregaard, Karsten.
 Return to sender : the moral economy of Peru's migrant remittances /
Karsten Paerregaard.
  pages cm
 Includes bibliographical references and index.
 ISBN-13: 978-0-5202-8473-9 (cloth)
 ISBN-13: 978-0-5202-8474-6 (paper)
 1. Emigrant remittances—Peru. 2. Peruvians—Foreign countries.
3. Peru—Emigration and immigration—Social aspects. 4. Peru—Emigration
 and immigration—Economic aspects. I. Title.
 HG3939.P34 2014
 332.042460985—dc23
 2014020175

Wilson Center

The Wilson Center, chartered by Congress as the official memorial to President Woodrow Wilson, is the nation's key nonpartisan policy forum for tackling global issues through independent research and open dialogue to inform actionable ideas for Congress, the Administration, and the broader policy community.

Conclusions or opinions expressed in Center publications and programs are those of the authors and speakers and do not necessarily reflect the views of the Center staff, fellows, trustees, advisory groups, or any individuals or organizations that provide financial support to the Center.

Please visit us online at www.wilsoncenter.org.

Jane Harman, Director, President, and CEO

Board of Trustees
Thomas R. Nides, Chair
Sander R. Gerber, Vice Chair

Public members: William Adams, Acting Chairman of the National Endowment for the Humanities; James H. Billington, Librarian of Congress; G. Wayne Clough, Secretary of the Smithsonian Institution; Sylvia Mathews Burwell, Secretary of Health and Human Services; Arne Duncan, Secretary of Education; David Ferriero, Archivist of the United States; John F. Kerry, Secretary of State. Designated appointee of the president from within the federal government: Fred P. Hochberg, Chairman and President, Export-Import Bank of the United States

Private citizen members: John T. Casteen III, Charles E. Cobb Jr., Thelma Duggin, Barry S. Jackson, Nathalie Rayes, Jane Watson Stetson

Wilson National Cabinet
Ambassador Joseph B. Gildenhorn & Alma Gildenhorn, *Co-chairs*
Eddie & Sylvia Brown, Melva Bucksbaum & Raymond Learsy, Paul & Rose Carter, Armeane & Mary Choksi, Ambassadors Sue & Chuck Cobb, Lester Crown, Thelma Duggin, Judi Flom, Sander R. Gerber, Harman Family Foundation, Susan Hutchison, Frank F. Islam, Willem Kooyker, Linda B. & Tobia G. Mercuro, Dr. Alexander V. Mirtchev, Thomas R. Nides, Nathalie Rayes, Wayne Rogers, B. Francis Saul II, Ginny & L. E. Simmons, Diana Davis Spencer, Jane Watson Stetson, Leo Zickler

I dedicate this book to my parents-in-law.

The Rhyme of the Remittance Man

There's a four-pronged buck a-swinging in the shadow of my cabin,
And it roamed the velvet valley till to-day;
But I tracked it by the river, and I trailed it in the cover,
And I killed it on the mountain miles away.
Now I've had my lazy supper, and the level sun is gleaming
On the water where the silver salmon play;
And I light my little corn-cob, and I linger, softly dreaming,
In the twilight, of a land that's far away.

Far away, so faint and far, is flaming London, fevered Paris,
That I fancy I have gained another star
Far away the din and hurry, far away the sin and worry,
Far away—God knows they cannot be too far.
Gilded galley-slaves of Mammon—how my purse-proud brothers taunt me!
I might have been as well-to-do as they
Had I clutched like them my chances, learned their wisdom, crushed my fancies,
Starved my soul and gone to business every day.

Well, the cherry bends with blossom and the vivid grass is springing,
And the star-like lily nestles in the green;
And the frogs their joys are singing, and my heart in tune is ringing,
And it doesn't matter what I might have been.
While above the scented pine-gloom, piling heights of golden glory,
The sun-god paints his canvas in the west,
I can couch me deep in clover, I can listen to the story
Of the lazy, lapping water—it is best.

While the trout leaps in the river, and the blue grouse thrills the cover,
And the frozen snow betrays the panther's track,
And the robin greets the dayspring with the rapture of a lover,
I am happy, and I'll nevermore go back.
For I know I'd just be longing for the little old log cabin,
With the morning-glory clinging to the door,
Till I loathed the city places, cursed the care on all the faces,
Turned my back on lazar London evermore.

So send me far from Lombard Street, and write me down a failure;
Put a little in my purse and leave me free.
Say: "He turned from Fortune's offering to follow up a pale lure,
He is one of us no longer—let him be."
I am one of you no longer; by the trails my feet have broken,
The dizzy peaks I've scaled, the camp-fire's glow;
By the lonely seas I've sailed in—yea, the final word is spoken,
I am signed and sealed to nature. Be it so.

—Robert William Service

Contents

List of Tables and Figures	xiii
Acknowledgments	xv
1. The Social Life of Remittances	1
2. Peru: Migration and Remittances	35
3. *Compromiso:* The Family Commitment	65
4. *Voluntad:* The Community Commitment	111
5. *Superación:* The Personal Commitment	153
6. After Remittances	195
References	209
Index	221

Tables and Figures

Tables

1.1.	Main Remittance-Receiving Countries by Amount of Remittances Received, 2012	7
6.1.	Selected Demographic Data on Mexico and Peru, 2010–2012	200
6.2.	Data on the Remittance Economies in Mexico and Peru, 2008–2012	201
6.3.	Remittance Distribution by Region in Mexico and Peru, 2009	201

Figures

2.1.	Annual Figures on Peruvian Migration, 1990–2012	41
2.2.	Migration from Peru to Five Continents, 2012	42

2.3.	Migration from Peru to Receiving Countries, 2012	43
2.4.	City or State of Settlement of Migrants from Peru, 2013	44
2.5.	Migration of Men and Women from Peru, 2009	45
2.6.	Migration from Peru by Sex, 1994–2009	46
2.7.	Gender Disparity in Migration from Peru, 1932–2006	47
2.8.	Migration from Peru by Age, 1994–2006	47
2.9.	Migration from Peru by Marital Status, 1994–2009	48
2.10.	Migration from Peru by Profession and Occupation, 1994–2009	49
2.11.	Migration from Peru by Income Group, 2006	50
2.12.	Region of Origin of Migrants from Peru, 2007	51
2.13.	Migration from Rural or Urban Areas of Peru, 2007	52
2.14.	Migration from Peru by Migrants' Place of Birth, 2010	53
2.15.	Remittances to Selected Developing Countries, 2012	54
2.16.	Remittances to Developing Countries as a Percentage of GDP, 2012	55
2.17.	Remittances to Peru from Selected Countries, 2009	55
2.18.	Peruvian Households Receiving Remittances and Those with Migrant Members, 2007	57
2.19.	Remittance Recipients in Peru by Sex, 2009	58
2.20.	Remittance Recipients in Peru by Age, 2009	59
2.21.	Peruvian Households Receiving Remittances and Those with Migrant Members by Income Group, 2007	60
2.22.	Peruvian Households Receiving Remittances by Region, 2006	60
2.23.	Remittance Recipients in Peru by Urban or Rural Residence, 2009	61
2.24.	Remittance Recipients in Peru by Region, 2009	62
2.25.	Use of Remittances by Recipients in Peru, 2009	63

Acknowledgments

Migration has been the topic of my research for many years. In two previous books, I explored how Peruvians migrate internally in Peru and internationally to other countries. The aim of this book is to examine how Peruvian migrants living in different parts of the world use their savings and experience as migrants to contribute to the well-being of their families in Peru as well as to the development of their regions of origin and new countries of settlement. The book's title, *Return to Sender*, refers to the money that migrants send to their relatives and communities in Peru. But even though the sending of remittances is the book's main theme, it also explores another less-documented aspect of migration: the many talents that Peruvian migrants mobilize to achieve their goals. The book is therefore not only a study of why and how migrants remit money home, but also an account of the ways they make their dreams come true and hereby enrich the surrounding society.

I am in debt to many people. Most of all, to the migrants who provided me with data for my study and who often shared their food with me or invited me to stay in their homes. In North Carolina, my thanks go to Elena Carlson Roncero for her hospitality and the many hours we have spent together. In Washington, D.C., Julio and Soledad Carranza invited me home on many occasions and introduced me to their lives as migrants. Cabanaconde's migrant community in Washington also received me with open arms. I am especially grateful to the late Romer Miranda and his family for letting me stay with them and presenting me to their fellow migrants. In Hartford, Connecticut, my thanks go to Hilmer Reyes and his family who offered me their hospitality and introduced me to Bolognesi's migrant community. In Spain, I am in debt to Chavica Dominguez and her family and in Chile I want to thank Carmen Irma and her family for their support and Lorena Nuñez Carrasco for introducing me to Aurora and Juan in Trujillo. In Peru, my thanks go as always to Teófilo Altamirano, my *compadre*, friend, and colleague, and to many others.

I initiated my writing on the book at the Woodrow Wilson Center in Washington, D.C., where I spent nine unforgettable months as a fellow. I want to thank the Center for the fellowship it granted me and all the wonderful people who surrounded me during the stay. I am especially indebted to my two interns at the center, Amy Parker and Raquel Mayer Cuesta, and to Woodrow Wilson Center Press director Joe Brinley for helping me find a publisher and to Shannon Granville for editing the book. In Denmark, I want to thank my former colleagues at the University of Copenhagen for their support.

Finally, I want to thank my wife, daughters, brother, late parents, and parents-in-law for the support they have provided me while writing the book.

Return to Sender

Chapter 1

The Social Life of Remittances

This book is about money: big money, more money than you can count or than Bill Gates will ever make. It is what Donald Terry has called "the case of the missing billions" (2005): the remittances that international migrants send home every year. In 2013, the world's 232 million migrants, representing a mere 3 percent of the total population, remitted $414 billion to developing countries, the second-largest capital flow in the world after private investment (World Bank 2013a).[1] Money, however, is not the research topic of this book or my reason for writing it. Although most migrants hope to make money in dollars, euros, yen, or other hard currencies, it is the well-being of their relatives and communities that is the true motivation for their adventurous travels to foreign parts, not the pursuit of personal wealth. In other words, money is merely the means to loftier goals.

---

[1] The World Bank predicts that the world's remittance flows to developing countries will reach $590 billion in 2014 (Monopatra, Ratha, and Silwal 2011).

My aim in writing this book is to shed light on the moral economy of remittance activities: that is, the motivating forces that drive migrants to remit money home and the meaning and importance that their families and communities attribute to their remittances. I explore the circumstances and tensions in migrants' lives that prompt them to remit money home and describe the predicaments and concerns that affect both ends of the remittance chain. This chain is, of course, influenced by broader general issues such as migration, globalization, and development; while the book's ethnographic contribution consists of describing the personal trajectories, family affairs, and social networks that shape migrant remittances, it is only by examining the wider economic and political contexts that the book can provide a full account of their importance.

Although the economic importance of remittances has been overlooked for a long time, the role of migrants in the world economy is gaining increasing recognition (e.g., "Weaving the World Together" 2011, 72–74). As a result, information on the numbers of international migrants and migrant remittances is plentiful, and studies of their economic and social impact on the sending countries—that is, migrants' countries of origin—have proliferated in the past decade. Recently, this knowledge has been put to use by consultants and scholars working in international institutions and development organizations, such as the World Bank, the Organisation for Economic Co-operation and Development (OECD), the International Organization for Migration, the International Monetary Fund, and the Inter-American Development Bank. These organizations have designed policies promoting remittances as a means of boosting growth in the developing world. The idea of channeling migrants' earnings abroad into investments at home has been welcomed by many sending countries and has paved the way for a new perspective on migration. Migrants, who were formerly regarded by many governments as "lost human resources" or even as "traitors" who had turned their backs on their home countries, are now heralded by the political leaders of sending countries in Asia, Africa, and Latin America as "saviors" and "heroes" in the hope that they can help solve domestic problems such as unemployment and underdevelopment.

Although this shift in the political view of migration represents an important step in the recognition of migrants' contribution to the economies of both the sending and the receiving countries, it has led many governments and international institutions to assume that remittances are free flows of capital that they can tap into whenever they need to. Indeed, few politicians and policymakers bother to ask why migrants remit in the first place. Why do some continue to remit for decades—some even throughout their entire lives—while others send money home only once or twice? And what makes migrants remit at particular moments in their lives and then stop remitting at others? More bluntly, what is the driving force behind remitting?

The book's message is that, just as business owners and corporate leaders have to know where the money that makes their businesses profitable comes from, so policymakers and politicians who promote remittances as a means of boosting development need to ask what makes their "clients" or "customers" invest. How long can they expect them to do it? What makes them expect that the money will keep flowing? In a review of the policy papers as well as the scholarly literature on remittances, it is surprising how rarely these questions are raised and how few researchers and policymakers have asked who "the goose that lays the golden egg" is and why "the goose" does it.

Classical economists, who believe that all economic activities serve utilitarian purposes, argue that remittances are driven by altruism, that is, that the recipient's use of remittances is identical with the migrant's own utility (Agarwal and Horowitz 2002).[2] But if this is the case, why is the second-largest capital flow in the world fueled by "irrational," altruistic behavior? In what terms, if not economic, do we account for such transfers? Other, more sociologically oriented economists, explain remittances as a "gift" from migrants to their relatives back home. Dilip Ratha, a World Bank expert in Washington, D.C., who is considered one of the founding fathers of the institution's policy of promoting remittances as a development tool, told me that it was his own personal experience as a migrant remitter that triggered the notion of remittances as gifts. He said, "I've been sending money to my mother in India on a regular basis for many years" and pointed out to me that "remittances are a gift" (Dilip Ratha, personal communication, December 2009). Of course, by using the term *gift* the World Bank expert touched the heart of my anthropological soul, which regards the act of exchange as a basic structure in human life. Indeed, few if any in my scholarly field would argue against this expert. As Marcel Mauss (1966) pointed out in his

---

[2] The meaning and importance of altruism in the study of remittances are an unsettled issue among economists. Referring to the works of Teichman, Evans, and Norman, Theodore Lianos and Jennifer Cavounidis write that if altruism is defined as devotion to the interest of another or as systematic unselfishness, guided by the principle of living for the good of others, "then it follows that acts resulting from a calculus of maximizing one's own utility are better described as egoistic rather than altruistic. Nonetheless, if others benefit from such behavior, it would be described as moral egoism" (2008, 121).

classic work, the gift is a carrier and extensor of social and cultural values that simultaneously creates obligations. But even so, what happens when your parents back home die or you become reunited with your family in the receiving country? Do these changes lead you to stop remitting, or do other family responsibilities then take over? And, perhaps more important, what does the migrant ask in return for the gift? Do hard-working migrants who remit most of their earnings to their spouses or children back home not expect the latter to use the money wisely? Do they not try to influence the household's decisions in their absence?

Most remittance studies and policies are directed toward the impact of remittances on migrants' home regions and their significance for developing-country economies. These studies and policies rest on the assumption that, as long as people migrate, money will keep flowing. This book questions this assumption and suggests that remittance flows fluctuate and change size and direction according to the needs of migrants and their relatives. Some migrants continue to remit to their aging parents for years, but others remit only once or twice in their lives, and some even receive money from their families at home.

To study the social life of remittances, I conducted an ethnographic inquiry into migrants' life trajectories and webs of relations and into the interactions and negotiations that tie them to their relatives and communities in their places of origin and the social meaning and moral value those relatives and communities attach to remittances. I review field data gathered between 1997 and 2011 among Peruvians in Argentina, Chile, Italy, Japan, Peru, Spain, and the United States to explore how migrants construe and fulfill their remittance commitments. Such engagements include their family commitments to support their parents, spouses, children, and other close relatives in Peru; their community commitments to finance development projects and religious events in their home regions; and, on a more irregular basis, their humanitarian commitments to aid other Peruvians when these fall victim to natural disasters and other misfortunes. To challenge the conventional picture of migrants as low-paid, unskilled family breadwinners whose only concern is to remit money home, I also examine migrants' individual commitments, that is, their dreams of achieving social mobility and making progress. By bringing migrants' personal talents and skills to the forefront, I illustrate the variety of ways in which they contribute to the development and welfare of the surrounding society, not merely as remitters but also as businessmen and women, entrepreneurs, artists, politicians, fund-raisers, managers, innovators, and leaders.

Remittances draw our attention because individuals who are poor and underprivileged are moving huge amounts of cash around the world. Yet, remittances do not flow like other forms of international capital but circulate between family and community members who are separated by national boundaries but who are nevertheless linked by relations of reciprocity and exchange. Remittances are therefore only the tip of the iceberg, the visible evidence of the many needs and demands that drive people to go abroad to work and save money and the personal efforts and sacrifices they make to send that money home to their relatives. Such endeavors have been the topic of my research for many years. In the late 1980s and early 1990s, I studied internal migration in Peru, which in the past 50 years has experienced a transformation from an underdeveloped, mostly rural society to a predominantly modern, urban society (Paerregaard 1997). Since 1997, I have followed Peruvians in their global odyssey in the Americas, Europe, and Asia and have documented how they form communities and create ties with other minorities and the majority population of these places (Paerregaard 2008a).[3] By focusing on remittances, this book brings me back to Peru and asks what commitments migrants make to their families and communities back home and how Peruvian society, the receiving societies, and the migrants themselves profit from these commitments.

Remittance Men and Women

The verb *remit* originates from the Latin word *remittere*, to send back. Although in modern English the word has many meanings, in this book *remitting* refers exclusively to the act of transmitting or sending money, with specific reference to the money that international migrants working in the developed world send to their home countries.

As already noted, migrant remittances represent the second-largest capital flow in today's globalized world, and in recent years they have become an important focus of the international organizations and aid agencies that promote economic development in developing countries. Yet bankers, financers, and wealthy individuals have remitted money for centuries, just as the

---

[3] In several of the receiving countries, the majority population speaks Spanish and shares historical and cultural background with Peruvians. Moreover, Peruvians have primarily settled in countries where the demand for cheap, unskilled labor is high, which offers them a unique opportunity to save money and send it home to their relatives.

wider society has made such transfers the subject of its moral appraisal. In the late nineteenth century and the first decade of the twentieth century, the younger sons of Britain's aristocracy, at a time when first-born sons inherited the estate through the law of entail, were often known as "remittance men." With few prospects for making a life of their own, these men went abroad to North America and Australia or the colonies, where they lived off the money sent by their families in England. While some prospered, others spent the rest of their days drinking, gambling, and wasting their time in other ways. Considered the black sheep of their families, these men became the subjects of literature such as Robert W. Service's poems "The Rhyme of the Remittance Man" (see the epigraph to this book) and "The Men That Don't Fit In," along with many others a century ago. Today's remittance economy is driven by constraints very different from the discriminating rules of inheritance that drove the younger sons of the British upper class into exile at the end of the nineteenth and beginning of the twentieth centuries. The "remittance man" in Service's poetry went abroad to live off his relatives' remittances; today's international migrants also travel to foreign places, but instead of receiving money they send it to their families back home. Remittance senders and receivers, in other words, have changed roles, and the "remittance man" is now acting as the provider rather than as the dependant. Moreover, remittances no longer aim to preserve the privileged position of the wealthy but to compensate for the lack of job possibilities and economic income of the underprivileged. Remittances continue to flow from the developed to the developing world, but their origin and aim have changed since the time of Service's "remittance man."

The bulk of today's remittances are sent by migrants from the developing world. Yet a brief look at the list of countries receiving remittances reveals that the remittance industry reinforces rather than restructures the unequal distribution of wealth in the world (table 1.1). In sheer numbers, India, China, the Philippines, and Mexico rank as the main receivers of migrant remittances, but they are closely followed by developed countries such as France and Germany, whose expatriate workers send home millions of dollars every year. Obviously, the contribution these workers make to the national economies of their home countries is relatively insignificant compared to the role that migrant remittances play in the economies of many developing countries. It is therefore these developing countries and not the wealthier countries that policymakers and development agencies have in mind when recommending remittances as a remedy for creating economic growth.

Table 1.1. Main Remittance-Receiving Countries by Amount of Remittances Received, 2012 (US$ thousand)

India	67,258	Nigeria	20,633
China	57,799	Egypt	19,266
Philippines	24,641	Bangladesh	14,085
Mexico	23,371	Germany	13,964
France	21,676	Belgium	10,111
	Peru: 2,788		

Source: World Bank 2013b.

At first glance, it seems plausible to assume that money sent by migrants from abroad brings wealth to the national economy just as foreign investments do. But unlike the latter, which is money invested by transnational companies or international organizations, the former are the earnings of migrants who have left the country to work and save money elsewhere. Although their remittances enrich their home country, they also represent a drain of human resources. Such a loss of labor is particularly salient in small countries like Haiti, the Kyrgyz Republic, Lesotho, Moldova, Nepal, Samoa, or Tajikistan. These countries are the most remittance-dependent countries in the world, where remittances constitute 20 to 48 percent of gross domestic product (GDP; see chapter 2) and where economic growth relies almost entirely on the continuous migration of a significant segment of the population (Pickert and Feilding 2006). Migrant remittances have also become a critical asset in the economy of countries with larger populations such as the Philippines, which encourages its citizens to take work in the global domestic service industries abroad (ERCOF 2010, xvi; see also chapter 6).

In many developing countries, however, the contribution of remittances to the national economy is less significant. Thus in Colombia, Ecuador, Mexico, and Peru migrants constitute 7 to 10 percent of the population, but because of these countries' size and relatively developed economies, remittances make up only a small percentage of their GDP (World Bank 2013b). It is the migration and the remittance economy of countries such as these and the effect that this economy has on the life of migrants and their families that are the topics of this book. Peru in particular offers an intriguing case study because the country's experience sheds light on some of the most contested issues in current debates on migrant remittances: their impact on inequality. Recent studies show that, compared to those in the rest of Latin America, Peru's remittances are extremely unequally distributed among the population owing to the diversity and dispersal of its migration (Fajnzylber and López 2007, 6; Acosta et al. 2006, 965). Unlike the migrations that are usually cited in the scholarly literature as examples of remittance economies (such as Egypt, Mexico, and Morocco), which are propelled by labor migrants from mainly poor rural and urban areas, Peruvian migrants come from a variety of social strata and regional groups. As a result, remittances are a critical source of income in the household economies not only of working-class families but also of middle-class families and make an important contribution to both the rural and the urban development of the country. Rather than reducing existing inequalities in Peruvian society, remittances amplify them and, even more relevant, create discord between migrants and nonmigrants and between migrant households and nonmigrant households.

Much of the research on remittances is conducted by economists using statistical data to measure the impact of the money that migrants send home on poverty in their countries of origin. The overall finding of these studies is that remittances contribute to the reduction of poverty on a national scale, although some economists question this conclusion by pointing to the negative effects that migration has on the supply of labor and on inflation in migrants' regions of origin. By contrast, the present study, which draws on qualitative research methods and ethnographic fieldwork, focuses on the importance of remittances for migrants and their household economies. Rather than examining the impact of remittances on poverty and development in migrants' home countries or regions, it seeks to understand how those flows shape existing gender, ethnicity, and class relations within and between their households and how these relations in turn influence the remittance flows. More specifically, it explores the constraints and exigencies that drive people to migrate and remit and the tensions and discrepancies that emerge when members of migrant families face each other as remittance senders and recipients. The book uses these insights to identify the moments in migrants' life courses when they start and stop remitting and examine how their families attribute social and moral value to remittances. It also widens the focus of migration and remittance studies by demonstrating how migrants make contributions and donations to the communities they are part of in their home country and how this engagement transforms relations of inequality and domination within these communities. Finally, it offers a review of the many ways in which migrants contribute to the sending as well as to the receiving countries not only by generating economic wealth but also by making use of their innovative, creative, and organizational skills to add social, cultural, artistic, and intellectual value to the surrounding society. In the spirit of Service's poems, this book gives voice to the modern world's remittance men and women and describes how they struggle to create a better life for themselves and others, despite the many obstacles they encounter along the way.

Debating Remittances

The topic of this book is far from new. Among the first to study remittances were anthropologists who documented Caribbean migration to England. In the 1960s and 1970s, Robert Manners (1965) and Stuart Philpott (1968) described the networks used by Caribbean migrants to get established in London and other cities and analyzed, in particular, how these networks served as mechanisms of control to make migrants remit even years after they had left home. In the following decades, anthropologists continued studying the migration-development nexus, but instead of examining and documenting the social meaning of remittances, they explored the roles that migrants assume as promoters of economic and social change upon their return to their home communities. Robert Rhoades's and Carminda Cavaco's studies of return migrants in Spain and Portugal are examples of this research (Cavaco 1993; Rhoades 1978; see also Gmelch 1980 and Brettell 2003). In the 1980s and early 1990s, migration studies changed focus, and the interest in understanding how remittances are negotiated and contested within migrants' family relations and how return migrants generate change gradually yielded to a broader perspective that investigated how economic and political structures shape migration and how migrant remittances contribute to growth (Reichert 1981; Massey et al. 1998). Inspired by globalization studies, anthropologists and other social scholars have renewed their interest in international migration in the 1990s and the 2000s, producing a growing body of literature that employs a transnational framework by which to scrutinize the ties that migrants create between the receiving and the sending societies (Levitt 2001; Levitt and Lamba-Nieves 2011).

As international migration and the money flows it generates reached new heights in the late 1990s, policymakers, international organizations, and development planners also began to pay attention to the importance of migrant remittances. Today these have become an issue of intense debate, not only among academics but also among consultants, planners, politicians, international organizations, and migrants' own associations (de Haas 2007b). Considering the huge amount of money circulating in the global remittance economy, it is hardly surprising that it breeds so many stakeholders and that these hold very different views of how remittances can be put to use. While some passionately recommend remittances as a way to stimulate development, others stubbornly argue against this idea. A third position has tried to carve out a stance in the middle by acknowledging the importance of remittances for migrant households while pointing out that these alone cannot produce development. Yet a closer look at the evidence and arguments these seemingly irreconcilable positions put forward reveals nuances that are often ignored in the debate. Thus within the first position (the optimists), one group of scholars and planners bases its claim on statistical data indicating that remittances reduce poverty in the sending countries, while another group argues that it is by empowering migrants politically in their homeland that remittances make their contribution to development. The arguments of the second group (the pessimists) and the data it draws on in their support are also at variance. One group of authors claims that migration causes dependence and therefore distorts development. By encouraging future migration, they argue, remittances are part of the problem rather than the solution to development in the sending countries. Using macroeconomic models, another group of pessimists contends that remittances deepen inequality and in some cases even generate poverty. Clearly, the claims for and against remittances are many and the methods and proofs used to sustain them diverse. In the following, I present the most important works referred to in the debate.

Remittances as Blessing

Some of the strongest arguments in favor of international migration come from economists using macroeconomic models. Among these are Richard Adams and John Page, who observe that "both international migration and remittances have a strong statistically significant impact on reducing poverty in the developing world." The authors base their argument on statistical data showing that "a 10% increase in the share of international migrants in a country's population will lead to a 2.1% decline in the share of people living on less than $1.00 per person per day" (2005, 1660). These results concur with the research of Acosta et al., who conclude that "for each percentage point increase in the share of remittances to GDP, the fraction of the population living in poverty is reduced by around 0.4%" (2006, 985).

The works of other economists provide further evidence for the positive contribution of remittances to development (Terry 2005; Ratha 2005). It is also supported by economic and sociological case studies showing that migrants' relatives direct some of the remittances they receive into productive activities, education, housing, and health (Vásquez-Alvarado, Barboza-Carrasco, and Matus-Gardea 2008; López-Córdova, Tokman, and Verhoogen 2005). In a study of remittance-receiving households in Mexico, Jim Airola found that "households that receive remittances expend a higher share of their household budget on durable goods, healthcare, and housing, and less on food than their observationally equivalent counterparts that receive no remittance income" (2007, 858). Miguel Jimenez, who also examined migrant remittances in Mexico, reaches the same conclusion: money from remittances stimulates development. In summing up his research, he states that "over the long term, this money might create a solid financial position and wealth for the household" (2009, 331). German Zárate-Hoyos's research, based on a Mexican income and expenditure survey from 1989, substantiates this observation. He proposes that "migrant households are rational economic agents that do not necessarily engage in conspicuous consumption" (2004, 654). Yet another study in Mexico conducted by Margarita Mooney offers evidence that remittances have a positive impact on development, although the author points out that their equalizing effect differs from region to region. This insight makes Mooney suggest that "migrants possessing adequate resources and appropriate family circumstances seek to demonstrate the economic gain they have achieved through migration by investing their remittances and savings" (2004, 60).

Scholars working in other parts of the world concur with the view that migrant households are rational agents that use remittances for productive purposes. Hein de Haas, who has studied Moroccan migration, contends that "there is increasing evidence [that] this pessimistic perspective (that migration has led to a passive and dangerous dependency on remittances) is founded on a rather poor empirical and analytical basis." He claims that "the idea that remittances are predominantly spent on excessive consumption has proved to be rather inaccurate" (2005, 1274). De Haas's conclusion resonates with the data of Gareth Leeves, whose research in Fiji and Tonga points to "a positive relationship between remittances and migration intentions" (2009, 174). Similarly, Sarah Bracking and Lloyd Sachikonye, who have examined remittances in Zimbabwe, find that these "are critical to alleviating household poverty in urban Zimbabwe" (2009, 215), while Susan Thieme and Simone Wyss who conducted an impact study of remittance in Nepal claim that remittances and international migration contribute to sustainable livelihoods in migrants' home region (2005, 59). Udaya Wagle, who also explored remittances in Nepal and their socioeconomic implications for the country's development, concludes that "increasing remittance income helped reduce both poverty and inequality by close to 4 per cent suggesting that the bottom strata of the population may have benefited equally if not more highly" (2012, 203). In a study of migration in Vietnam, Wade Pfau and Long Thanh Giang (2009) reached a similar conclusion: remittances reduce both inequality and poverty. Positive effects of remittances are also reported in other developing countries such as Jordan, where a study by Wael Mansour, Jad Chaaban, and Julie Litchfield (2011) shows that remittances improve educational attendance in the sending areas. Interestingly, Tineke Fokkema, Eralba Cela, and Elena Ambrosetti find that remittances sent by second-generation migrants with parents from Morocco, Turkey, and the former Yugoslavia also contribute to the development of the sending countries. Their research reveals that remittances are the result not only of an altruistic behavior aimed at improving the welfare of parents at "home" "but also of the desire to invest in the ancestral country" (2013, 25). Indeed, such a positive relationship may be found in both the sending and the receiving countries. In a study of the impact of migrant remittances on the US economy, the OECD states, "Remittances yield surprising benefits to the US economy, primarily in sectors where it is most needed" (2009, 13). In other words, from an economic perspective both the developed and the developing world profit from migrant remittances.

Some of the most optimistic prognoses about the development effects of labor migration do not come from economists using macroeconomic models but from sociologists influenced by the so-called new economics of labor migration (Stark 1991). One of the pioneers of this school is Douglas Massey, who has conducted extensive research on US-bound migration from rural Mexican communities and its importance for their development. Massey and his colleagues use their data to take issue with migration studies that question the positive effect of remittances on development. "These studies show that migrant remittances are rarely invested in productive activities, but they take a very narrow view of what constitutes 'productive,'" they write (Massey et al. 1998, 273). They then go on to criticize the pessimists for ignoring the indirect, second-round effects on household incomes and employment, a conclusion other scholars who have studied the multiplicative effects of remittances support (Julca 2011; Mazzucato, van den Boom, and Nsowah-Nuamah 2008). The hypothesis of Massey and others of this school of thought is that rural families use migration as a form of self-insurance and a strategy for economic survival and that when migrating they draw on their social networks, one of the few resources they command in crossing international borders and finding work in their new environments. However, as Alejandro Portes explains, "The cumulative effects of networks over time would lead, in these circumstances, to the desolate extremes portrayed by some ethnographic studies—'ghost towns' and 'tinsel towns'" (2008, 23).[4]

The most ardent protagonists of remittances, however, are not academic scholars but international organizations, aid agencies, and the governments of the sending countries. The idea of promoting international migration and migrant remittances as a means for speeding up the development process in Asia, Africa, and Latin America was conceived in the World Bank and other organizations in Washington, D.C., in the late 1990s at a time when international migration was gaining momentum. Having regarded migrants with suspicion in the past, sending governments began to change their rhetoric by inviting their migrant populations to invest their capital and savings in their country of origin. The World Bank, the Inter-American Development Bank, the International Organization for Migration, and other institutions soon responded to the revised image of international migrants and started proposing policies and designing strategies to enable sending countries to profit from migrant remittances. This recent trend within international development has prompted Devesh Kapur to ask whether remittances are a new development mantra (Kapur 2008). Kapur and John McHale suggest that "within the development community, remittances strike the right cognitive chords. They fit with a communitarian, 'third way' approach—neither inefficient socialism nor savage capitalism—and exemplify the principle of self-help" (2003, 50). In other words, in the eyes of development organizations remittances constitute the perfect blending of neoliberal individualism and communitarian awareness that offers international institutions an alternative to conventional aid practices and encourages developing countries to use their own resources to boost economic growth.

In the 2000s, this new development paradigm gained ground primarily in Latin America, which receives over 65 percent of all official international remittances in the developing world (Adams 2006, 420–21), as well as in Asian and African countries such as the Philippines and Morocco. In the same period, many international organizations promoting development and migration have placed remittances at the top of their agenda, using catchy

---

[4] In a review of the new economics of labor migration (NELM), Mariano Sana and Douglas Massey state, "Mexico provides an ideal setting for the operation of migratory mechanisms postulated by NELM" but also that "this narrative, however, appears not to be readily applicable to other countries where key assumptions, such as family stability and cohesion, do not hold" (2005, 525).

titles and headlines such as "From a Zero-Sum to a Win-Win Scenario," "Closing the Distance," "Many Happy Returns," "Tapping the Diaspora," and "Leveraging Remittances" (Agunías 2006, 2009; Johnson 2010; Ketkar and Ratha 2010; Ratha 2007). In the words of Stephen Castles and Raúl Wise, "Migrants are being redefined as 'the heroes of development'" (2008, 3). Certainly the sudden discovery of remittances has given rise to a new development mantra, but, as Terry reminds us, "it is not an exaggeration to say that the transfer of remittances represents the ultimate in family values: hard work, thrift, sacrifice, and hope for a better future." Terry concludes by noting that "underlying all of them is one basic fact: it's their money" (2005, 12). In the new "gold rush" in international development, therefore, we should not forget that the source financing development is not wealthy governments and countries in the developed world but hard-working migrants who go abroad not to sponsor the development projects of their home governments but to save money, buy food for their families, and pay for their children's education. Extra household income remittances make an important difference to migrant families, but as a policy instrument they often provide many governments with a welcome opportunity to cover up inefficiency.

Remittances as Curse

Remittances exceed total official development assistance and amount to more than half of total foreign direct investment in developing countries (Maimbo and Ratha 2005, 20). Why not make them work in the service of a good cause and design policies that facilitate their continuous flow and encourage their use for the development of migrants' home regions? Essentially, this is the argument made by Maimbo and Ratha. But just as the optimists regard remittances as an overlooked resource in development policies, the pessimists see them as the symptom of the very problem that such policies are trying to solve. Even though they gloss over a broad spectrum of stances and viewpoints, this position agrees on the following: remittances widen the gap between rich and poor, enhance structures of dependence, and place the responsibility for development on the powerless (the migrants) instead of on the power holders (their governments). Finally, most pessimists concur that people rarely invest remittances in productive activities but spend them mainly on basic needs. One of the first scholars to articulate this skepticism was Joshua Reichert, whose area of research is US-bound labor migration in a Mexican village. Reichert argues that labor migration and the dream of making money in the United States are a self-fulfilling prophecy that over time will drive everybody to migrate. In other words, rather than stimulating development, labor migration curbs it. Or, as Reichert puts it, "The phenomenon of seasonal U.S. migration tends to perpetuate itself—a process that I refer to as the migrant syndrome." He sums up his argument by stating that "while migration provides temporary relief from rural poverty through the growth of individual household economies, it has failed to effect the kind of overall structural transformation needed to ensure the long range viability and autonomy of sending communities" (1981, 64).

Reichert's argument that labor migration (and with it remittances) perpetuates itself and discourages rather than encourages structural transformation in the sending communities has inspired the work of many other scholars. David Ellerman asserts that "there is nothing more permanent than 'temporary' migration" and points out that "the poorest of the poor are not the typical migrants" (2005, 618). In conclusion, Ellerman notes that "migration often seems to work in a similar way as a safety valve to relieve the pressure of a pressing problem rather than to resolve it" and adds that migration "relieves the pressure to change the structural barriers to development." In a warning against using remittances as a remedy to foster development, Ellerman contends that "many governments in developing countries have now discovered the 'oil-well of remittances' that might help them to paper over problems and pay the costs of not changing" (2005, 620). Ellerman's critical thoughts are shared by Leigh Binford, who, on the basis of a study of Mexican migration, claims that the debate around remittances and development has been misconstrued as a result of a narrow focus on economic issues on the one hand and migrant agency and household strategies on the other (2003, 307). The author claims that "by focusing so heavily on agency and backgrounding structure, many contemporary researchers come dangerously close to glorifying household economic strategy-making that is more structurally constrained now than at any point in recent memory" (2003, 323). Binford concludes that "migrant labor makes a small, but no less real contribution to widening the economic gap between Mexico and the United States. That economic gap remains an important spur to present and future migration" (2003, 317).

In a review of the work of Massey and other scholars subscribing to the new economics of labor migration, Portes follows up on this critique by stating that "authors of this school tend to neglect another and less positive consequence of social networks, namely that the cumulative processes of out-migration that they facilitate may end up emptying sending areas of the able-bodied population and weakening their productive structures" (2009, 8). Portes also notes that "there is no precedent that any country has taken the road toward sustained development on the basis of the remittances sent by its expatriates" (37). Castles and Wise share Portes's skepticism and assert that "where governments rely on 'remittances-led development' the outcome is likely to be structural dependence on further migration and remittances: a vicious circle of decline, rather than a virtuous circle of growth" (2008, 10). In their view, policies relying on migrant remittances lead to further migration and eventually to more rather than less dependence on remittances. As de Haas concludes from his study of migration and development in remittance-receiving countries, "The important point here is that migration was not the factor that triggered development but, rather, that development by structural political and economic reform *unleashed the development potential of migration*" (2012, 19, italics in the original).

Voices critical of remittances, however, do not all come from anthropology and sociology. Economists too express doubts concerning the prospects that migrants' savings will necessarily bring prosperity and growth, though for reasons different from those proposed by anthropologists and sociologists. Abdih et al. claim that remittances give rise to a moral hazard problem because they "allow households to purchase the public good rather than rely solely on the government to provide that good" (2011, 664). According to the authors, the government can then free ride and appropriate more resources for its own purposes, which opens the door for more corruption. Chami et al. also find that remittances are a questionable source of income: they define them as "unrequited, nonmarket personal transfers between households across countries," to be distinguished from official or private capital flows because of "the presence of familiar relationships" (2008, 3). Because of this particularity, they argue, it is troubling that the statistics used to measure remittances include workers' remittances and employee compensation, as well as migrants' transfers.[5] Only the former category is

---

[5] According to Chami et al., three components of the balance of payments are employed in compiling statistics on remittances: "The first component, *workers' remittances*, records current transfers by migrants who are employed in, and considered a resident of, the countries that host them. The second component, *employee compensation*, is composed of wages, salaries, and other benefits earned by individuals in countries other than those in which there are residents for work performed for and paid for by residents of those countries (typical examples include earnings of seasonal workers and embassy employees). Finally, the third component, *migrants' transfers*, are contra-entries to the flow of goods and changes in financial items that arise from individuals' change of residence from one country to another" (2008, 4).

included in the notion that scholars and policymakers have in mind when examining remittance flows. Conversely, the latter two categories account for compensations and, to a smaller extent, transfers directed toward Europe, which explains why France, Germany, and other developed countries figure among the world's main recipients of remittances (2008, 5).

Scholars working in other parts of Mexico, a country often regarded as a model for studying remittances, have offered more examples of the negative economic impact. R. C. Jones, a geographer who conducted a household survey in the state of Zacatecas, reports that "interfamilial inequalities are found first to decrease and then to increase as a place's migration experience deepens" (1998, 8). These observations are shared by Alejandro Canales, who points out that in Mexico "remittances have a very limited impact on development promotion and poverty reduction, because, essentially, they are constituted by a salary fund that is transferred between households of similar socio-economic conditions" (2007, 386). Agustín Escobar Latapí also provides evidence that remittances enhance rather than diminish inequality. He contends that "to enhance its development impact, migration should diminish" (2009, 103) and suggests that "working in Mexico must become more rewarding" (2009, 105). By the same token, Zárate-Hoyos points out that remittances "in developing countries seem to increase inequalities while in developed countries they have the opposite effect" (2008, 31), a position shared by scholars studying remittances in other parts of Latin America (Pribilsky 2004). Zárate-Hoyos sums up this point by stating that "there is insufficient evidence to prove that remittances are an effective development tool against poverty in developing countries" (2008, 35).

Research on the use of remittances adds fuel to this skepticism. A study by Alejandro Dias Garay and María Juárez Gutiérrez in the state of Guerrero, one of the major remittance-receiving states in Mexico, showed that "of all family remittances received, 91% go to basic home necessities, food and health; in smaller proportion, to clothes and shoes as well as house improvements" (2008, 127). Similar observations have been made in western Mexico, where Jesús Arroyo Alejandre and Isabel Corvera Valenzuela found that "the major part of the remittances are used to maintain the family, then they are used to buy a family house and a small percentage goes to savings and another even smaller to the formation of productive companies" (2003, 53). Luin Goldring agrees with Arroyo Alejandre and Corvera Valenzuela and states that "in Mexico, remittances are largely used as income, most income is used to cover recurrent expenses and education, and only a small share goes to savings and investments" (2004, 806).

Alejandra Cox-Edwards and Eduardo Rodríguez-Oreggia, who used a propensity score-matching analysis to study remittances in Mexico, bring this point home when claiming that, "if as suggested by the findings here, the flow of persistent remittances basically replaces lost income, with no significant surplus to alter labor supply price, or to be invested, policy makers must re-think their strategies to foster business creation among migrant families" (2008, 1012).

Scholars studying the impact of remittances in other parts of Latin America also question their poverty and inequality-reduction effect. Matthew Taylor, Michelle Moran-Taylor, and Debra Ruiz argue that in Guatemala "migration creates a new class of elite, a new elite, who accumulate land and capital with their migrant earnings." They conclude that "remittances do not help Guatemala's poorest who cannot afford to migrate in the first place and migration therefore perpetuates the inequities there" (2006, 59). A similar conclusion is drawn by Ximena Soruco, Giogina Piani, and Máximo Rossi, whose study of remittances in the highlands of Ecuador showed that a new group of nouveaux riches had emerged that made local people "consider emigrants and their families to be arrogant" (2008, 24). While remittances improved the living standards of migrants' families, they had a questionable effect on education in the area. Thus Soruco, Piani, and Rossi found that "remittances from emigrants have a positive impact on elementary school education but a negative effect on high school and university education" (2008, 22). Acosta et al., whose research on the impact of remittances covered most of Latin America, provide more evidence for this observation. Their data reveal that remittances have reduced poverty headcounts in only 6 of the 10 countries for which they have data, the exceptions being Mexico, Nicaragua, Paraguay, and Peru, and that they have reduced poverty gaps in only three cases, namely, Ecuador, Guatemala, and Haiti (2006, 982). The authors therefore suggest that "remittances do not have a significant inequality-reducing effect, but they do appear to reduce poverty headcounts significantly" (2006, 985). Overall, however, they conclude that "these results suggest once again that in the case of Latin America, remittances do not reduce poverty" (2006, 973). Studies in Africa substantiate this observation. Valentina Mazzucato, Bart van den Boom, and N. N. N. Nsowah-Nuamah, who examined the impact of remittances on inequality in Ghana, conclude that "remittance shares are skewed towards the richest quintile" and that "remittances from abroad directly to the poor are rare" (2008, 113). Clearly, the arguments against using remittances to boost development are as compelling as those in favor.

Remittances as Fact

Research on remittances and their impact on poverty, inequality, and development is abundant. Most of it is concentrated in Latin America, the continent that receives the bulk of the world's remittances and over which scholars are deeply divided on whether or not remittances contribute to growth and prosperity. As Luis Guarnizo points out, debates on whether or not family remittances have a positive effect on communities and on the development of the countries of origin "still remain unsettled" (2003, 675). De Haas (2012) shares this observation; he finds that the scholarly discussion on the relation between migration and development—not just in Latin America but also in other parts of the world—moves like a pendulum between an optimistic and a pessimistic view. As already discussed, the disciplinary methods and theories that produce the scholarly insights informing this debate are multiple, and the arguments scholars in each camp bring forward also vary. Indeed, even within individual disciplines such as economics, sociology, or anthropology, scholars are divided in their views of remittances, a bewildering fact that is magnified by their apparent use of similar research methods and data samples to reach opposite conclusions. The diversity of ways in which scholars conceptualize remittances and examine their effects leaves many baffled. Nevertheless, it also illuminates the complexity of the issue and guides us toward a more pragmatic understanding of remittances that recognizes their significance for family households as a source of both economic income and social change.

In the following, I focus on two aspects of migrants' remittance practices with important implications for themselves as well as their families: (1) the new family roles that emerge when household members go abroad and start remitting home; and (2) the moral and political value that migrant families and the surrounding society attach to remittances. As the authors falling within the third position contend, even though remittances do not always produce the expected results, they have a critical impact on the lives of migrants, their families, and their communities economically, morally, and socially.

Understanding remittances as part of a wider social context of family and community relations brings the debate beyond the narrowly optimistic or pessimistic viewpoints already discussed (see Levitt 2001). As Susan Rose and Robert Shaw point out, "The issues are far too complex to characterize remittances simply as positive or negative—or as productive or unproductive" (2008, 81). Jeffrey Cohen, who studies Mexican-US migration from rural Oaxaca in southwest Mexico, also argues against "the unidimensional theories of remittances practices, with a strict focus on either dependency or development" and suggests that by exploring remittance practices as part of a household's planning "we begin to move beyond the limits of dependency and developmental frameworks." Cohen's aim is to reach a "realistic perspective" that recognizes that "remittances cannot resolve social inequalities, nor do remittances necessarily lead to growth, but at the same time acknowledges that many migrants have few alternatives to sojourns" (2005, 89). Acknowledging that remittances offer no silver bullets to solve the problems of the developing world but are often the only alternative to unemployment and declining living conditions is an approach shared by Nicholas van Hear, who studies remittances in Ghana and Sri Lanka. Van Hear contends that migration is a strategy to access new sources of income and that remittances should be understood as part of an exchange in return for the outlays or investment of the household in the migration of some of its members, and therefore suggests that research on remittances needs to look at household planning (2002, 202–3). Remittances are two-way exchanges, van Hear claims, because, "like other household strategies, migration involves outlays or investment, and there is an expectation of return from that investment" (2002, 206).

Using household planning as an analytical lens for exploring remittances sheds light on the specific needs that trigger the decision to migrate and also offers a more nuanced picture of why migrants remit. In their study of labor migration in a London hotel and hospital, Adina Batnitzsky, Linda McDowell, and Sarah Dyer found that remittances serve as "a social mechanism through which migrants are able to fulfill multiple obligations to families and places of origin, while also enhancing their own economic status and future" (2012, 140). In a similar vein, based on microlevel research on remittance behavior among Brazilian immigrants in North America, Franklin Goza and Igor Ryabov report that "family obligation measures were the driving force behind remittance activity" in the United States (2010, 179). Perhaps even more important, viewing remittances through a household lens helps us unpack the gender and class aspects of the remittance economy and brings to the fore the relations of negotiation and contestation that shape migrants' remittance practices. Thus in Cohen's research, "migrant men tended to remit at a higher rate than migrant women" (2010, 155), which resonates with the findings of studies in the rest of Latin America (Bendixen and Onge 2005, 48), as well as the Philippines (Semyonov and Gorodzeisky 2005, 63). Such a gender bias may also be true in other parts of the world, but women nevertheless make greater sacrifices to remit. The United Nations Development Programme's *Human Development Report 2009* informs us that "women tend to send a larger proportion of the income home, on a more regular basis, though their lower wages often mean that the absolute amounts are smaller" (2009, 74), an insight that coincides with the findings of other remittance studies. In their global review of migrant remittance practices, Asmita Naik, Jobst Koehler, and Frank Laczko found not only that women have a greater propensity to remit a larger proportion of their income and send money home more regularly but also that they "earmark remittances for food and clothes" (2008, 61).

Jason Pribilsky also confirms the importance of examining how gender influences remittances in his investigation of how Ecuadorian men and women renegotiate their family roles in a migration context. His research shows that the wives of migrants worry "that their husbands might be holding back remittances and not sending all they could," but that this drawback needs to be held up against the fact that "in their roles as remittance managers women often occupy better positions than non-migrant wives to demand portions of their husbands' earnings" (2004, 328–29). Pribilsky also reports that "many women told me how their experiences as remittance managers made their husbands become better listeners and allowed themselves more room to disagree actively with their spouses" (2004, 329). Other studies conclude that even though labor migration and the remittance economies it generates offer nonmigrants new room to maneuver, they also create worries. Thus in their research on the meaning of migration among Honduran women whose husbands migrate to remit money home, Sean McKenzie and Cecilia Menjívar found that "many women came to associate the men's 'economic' migration with elevated levels of tension, even when they received money and gifts" (2011, 77). Moreover, studies of the effect of remittances on gender relations reveal that remittances rarely make up for unequal relations within the household. Thus Ann Vogel and Kim Korinek, who have examined how migration contributes to educational spending in Nepal, report that "remittances flows do not appear to provide incentive to 'correct' gender bias in human capital investment" (2012, 93). In other words, migrant money and its use are highly sensitive to gender relations and household needs. By the same token, Jørgen Carling asserts that remittances can be a source of tension between family members and that "the migrant has an upper hand in having earned the money, but this could be overshadowed by other aspects of the relationship." To understand these aspects, Carling argues, we need to scrutinize "how the sending of remittances shapes, and is shaped by, relations between senders and receivers" (2008, 55), an approach that Lisa Åkesson has employed in her studies of migration in Cape Verde. She observes that "migrants often have obligations to several households," which "have reduced the risk that remittances will exacerbate inequality" (2009, 395), as is often reported by scholars studying migration in such places as Mexico, where remittance receivers tend to be concentrated in the same households.

Variations in household compositions and family structures can also be found within Latin American countries, as Mariano Sana and Douglas Massey show in their comparison of remittances in Mexico and the Dominican Republic. According to the authors, their "results thus support the idea that remittances are more oriented toward investment in Mexico and more devoted to family maintenance in the Dominican Republic" (2005, 523). Finally, class and economic status are critical parameters in the assessment of the impact of remittances on household economies. Thus Sónia Parella and Leonardo Cavalcanti found that among Peruvian and Ecuadorian families in medium-high sectors, "the migrant projects do not correspond so much to family strategies but rather to individual motivations, the individual desire to *superación*" (2006, 252).[6] By focusing on the relationship between senders and receivers and, in particular, by taking into account the gender dimensions, the social and economic status of the remittance households, and the family structures of the sending countries, we begin to understand the wider social and economic context of which remittances are a part and the many agendas and interests at stake in remittance practices.

The second aspect of importance in assessing the significance of remittances for migrants and their families is their political and moral implications. The emergence of remittances as a development mantra among international organizations and policymakers has changed the image of migrants. Formerly viewed as "lost human resources," many governments now recognize the economic value of their migrant populations and design policies to ease their contact with their home country. Some governments even encourage their populations to migrate to support their families at home, while others create programs that facilitate so-called collective remittances, that is, money collected by migrant organizations to invest in development projects in their home areas. Whether these policies try to capture individual or collective remittances, their goal is the same: to make

---

[6] As I shall discuss in further detail in chapter 5, *superación* refers to migrants' personal struggle to achieve social mobility and improve their individual lives.

migrants send home their savings. As Peter Hansen found in his study of Tanzanian remittances, "Remittance and diaspora policies are not based on actual knowledge but, rather, on magical beliefs surrounding the flow and manipulation of material wealth and human resources" (2012, 88). Alex Julca brings this point home by concluding that "governments at origins often become 'addicted' to remittances" (2011, e45). In other words, rather than supporting migrants in their struggle to improve their lives, governments, nongovernmental organizations, and other organizations view them as instruments for political aims. However, such policies can easily be a double-edged sword. Many migrants continue to feel attached to their country of origin for many years, a feeling fueled by their concern for the well-being of their relatives and fellow countrymen. Yet they find it troublesome to see their hard-earned income portrayed as an unlimited source of wealth that not only families but also governments may tap into to finance public investments. As Susan Eckstein, who studies remittance activities among Cubans in the United States, points out, "Income-sharing has come to be seen as a duty, as an imperative," which has created the image of Cuban migrants as rich and powerful. "Cubans now see those living abroad as superior regardless of their source of income," Eckstein concludes (2010, 14). While the politics to capture migrant remittances have improved the image of Cuban migrants, who were formerly called "traitors" but are now regarded as "saviors," they also impose a duty on them to spend their money in Cuba. In a study of African migrants and their home associations, Claire Mercer, Ben Page, and Martin Evans found a similar ambivalence in the new rhetoric that governments and international organizations employ to channel migrant money into development. The authors sum up the results of their research by stating, "We do not therefore conclude that transnational diasporas have little to contribute to the development of home, but we do suggest that entrenching their role in development may place undue burdens on them" (2009, 157). Research on remittance sending among low-paid workers in London supports this view, providing evidence of the many sacrifices migrants must make to send money to their families back home (Datta et al. 2007). Development policies based on migrant earnings thus portray remittances as a moral imperative and create an image of migrants as breadwinners not only for their own families but also for their home countries. Terry brings this point out in his definition of remittances as "private transactions between private parties," stating that "remittances amount to the hard-earned gains of hard-working people. The money rightly belongs to them and their families." He concludes, "It's their money" (2005, 12).

But besides forcing the moral burdens of financing development onto the shoulders of migrants, remittance policies also empower them, though unwittingly for the most part. As James Scott concludes from his study of resistance (2009), policies intended to submit people to political control often have the opposite effect. By reaching out to migrants and requesting their economic support, political leaders in the sending countries not only acknowledge them as legitimate members of their home societies but also give them a voice with which to influence the development of their countries of origin. Kapur argues that "it is possible to view remittances as a political weapon of the weak" (2008, 350) and suggests that "in lieu of political voice, migration becomes an exit strategy, and remittances either fuel further exit or empower political voice by making resources available to new groups" (2008, 50).

This scenario has emerged in Mexico, where the government has for several years pursued a policy encouraging the country's huge migrant population in the United States to pool their savings and use them to sponsor rural development in their home towns (Orozco 2002). The cornerstone of this policy is a program called 3x1 (see chapter 6), in which the local, national, and federal governments in Mexico each provide an equal share of the investments migrants make in their community of origin (García Zamora 2005; VanWey, Tucker, and McConnell 2005). The 3x1 program has made the country a role model for using so-called collective remittances, or "migrant philanthropy" as some prefer to call them (Waldinger, Poplin, and Aquiles 2008, 844), and for fostering growth even though its impact on development is disputed. Manuel Orozco and Katherine Well, who study hometown associations (HTAs) and collective remittances, report that "in Mexico, hometown associations are playing an increasingly important role in transnational development. Yet, their influence is limited. To exert a greater positive effect, HTAs must achieve improved contact with community stakeholders in order to learn about development priorities"; but often such conversations are difficult to establish and maintain (Orozco and Well 2005, 157–58). Moreover, according to Jonathan Fox and Xochitl Bada, many HTAs suffer from a "lack of capacity in project supervision and a poor understanding of their role as public accountability actors" (2008, 452). Even though the 3x1 program has been heralded by international organizations and is often held up as proof that remittances can make a difference, its achievements in promoting rural development in Mexico are limited. Indeed, Fox and Bada estimate that "this programme represents a tiny fraction of Mexico's overall social investment spending" (2008, 456).

However, Fox and Bada also draw our attention to an often neglected achievement of the 3x1 program: the political empowerment that migrants attain in their role as remittance senders. They argue that "while exit may sometimes weaken voice ... exit can also reflect the *prior weakness* of voice" (2008, 440). They further contend that migrants have used their new power to gain influence in the local and regional politics of their home areas. As evidence for the empowering effect of remittances, Fox and Bada point to the capacity of HTAs to mobilize and lobby, which has increased "the voice and standing of the outlying communities vis-à-vis the municipal authorities" (2008, 451), and praise the program for allowing the HTAs "to bolster the representation of their often-subordinated home community within municipal, state and federal politics" (2008, 452). This observation resonates with the findings of Sergio Soto Priante and Marco Velázques Holguín, who see the explosive increase in migrant organizations registered as HTAs as an indication of the 3x1 program's success. The authors report that "the program has prompted the creation of new migrant clubs and the reactivation of others from 20 registered before the program was introduced in 2002 to more than 800 in 2005" (2006, 14). In the same period, the amount of money allocated to projects under the 3x1 program increased from 429,000 pesos to 503,000 pesos (2006, 17). Soto Priante and Velázques Holguín claim that these projects have limited value in improving the infrastructure in migrants' home areas but have had "a stimulating effect on the trust of the local communities in their own agency capacity" (2006, 16). They conclude that "the main achievement of the 3x1 program is the social learning that is based on an alternative concept of development more based on social change than the logic of the market and that implies a social politic that includes a wider vision of the simple accounting of remittances, clubs and works" (2006, 10).

Several scholars assert that a "migrant civil society" has emerged in the wake of the 3x1 program (Waldinger, Poplin, and Aquiles 2008, 845; Fox and Bada 2008, 843), a term that Fox and Bada define as "migrant-led membership organizations and public institutions," of which HTAs are the most common (2008, 843). Goldring elaborates on this phenomenon and points out that "most collective remittances have been made under a model that bears more resemblance to charitable donations than profit-oriented investments" (2004, 823). He therefore suggests that we call collective remittances and the projects carried out with them lived examples of social citizenship, because they facilitate (or substitute for) "the state's traditional responsibilities," and of substantive (or de facto) citizenship because "working on projects involves political participation under conditions in which migrants are not covered by a legal framework that explicitly provides for or acknowledges their full political rights in Mexico" (2004, 826). Understanding HTAs as forms of migrant civil society and collective remittance and the projects carried out under the 3x1 program as examples of social or substantive citizenship thus highlights the political power that poor and marginal people gain by emigrating and using their remittances to claim continuous membership of their home country during their absence. This insight resonates with Thomas Lacroix's study of HTAs among North African and North Indian immigrants in France and England, which concludes that collective remittances can play a critical role not only in migrants' relation to the home country but also in their integration in the receiving society (2013).[7]

By using HTAs and collective remittances to negotiate with inefficient and corrupt political leaders in their home regions, Mexican migrants have paved the way for new forms of citizenship. However, their experience is unique partly because the vast majority of migrants are concentrated in one country (the United States) and partly because this country shares borders with Mexico, which reduces the cost of migrating (Sana and Massey 2005). By contrast, the migrant populations of most sending countries are scattered in several migrant destinations, and collective remittances therefore do not reach the same volumes as in Mexico. Furthermore, migrants' communications with their home communities are often irregular, and their organizations may represent only a small proportion of the migrant population. Valentina Mazzucato and Mirjan Kabki, who study migrant institutions and remittances in Ghana, report that "HTAs do not represent the totality of migrants from a certain region living in a particular receiving country. They are thus not the democratic institutions they are made out to be" (2009, 245). In their research, the authors also observed that "some HTA development projects are conceived with little consultation of local leaders and population" and that migrants represent only certain constituencies within their communities (2009, 245–46). It is therefore premature to draw conclusions about the political empowerment that migrants gain by pooling their money in collective remittances, and on the basis of the Mexican experience it is fair to suggest that, although programs such as 3x1 provide

---

[7] Jørgen Carling and Kristian Hoelscher's study of immigrants' capacity and desire to remit in Norway support Lacroix's point that migrants' inclination to remit is closely related to their situation in the receiving society. Although they conclude that economic integration is important for migrants' capacity to remit, however, Carling and Hoelscher add that migrants' sociocultural integration "appears not to have significant effects on remittance-sending" (2013, 939).

migrants with more room to maneuver, the cost of migrating is often much higher than the agency attained. Indeed, in the case of Peru, collective remittances receive far less political attention than in Mexico, and even though migrants from rural areas in Peru have formed HTAs in several parts of the world to support their home communities, their contributions make up only a small percentage of that country's total flow of remittances (see chapter 2). As Paolo Boccagni concludes from his research on collective remittances among Ecuadorians in Spain, "The notion of collective remittances far overestimates the facts" (2010, 197). Nevertheless, as I shall discuss in chapter 4, collective (as well as individual) remittances do have an important empowering effect on Peruvian migrants (and sometimes also their relatives in Peru), who convert them into social and cultural capital and gain influence in their home communities.

Concept, Approach, and Method

In this book, I am especially inspired by the third approach—which I have labeled "remittances as fact"—because it helps me inquire into the social anatomy of Peruvian migrant remittances. Such an inquiry includes investigating the moments in migrants' lives when they start remitting, the changes this causes in the relations between migrants and their families, the economic and moral importance that senders and recipients attach to remittances, and finally the circumstances that prompt migrants to stop remitting. Peruvian migration is a particularly relevant case through which to scrutinize these questions because of the migrants' social diversity and physical dispersal. Most migrants come from urban areas and belong to the middle classes. Their remittances are therefore critical because they constitute a substantial contribution to the household economy of their families in allowing them to maintain their standard of living. However, even more important is that moral value is placed on remittances by migrants' families as well as by more remote relatives, neighbors, friends, and others, a value that may be used to reinforce class distinctions. Remittances are not merely spent on daily needs but indexed as symbols of status and power, read into a geographical hierarchy of migration destinations, and ranked according to migrant earnings and saving capacity. In this mapping, remittances from Japan, a country with high salaries, are considered more prestigious than remittances from Argentina and Chile, where salaries are low. Italy, Spain, and the United States, where salaries are lower than in Japan but higher than in Argentina and Chile, rank in the middle. Though in smaller numbers, migrants from rural areas also remit to their families and, more irregularly but in much larger amounts, to their communities. Most of these remittances are used to sponsor prestige-producing activities such as fiestas, although migrants also donate money for charity work and other philanthropic aims. In fact, quite a few migrants who lived in Peru's cities before emigrating were born in the country's rural highlands but moved to urban areas to find work. Many of these rural-urban migrants maintain ties to their communities of origin, although few plan to return there to live. Once they embark on international migration, however, their primary point of reference in Peru is the city where their close relatives live and not their home community. Similarly, it is the family they have left behind in Peru's urban shantytowns rather than the population of their regions of origin that benefits from their remittances.

Another aspect of Peruvian remittances of relevance to this study is gender. Since women as well as men migrate, both sexes are active remittance senders as well as recipients, which makes Peru an interesting case study for observing how remittances and gender relations mutually shape each other. Finally, I scrutinize family relations. The remittance is a gift, but like all gifts it requires something in return. I explore the intricacies of such reciprocity by examining the social life of Peruvian remittances, that is, taking into account how migration is planned and practiced within Peruvian households, how migrants communicate with their families during their absence, how remittance senders and recipients negotiate their individual needs and define their common objectives and, finally, how they organize, conduct, and audit the remittance transactions. Inspired by Peggy Levitt (2001), who broadens the conventional understanding of the term *remittances* to include what she calls *social remittances*, I explore remittances as the commitments migrants make to their relatives, to their communities, and, let us not forget, to themselves and scrutinize migrant remittance activities as the moral economy that grows out of these commitments. More specifically, I view the transference of migrants' money as part of an ongoing exchange of services and meaning between migrants and the members of their families and community. Most of the existing scholarly literature and policy papers focus on the pecuniary dimension of remittances and distinguish the money migrants remit to their households from the donations they give, the fees they pay to their home communities, and the savings and investments they make to buy a car, build a new house, or set up a business, for example. By contrast, I argue that such money transfers are all driven by the commitments migrants make upon their departure. Because these commitments often overlap, we need to study them within the same analytical framework. From the standpoint of development policy and statistics, such a broad definition of migrant money transfers runs the danger of ignoring their specific purpose and use and of encouraging policymakers to assume that a remittance, a donation, a fee, or an investment is fungible and thus arrive at the wrong policy decision. Yet, from an anthropological perspective, it is precisely this fungibility in real life that makes remittances such an interesting object to study. We can capture the social and moral complexity of this economy only by exploring how migrants' many commitments are negotiated and contested and then scrutinizing how their money is then separated out into family remittances, community donations, and personal savings and afterward received and attributed different meanings and eventually spent in their home countries.

Analytically, I have three ways of approaching remittances:

- A phenomenological approach that focuses on individual remittance transactions and asks, *What is the social biography of the remittance?* To answer this question, we need to know when the idea of remitting was conceived, how the money to be remitted was earned, who sent the money, what its itinerary was, how it was transferred, who received it, how was it distributed, who spent it, and how was it spent.[8]
- A process-oriented approach that investigates how remittance transactions are repeated over time and in space and asks, *What is the life course of remittance flows?* Here the required information is when and how money transactions accumulate and take the forms of remittance flows, what their frequencies and fluctuations are, what their pathways are, how long they last, who takes part in them, and which networks facilitate them.
- A structural approach that documents the economic and social context of the remittance flows and asks, *What is the moral economy of remittances?* This question can be answered only by inquiring into the migration practices that produce the remittance flows, the stakeholders in the flows, the interests that drive them, the constraints the senders face, the opportunities they provide to the recipients, the conflicts they generate, and the meaning and significance of their use and consumption.

Together, these three approaches offer a comprehensive perspective on how migrants develop remittance flows at different societal levels—the

---

[8] On the notion of the biography of things, see Kopytoff (1986).

individual, the household, and the extra-household and community—and thus unpack the various elements that shape the social life of remittances. The first aim of such an inquiry is to identify the circumstances in the lives of migrants that prompt them to remit and then to stop remitting. The second aim is to explore the factors in the sending and receiving context that make single money transactions take the form of remittance flows and over time make them grow, peak, and eventually dry up. Finally, I assess the social and moral importance that different social actors attribute to remittances and give examples of the many ways that migrants contribute to the receiving and sending societies. To capture the concerns and needs that prompt migrants to remit and to describe ethnographically how remittance flows evolve over time and in space, I employ the term *commitment* to conceptualize migrants' motivation to remit. In my analysis, commitments refer to the agreements migrants make with their relatives and communities to support them during their absence. Rather than an individual promise made by migrants to families and friends upon their departure, a commitment is a pledge tied to specific relationships of trust and responsibility between remittance senders and recipients. As these relations undergo changes during the migration process, migrants' commitments need to be recurrently reaffirmed and sometimes revised. But even when commitments become subject to tensions and conflicts, migrants rarely break them. Failing to help your elderly mother or support your children or turning your back on your community is simply not an option. Indeed, many migrants regard their commitments as an oath, implying a strong sense of accountability not only to others but also to oneself.

I develop my analysis by distinguishing three kinds of commitments that migrants make to pursue their goals. The first is the *compromiso*, which literarily means *commitment* and which covers migrants' individual pledges to support their relatives while they are gone. As breadwinners, most migrants consider this support to be their contribution to the household to cover basic needs similar to the contributions they made before emigrating. Migrants also make *compromisos* to single family members, often for a specific period of time to pay for something like education, for example. Finally, they send money in response to special requests from close as well as remote relatives when they fall ill or urgently need help for other reasons.

The second commitment is *voluntad*, which means "social volition" and refers to the donations migrants give to their communities of origin. Often such donations are given by migrants from rural areas to their villages or hometowns, but migrants from urban areas also donate money to religious institutions and charitable organizations. Some migrants also form hometown associations in the receiving society that make collections that are pooled and remitted as so-called collective remittances. These are sometimes invested in local infrastructure or schools, but they are also used to build or restore churches, soccer stadiums, and the like. Most commonly, however, *voluntad* is a commitment to spend large amounts of money on fiestas or other activities that yield prestige.

The third commitment is *superación*, meaning "overcoming" or "surpassing" or, as it is often called, *superarse*, that is, "to overcome or surpass oneself." This is the commitment that people make to themselves regarding their individual efforts to achieve social mobility. Among migrants *superarse* often comes last in their many endeavors to help others and contribute to the wider community. Yet although the dream of saving money, getting an education, buying a car, and the like may never come to anything, it is the aspiration to create a better life for themselves that inspires many migrants to embark on a journey to foreign places.

The book draws on two sources of information. In chapter 2, I use quantitative data from Peru's Instituto Nacional de Estadistica e Información (INEI) to examine Peruvian migration and remittances. INEI's sources and methodology are discussed in detail in the chapter. The second source of information is my own ethnographic data gathered among Peruvians in Argentina, Chile, Japan, Peru, Spain, and the United States between 1997 and 2010. Working with data across such a broad time span poses a methodological challenge insofar as migration flows shift routes and destinations and the remittances they produce change intensity and direction. However, long-term fieldwork has also allowed me to observe how migrants' activities and the events in which they participate develop over time and—of particular importance to this book—how remittance flows commence, peak, and come to an end. I have chosen the following sites for my multisite data collection: Hartford, Connecticut; Los Angeles, California; Paterson, New Jersey; Miami, Florida; Washington, D.C.; Barcelona, Spain; Buenos Aires, Argentina; Isesaki, Japan; and Santiago, Chile. In these sites, I mapped out migrant institutions and practices and interviewed community leaders (editors of Peruvian newspapers, leaders of associations, consulate officials, and representatives of business communities, among others). The data also comprise formal as well as informal interviews with more than a hundred migrants of both sexes and from different social strata, as well as a dozen extended case studies that followed the movements of migrant families in different locations over a period of several years with the aim of scrutinizing the networks they create, the livelihood strategies they pursue, and the remittance activities they engage in. Together with some of the informal interviews, these extended case studies constitute the main source of the data I examine in chapters 3 and 5, in which I review individual life trajectories and discuss how these frame migrants' remittance activities and their struggles to make progress in their new environments. Both chapters briefly introduce the reader to the persons I interview and the circumstances of our encounters. Last, I participated in migrant family reunions and attended meetings and activities organized by migrant organizations in selected localities. My analysis of migrants' community commitments in chapter 4 draws heavily on the observations made during these events but is also informed by the personal interviews I conducted with migrants and community leaders.

Structure of the Book

The book is divided into six chapters. Following this introductory chapter, chapter 2 offers an overview of Peruvian migration. This includes an account of the principal waves in Peru's contemporary emigration and a description of the receiving contexts in the many countries where Peruvians settle. The chapter also presents the most recent data on Peruvian migration and remittances, including information on the gender, age, origin, and destinations of migrants and on remittance recipients according to income, region, and other factors. The chapter serves as a contextual framework for the ethnographic analysis in the following three chapters.

Chapter 3 examines the *compromiso*, which I call the family commitment. It consists of 10 case studies of five females and five males who fulfill the role of either remittance sender or remittance recipient and whose stories in different ways illustrate the dilemmas and exigencies that produce family remittances. The chapter is divided into three subsections. The first subsection describes four cases of solo migrants, that is, those who are the only members of their family to migrate and whose commitments are confined to particular relatives and specific needs. The next subsection discusses two cases of migrants whose commitments involve several relatives and whose remittance engagements change volume and course in response to changing family relations. In the last subsection, I present four cases of migrants whose remittance commitments have been either fulfilled or interrupted by occurrences in their own lives or in the lives of their relatives. The subsections illustrate three important sequences in the social life of remittances: the first shows how remittance flows gain momentum; the second, how they peak; and the third, how they come to an end.

Chapter 4 addresses the second of the three commitments: *voluntad*, or as I also call it, the community commitment. It describes three case studies, each discussing the donations and contributions that migrants make either individually or collectively to their home villages. The cases illuminate three different ways in which migrants commit themselves to *voluntad*. In the first case, migrants go abroad on labor contracts and return after three years. Meanwhile, they pay a fee to preserve their membership in the community and to claim their rights to land when they come home and settle. The second case shows how migrants who mostly travel by illegal means and have formed strong migrant organizations send collective remittances to help their home communities but use their savings mainly to sponsor huge fiestas in the village. Finally, the third case demonstrates how long-term legal migration has created a well-organized migrant community able to assemble collections and send remittances to improve infrastructure and finance the construction of a computer center and a church.

In chapter 5, I examine the meaning and importance of *superación* or the personal commitment. This chapter briefly discusses 18 cases showing what migrants do with their lives once they have fulfilled their family and community commitments. The chapter is divided into five subsections. The first, entitled "Migrants as Savers," describes how migrants save for their retirement; the second, "Migrants as Investors," tells how they invest in economic activities; the third, "Migrants as Entrepreneurs," depicts how they start new businesses; the fourth, "Migrants as Innovators," traces how they make career shifts; and the fifth, "Migrants as Transformers," relates how they engage in politics. This variety of endeavors, activities, and engagements demonstrates how migrants make plans for their future, save capital to invest, use their skills to achieve mobility, rethink their talents to create new ideas, and mobilize their fellow migrants to change society—in short, examples of the many ways in which migrants enrich the world in both the sending and the receiving societies.

The conclusion in chapter 6 sums up the insights pursued in the three earlier chapters and discusses their implications for our understanding of migration and the contribution remittances make to migrants' home countries. It reviews three models for remittance-driven development policies (the European, Mexican, and Philippine models) and uses these as a comparative framework for discussing the particularities and commonalities of Peruvian migration and remittance practices. It also considers how my data supplement the existing literature on this topic and how they add new knowledge to the debate on remittances. Finally, the chapter uses my study to highlight other ways in which migrants contribute to a better world.

Chapter 2

Peru: Migration and Remittances

To understand the remittance practices of Peruvians requires that we know who the migrants are, where they migrate, why they migrate, and how they migrate. This chapter seeks answers to these questions by analyzing the available information on Peruvian migration and remittances. Until recently, such knowledge was scarce and relied on a variety of sources such as census data from the receiving countries, statistics provided by international organizations, surveys conducted by a few research projects in Peru, and sporadic head counts made by Peruvian embassies and consulates. Needless to say, figures on Peruvian migration are many, and they rarely converge. However, in 2007 Peru's INEI (Instituto Nacional de Estadística e Información), in cooperation with the Dirección General de Migraciones y Naturalización (DIGEMIN), MIGRACIONES (Superintendencia nacional Perú) and the International Organization for Migration (IOM), began producing its own data on population movements and money flows, among many other issues. Even though INEI retrieves these data from several sources employing different methodologies, they provide useful and reliable information on

Peruvian migration and remittances.[1] However, household surveys such as those provided by INEI often face difficulties in measuring remittance transfers, as opposed to migration in general, and it can be hard to determine the exact percentage of migrants who remit and, in particular, the number of households they remit to. Another problem is that INEI's database on international migration provides information only on migrants' movements at the moment they leave Peru, which makes it impossible to reconstruct their previous migration movements within Peru and thus to identify a broader pattern of step migration in which migrants first move from the countryside to the city and then embark on international migration. As I shall point out below, some of Peru's international migrants may actually come from the country's rural highlands even though the statistics provided by INEI indicate their origin as one of the country's urban centers.

This chapter draws on INEI's database to discuss the most prevalent features of Peruvian migration and remittances. It is divided into four sections. In the first section, I briefly introduce the reader to Peru's contemporary migration history. In the second and third sections, I then discuss migration and remittances in more depth and illustrate my arguments with 25 charts. In the final section, I summarize the main conclusions of the chapter.

History of Peruvian Migration

Ever since the Spanish conquest, Peru has been a country of immigrants, receiving fortune hunters, settlers, and exiles from Europe; enslaved laborers from Africa; and contract workers from Asia. It was only in the last half of the 20th century that Peru changed from an immigrant to an emigrant country and that Peruvians began going abroad in large numbers (Altamirano 2006; Paerregaard and Berg 2005; Paerregaard, Takenaka, and Berg 2010;

---

[1] INEI's database on migration and remittances draws on the following sources (INEI, IOM, and DIGEMIN 2010, 71–75): (1) national census material (Peruvian censuses were conducted in 1940, 1961, 1972, 1981, 1993, 2005, and 2007); (2) monthly police records on Peruvians leaving and entering the country; up to 1993, these were a simple registration of how many left and entered, but from 1994 the police have kept more complete records on migration, for example, registering the country of residence of the 231,085 Peruvians who declared they live outside Peru and who hold resident visas in these countries (INEI, IOM, and DIGEMIN 2010, 34); (3) the national register of identification called RENIEC (Registro Nacional de Identificación y Estado Civil), where Peruvians' place of residence (whether at home or abroad) is registered; and (4) a national survey of Peruvian households called ENOHA (Encuesta Nacional de Hogares), which was conducted among 95,469 individuals and 22,204 households in 2007.

Paerregaard 2008a). The first important wave of migration occurred in the early 1930s after a failed coup in 1931 that prompted a group of political refugees to go into exile and settle in US cities such as Chicago and New York. In the aftermath of World War II, Peru experienced an economic boom, but as educational possibilities in Peru were still few, middle- and upper-class families sent their sons to Argentina or Spain to study, where they obtained academic degrees in medicine, law, and other professions. In Madrid, Barcelona, Buenos Aires, La Plata, and other cities, these men formed migrant associations, and over the years quite a few married local women and settled abroad. Simultaneously, women from Quechua-speaking rural areas in the Andean highlands started to migrate to southern Florida and other places in the United States, where they found work as domestic servants; and in the late 1950s, males from Lima's working-class neighborhoods (such as Surquillo, La Victoria, and Callao) traveled to Paterson and other cities in New Jersey to work in the booming textile industry. In this period, New York and Chicago also emerged as magnets for Peruvian migration, and when unemployment grew because of the economic crisis in the 1970s and the textile workers of New Jersey were laid off, many migrated to Los Angeles and other cities in California. During the 1970s and early 1980s, Miami received a growing number of migrants from Peru's rural Andean areas, particularly from the departments (now regions) of Ancash, Junín, and Ayacucho; and in the years that followed, the city also emerged as the destination of middle- and upper-class Peruvians, mostly from Lima, who fled the economic and political problems the country faced in the 1980s. This middle-class exodus continued under the Fujimori regime (1990–2001), extending to other US cities such as Dallas; Houston; Washington, D.C.; and San Francisco.

In the late 1980s, Peruvian migration started to change direction toward Europe, Asia, and the Americas, and in the 1990s a number of new destinations emerged (Paerregaard 2008a). The geographical shift in Peruvian migration occurred in response to push as well as pull factors. On the one hand, in the late 1980s and early 1990s Peru's unemployment and inflation skyrocketed, as the country sank deeper into a morass of economic depression and political conflict during the government of Alan García (1985–90). Impoverishment and emigration rates continued to grow after the Fujimori government (1990–2001) introduced a neoliberal policy in 1990. In 1986, though, the United States implemented the Immigration Reform and Control Act, which legalized roughly 3 million undocumented immigrants but at the same time tightened the country's border controls. As a result, it became more difficult for Peruvians and other Latin American immigrants to enter the United States. The 1996 immigration act made it even harder to cross the US-Mexican border, and since the terror attacks in 2001 many Peruvians have felt they are victims of the increasing criminalization of illegal migration in the United States.

The shift in Peruvian migration toward new destinations was also driven by other pull factors. In the late 1980s, the governments in Italy, Japan, and Spain passed new immigration laws to encourage the immigration of foreign unskilled workers (Paerregaard, Takenaka, and Berg 2010). The laws, which were a response to the falling birth rates and the growing need for labor in domestic work and manufacturing in the three countries, made it easier for foreigners to enter countries, a change that favored Peruvian and other Latin American immigration in particular. Thus, since 1990 Latin Americans have been allowed to apply for work permits within specific occupations in Spain. The same year Japan invited descendants of Japanese emigrants, including Peruvians and Brazilians, to take up temporary work in Japan to satisfy the demand for labor, mostly in manufacturing industries. Subsequently, large numbers of Peruvians, mostly males, have migrated to Japan to do factory work, whereas Peruvian women have migrated to Spain (and lately Italy) to do domestic and care work. Whereas the number of migrants in Japan has remained relatively stable in the 2000s, Italy and Spain have continued to attract growing numbers of Peruvians who either migrate through family reunification, obtain one of the annual work permits that the Italian and Spanish governments grant to foreigners, or benefit from the amnesties that these European governments recurrently offer to undocumented immigrants. However, the economic crisis in southern Europe has left many migrants in Italy and Spain unemployed, and in future years the wave of migration is likely to change direction again, as young Spaniards and Italians start migrating to Latin America in response to the gloomy prospects for finding work in their home countries.

In the second half of the 1990s, Argentina and Chile also became important destinations for Peruvian migration. The two countries emerged as magnets for Peruvian migrants at a time when it was more difficult for them to find work in Italy, Japan, and Spain, while the demand for unskilled labor and especially for domestic workers in Argentina and Chile was growing rapidly (Paerregaard 2012b). From a gender perspective, the migration flow toward Argentina (from 1994) and Chile (from 1997) resembles the sudden inflow of Peruvians that Italy and Spain experienced in the early 1990s. Thus, the women who found employment as domestic workers for either Argentine and Chilean families or Spanish and Italian families have spearheaded both waves. However, from a class perspective the two waves of migration differ in a number of respects (Paerregaard 2007). Peruvians can reach Argentina and Chile by bus in two to three days and are allowed to enter the two countries on a tourist visa, which can later be overstayed. Argentina and Chile therefore attract migrants from Peru's impoverished urban areas who cannot afford the investment that travel to Italy and Spain (or other destinations) requires. Indeed, to these migrants Argentina and Chile represent a last resort in a situation where all other migratory options have been ruled out.

In the past decade, the amnesty programs offered by the governments of Argentina, Chile, and Spain have improved the situation of many Peruvians and other Latin Americans in those countries.[2] In Spain, which has experienced explosive immigration in the past decade and now has an immigrant population of more than 5.5 million (about 12 percent of the total population) (INE 2009), the government granted an amnesty to 700,000 undocumented immigrants in 2005, including many of the 138,000 Peruvians living in the country (Ferrero-Turrión and López Sala 2010). Latin American immigrants in Spain, comprising mainly Ecuadorians, Bolivians, Colombians, Argentines, and Peruvians, also have the right to apply for Spanish citizenship after two years of legal residence and to seek family reunification with their parents and children (Aparicio 2007; Merino Hernando 2004). In Argentina, Peruvians constitute the third-largest immigrant group of almost 150,000 (DNM 2010, 3). Although the country's migrant population of 1 million is much smaller than Spain's, the Argentine government is increasingly recognizing immigration as an important issue. In 2005, it launched the Patria Grande program, offering stay and work permits to undocumented immigrants from Peru and other neighboring countries who entered Argentina before 2006 (DNM 2010). In Chile, immigrants still make up a tiny percentage of the population, and in 2009 only 352,000 foreigners were living there (Departamento de Extranjería y Migración 2010). The number of immigrants is small, but in 2007 the Chilean government granted amnesty to the Peruvian community of 130,000 migrants, who constitute the country's largest foreign minority. The following year more than 15,000 undocumented Peruvians registered and obtained legal stay permits in the country (*La República* 2007).

---

[2] Unlike immigrants in Argentina, Chile, and Spain, Italy, whose foreign-born residents constitute 7 percent of the country's total population, has not granted amnesty to its immigrants recently. Officially, the number of Peruvians, who make up the second-largest Latin American immigrant group in this country, is estimated to be 83,000 but is likely to be much higher (Istat 2010).

Most Peruvians migrate to places where they already have social networks in place to help them find work and housing upon their arrival and navigate everyday life in a new context. However, the destinations to which Peruvians migrate are often perceived as forming a hierarchy. In this hierarchy, the United States still represents to most Peruvians a unique opportunity to study, do business, and work to save money. Similarly, Japan is regarded as a haven by many because salaries are generally higher than in other countries, while Italy and Spain are preferred destinations because Peruvians find it easy to adapt to the local language and culture. Conversely, Argentina and in particular Chile are thought of as last resorts because salaries there are comparatively low and migrants' prospects for improving living conditions for themselves and their children in a shorter period of time are lower.

The choice of destination also reflects migrants' economic and social status in Peruvian society. In Japan, only Peruvians of Japanese descent and their spouses are allowed in without many visa restrictions. In more recent years, migration to Italy, Spain, and the United States has required special skills or connections, and unless migrants already have relatives in these countries to sponsor them, they have to resort to paying smugglers to cross the borders. In contrast, Argentina and Chile are viewed as discount destinations pursued by migrants who have neither the connections, the necessary skills, nor the means to pay for illegal travel to these other countries. Within this migration hierarchy, however, there is always room for maneuver. Migrants often migrate to Argentina and Chile to save money to go to Italy or Spain at a later time; likewise, some Peruvians of Japanese descent migrate to Japan with the aim of obtaining tourist visas or work permits in the United States. These patterns of migration often result in reinforcing or recreating socioeconomic divisions within Peru, because migrants with resources are more likely to end up in destinations that allow for faster social mobility.

Peruvian Migration: Dispersal and Diversity

Peruvian migration grew steadily in the second half of the 20th century, but it was not until 1990 that it started to gain momentum. Figure 2.1 demonstrates the explosive growth of Peruvian emigration from 1990 to 2009. In this period, the number of Peruvians who left their country of origin grew fivefold, rising from 46,596 in 1990 to 235,461 in 2008. As a result, a total of 2,572,352 Peruvians emigrated without returning between 1990 and 2012 (INEI, IOM, and MIGRACIONES 2013, 15) at an average annual rate of

101,905 (INEI, IOM, and DIGEMIN 2010, 14). As the figure reveals, this growth has been generally stable but had also fluctuated, with decreasing numbers that are closely related to recent economic and political change in Peru. In the late 1980s, Peru suffered from hyperinflation and a falling gross domestic product (GDP) that set off Peruvians' current exodus. The Fujimori government that took power in 1990 initially fueled this migration by introducing neoliberal policies that slowed the galloping inflation but left thousands of people without jobs or the means to earn a living. Whereas a short period of hope in 1993 briefly relieved the pressure, migration reached new heights in 1994. That same year, however, Fujimori's reforms started to pay off, and Peru's economy soared with a growth rate as high as 12 percent. In response, the number of migrants dropped dramatically in 1995 and stayed low for a couple of years, until the tide once again turned and Peru faced new economic difficulties in 1997. Although Peru's economy slowly recovered in the years that followed, corruption and instability under the Fujimori regime left the country in political limbo for several years, triggering a new wave of emigration.

In 2001, Peru elected a new government, generating hopes of a better future, and since 2004 it has performed extremely well economically, producing an average annual growth rate of 6.9 percent (WDI 2013). Nonetheless, years of economic mismanagement and political instability had made Peruvians distrust the country's ability to recover, and many therefore continued to leave the country. Indeed, it was only in 2008 that the migration

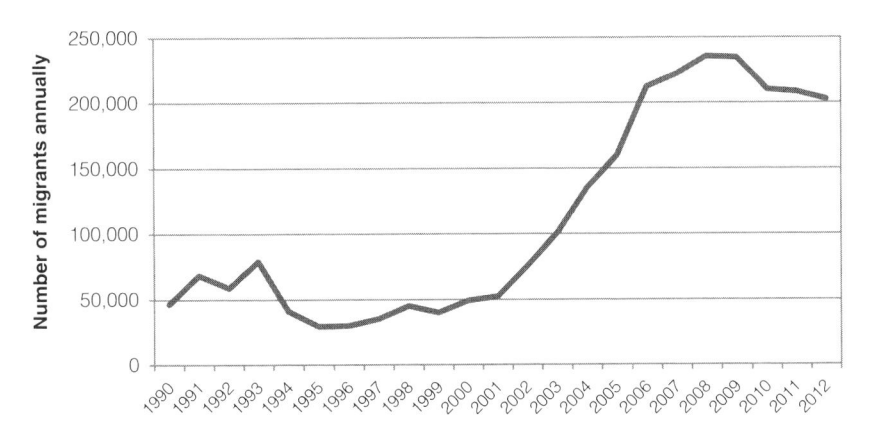

Figure 2.1. Annual Figures on Peruvian Migration, 1990–2012
Source: INEI, IOM, and DIGEMIN 2010, 14; INEI, IOM, and MIGRACIONES 2013, 22.

curve peaked. While this paradox of simultaneous explosive growth and migration may be an indication that chronic migration takes years of progress to bring to a halt, it can also be read as a sign that Peru's newly gained prosperity is encouraging many Peruvian migrants to combine permanent migration with more prosperous economic activities within Peru.

As Peru's economic and political crisis increased in the 1990s, the country's working and middle classes began to use migration as an alternative way of making a living and achieving social mobility, creating an ideology of migration: living in Miami, Madrid, or Buenos Aires is better than living in Lima. It has taken a decade of growth and stability to challenge this idea and make Peruvians believe that staying home can also bring something good.

The migration curve now has peaked. Yet a large number of Peruvians continue to migrate every year, and return migration is still very small. In 2012, the number of Peruvians living outside Peru (2,572,352) constituted 8.8 percent of the country's total population, which was estimated at 30 million that year (World Bank 2013). As figure 2.2 illustrates, their destinations are many and include countries on several continents. The principal destinations are North America, South America, and Europe, which respectively receive 33.7 percent, 30.8 percent, and 29.6 percent of Peruvian

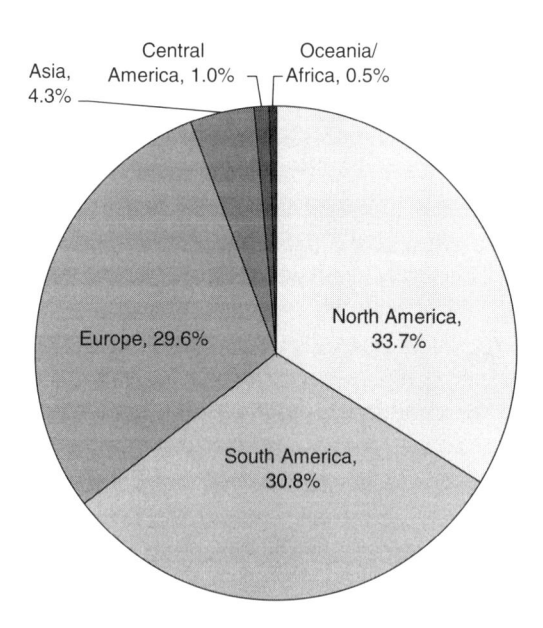

Figure 2.2. Migration from Peru to Five Continents, 2012
Source: INEI, IOM, and MIGRACIONES 2013, 28.

migrants. Asia and Central America, by contrast, have received only very small proportions of Peruvian migration, the former 4.3 percent and the latter 1.0 percent. Finally, merely 0.5 percent of Peruvian migrants have settled in Africa and Oceania.

Figure 2.3 shows the distribution of Peruvians to the major countries of settlement. It underscores the migration pattern of figure 2.2, which is one of global dispersal. Yet even though Peruvians are scattered on several continents, they tend to concentrate in certain countries and regions. The United States has received almost a third of all Peruvian migrants, at 31.4 percent; together, Spain (15.4 percent) and Italy (10.2 percent) make up more than a quarter; while Argentina at 14.3 percent and Chile at 9.5 percent together almost receive a similar number of migrants. In Asia, however, the bulk of Peruvian migrants live in Japan (4.1 percent). Other South American countries such as Venezuela (3.7 percent) also receive Peruvians, but trail behind with much smaller numbers. The rest (11.6 percent) are distributed among such countries as Australia, Bolivia, Brazil, Canada, Ecuador, France, Germany, Mexico, Switzerland, and the United Kingdom. This pattern of dispersal and concentration is the outcome of the migration waves of the 1990s and 2000s, which directed Peruvians away from the United States toward other parts of the world: Argentina, Chile, Italy, Japan, and Spain.

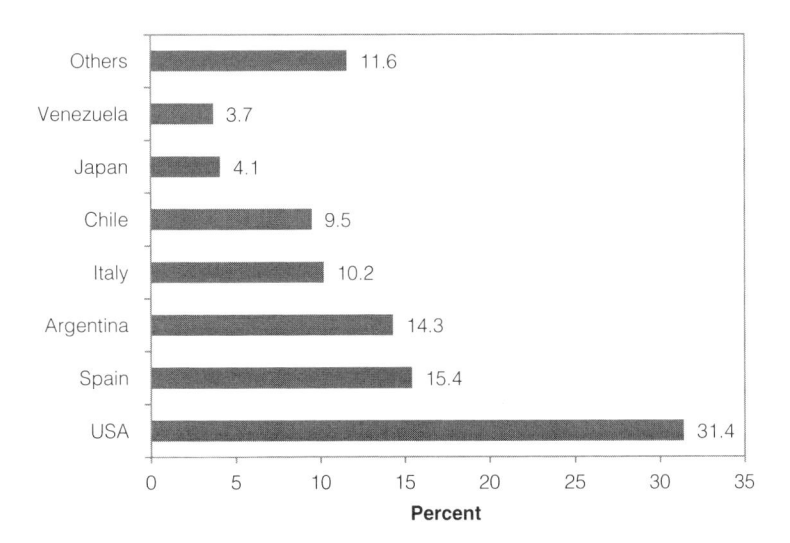

Figure 2.3. Migration from Peru to Receiving Countries, 2012
Source: INEI, IOM, and MIGRACIONES 2013, 28.

Concentration within global dispersal can also be observed in figure 2.4, which shows Peruvians' preferred cities, states, and regions of settlement. Although 33.6 percent of all migrants are listed under the rubric "Other cities/states," a remarkably high percentage of Peruvians live in cities such as Buenos Aires (10.7 percent) and Santiago (8.0 percent), two cities where Peruvians constitute the largest immigrant groups, and Madrid (7.7 percent); in New York (4.7 percent) and New Jersey (4.7 percent), where such cities as Paterson, Passiac, Elizabeth, and Bergen have been the center of Peruvian migration; Miami (4.6 percent); Milan (4.5 percent); Barcelona (4.0 percent); Los Angeles (3.3 percent); Virginia (2.0 percent), where many Peruvians working in the Washington, D.C., area live; San Francisco (1.7), Peruvians' second city of residence in California; Lazio (1.5), a city close to Rome, Italy's capital; Caracas (1.4 percent), Venezuela's capital; Maryland (1.3 percent), another neighboring state of Washington, D.C.; Córdoba (1.3 percent), another Argentine city; Turin (1.2) in northern Italy; La Plata (1.2 percent), a neighboring city to Buenos Aires; Connecticut (1.0 percent), where the state capital of Hartford is the center of settlement of Peruvian migrants; Montreal

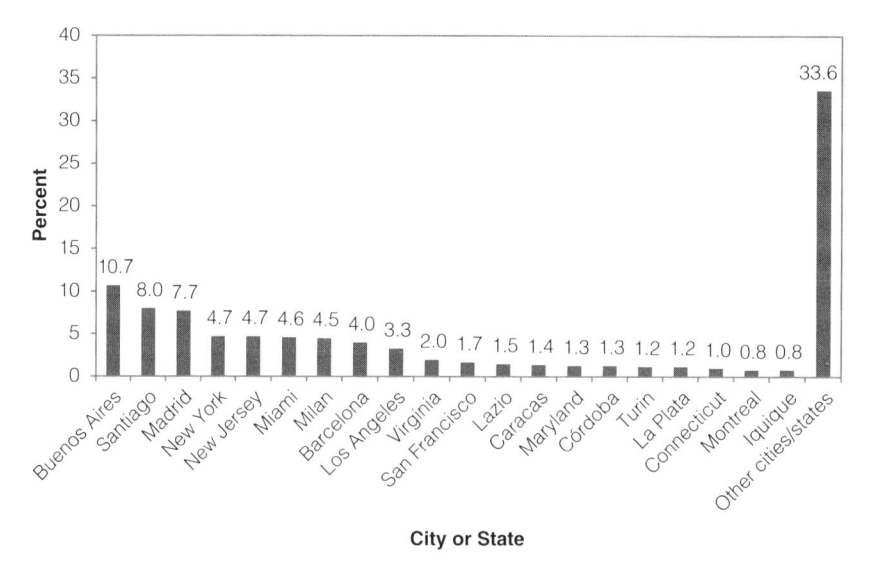

Figure 2.4. City or State of Settlement of Migrants from Peru, 2013
Source: INEI, IOM, and MIGRACIONES 2013, 29.

Note: Buenos Aires, La Plata, and Córdoba in Argentina; Santiago and Iquique in Chile; Madrid and Barcelona in Spain; New York, New Jersey, Miami, Los Angeles, Virginia, San Francisco, Maryland, and Connecticut in the United States; Milan, Lazio, and Turin in Italy; Caracas in Venezuela; Montreal in Canada.

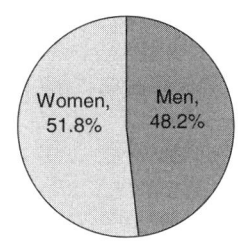

Figure 2.5. Migration of Men and Women from Peru, 2009
Source: INEI, IOM, and DIGEMIN 2010, 20.

(0.8 percent) in Canada; and Iquique (0.8 percent) in northern Chile. The figure illustrates that Peruvians tend to settle in the capital and a few other big cities in the countries to which they migrate, a pattern that is particularly salient in Argentina, Chile, Italy, and Spain. In the United States, Peruvians settle in larger urban areas, but these are many and include such cities as Miami, Florida; New York, New York; Los Angeles and San Francisco, California; Washington, D.C.; Paterson, New Jersey; and Hartford, Connecticut. Peruvians' dispersal is even more prevalent in Japan, where they live scattered in many cities both north and south of Tokyo.

Peruvian migration is not only scattered but also diverse. Figure 2.5 shows that in 2009 both sexes migrated in large numbers but that more women than men emigrated. This is hardly surprising considering that there were more women (50.3 percent) than men in the 2007 census (INEI 2007), but compared with other international migrations (such as Mexican migration), the dominance of Peruvian female migrants is noteworthy. Figure 2.6 shows that this gender pattern was prevalent throughout the 15-year period between 1994 and 2009, except for 2005, 2006, and 2007, when more men than women emigrated. Notwithstanding these years, female migrants are clearly the majority, but interestingly their dominance varies from year to year. These variations reflect the spearheading role women play in Peruvian migration. In 1990, Peruvian migration changed direction, and the pioneers of this new wave were women migrating to such countries as Italy and Spain, where domestic labor was in high demand.[3] Peruvian males, however, quickly follow their female relatives (or rather, the latter were quick to help the former to migrate), and in 1994, the first year registered in figure 2.6, women and men emigrated in almost the same numbers. Yet in the same year, Argentina emerged as a new magnet for Peruvian migration,

---

[3] Japan, however, was still the preferred target of Peruvian men.

46   *Peru: Migration and Remittances*

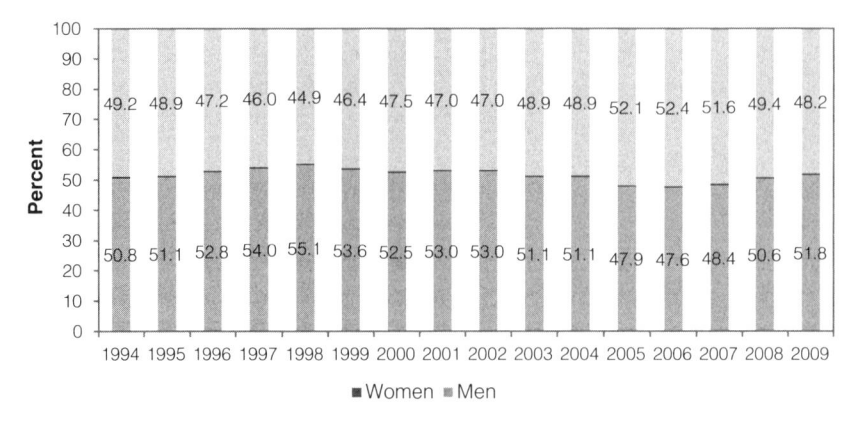

[Bar chart showing percentages of Women and Men migrants from Peru, 1994-2009:
1994: Women 49.2, Men 50.8
1995: Women 48.9, Men 51.1
1996: Women 47.2, Men 52.8
1997: Women 46.0, Men 54.0
1998: Women 44.9, Men 55.1
1999: Women 46.4, Men 53.6
2000: Women 47.5, Men 52.5
2001: Women 47.0, Men 53.0
2002: Women 47.0, Men 53.0
2003: Women 48.9, Men 51.1
2004: Women 48.9, Men 51.1
2005: Women 52.1, Men 47.9
2006: Women 52.4, Men 47.6
2007: Women 51.6, Men 48.4
2008: Women 49.4, Men 50.6
2009: Women 48.2, Men 51.8]

Figure 2.6.   Migration from Peru by Sex, 1994–2009
Source: INEI, IOM, and DIGEMIN 2010, 20.

which once again became a primarily female activity satisfying the need for domestic workers. A similar change occurred in 1997 and the years that followed, when Chile experienced rapidly growing Peruvian immigration. In the 2000s, southern Europe and the Southern Cone countries continued to be Peruvians' preferred destinations, and from 2002 males had almost caught up with females in the migration statistics. Arguably, the male dominance between 2005 and 2007 is evidence of a stabilization of Peruvian migration, which in countries such as Italy and Spain is facilitated through family reunification and migrant networks. Curiously, since 2007 more women than men have been emigrating, although in smaller numbers than previously.

Figure 2.7 offers an unusually rich documentation of gender disparity in Peruvian migration from 1932 to 2006. INEI does not provide information on the sample used for this chart, which is presumably based on police records of Peruvians leaving and entering the country. According to the figure, in the 1930s, 1940s, and 1950s men clearly predominated in Peruvian migration, which was insignificant in those years.

However, from the late 1950s male dominance decreased, and from the mid-1960s on more women than men emigrated. At that time, Peruvian migration to the United States was growing, and—as happened 30 years later when Peruvians started to migrate to Argentina, Chile, Italy, and Spain—women took the lead. As in the 1990s, it was the demand for domestic labor that initially propelled Peruvian migration. Even though many males soon followed their fiancées, wives, sisters, or mothers, women have predominated in Peruvian migration in the past five decades, except from 1977 to 1986 when men were predominant.

Peru: Migration and Remittances 47

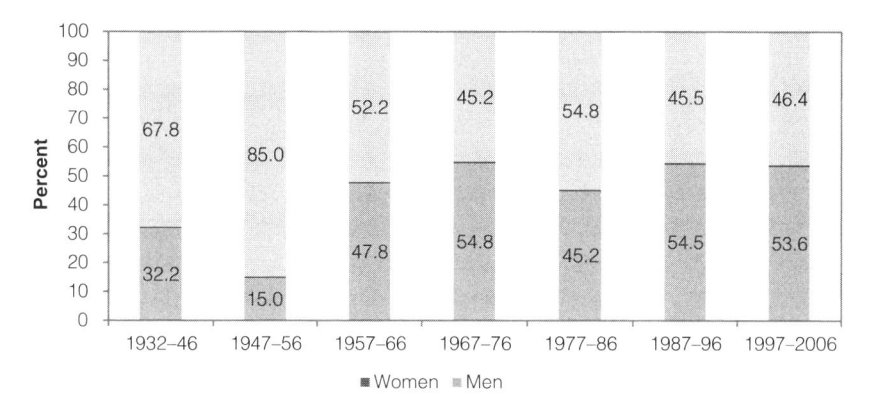

Figure 2.7. Gender Disparity in Migration from Peru, 1932–2006
Source: INEI and IOM 2008, 39.

Figure 2.8 illustrates migrants' distribution by age. It shows that the majority (50.8 percent) of migrants are between 20 and 40 years of age, a sign that migration is driven by a need to find work and that Peruvians emigrate even as they grow older. However, the relatively high number of migrants older than 40 (30.7 percent) also suggests that many travel as the relatives of other migrants seeking family reunification. The relatively low

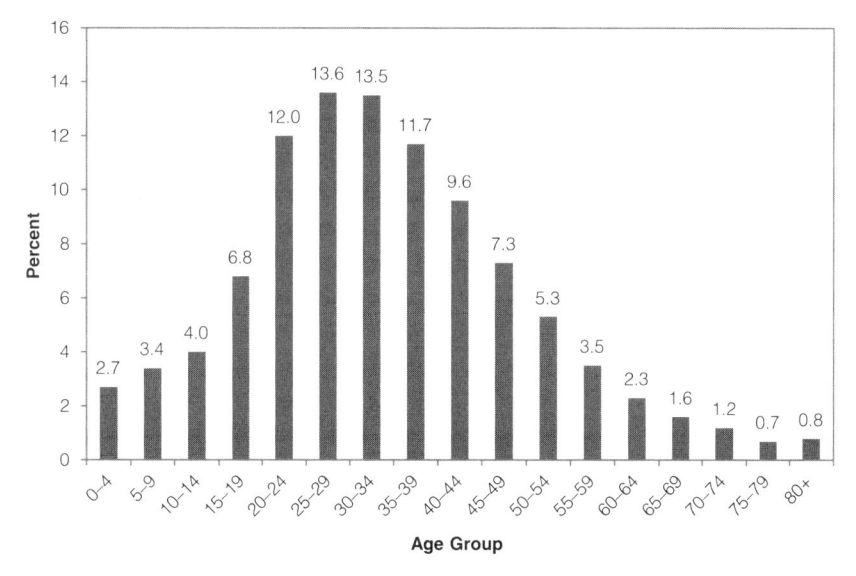

Figure 2.8. Migration from Peru by Age, 1994–2006
Source: INEI, IOM, and DIGEMIN 2010, 21.

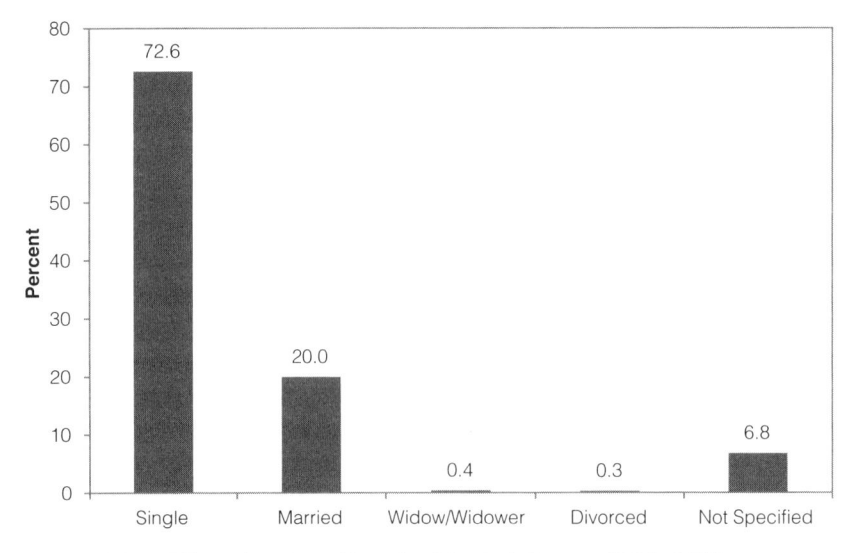

Figure 2.9. Migration from Peru by Marital Status, 1994–2009
Source: INEI, IOM, and DIGEMIN 2010, 24.

number of migrants under 20 (18.5 percent), however, shows that migrants often leave their children behind with relatives and wait to apply for family reunification until the children finish schooling.

According to figure 2.9, almost three quarters of all migrants (72.6 percent) were single at the time they left Peru, while only a fifth (20 percent) were married. The number of divorced migrants is close to zero percent (0.3 percent) while 0.4 percent are widow or widowers and 6.8 percent are not specified. These data seem inconsistent with the fact that more than 50 percent of all migrants are between 20 and 40 years of age, as shown in figure 2.8. A possible explanation for this puzzle is that Peruvians who are single are more inclined to migrate. Another, perhaps more likely, explanation is that migrants tend to answer "single" rather than "divorced" when asked for their marriage status, a behavior that can be attributed to cultural prejudices. Finally, many Peruvian couples are *convivientes* (that is, they live in partnerships and form families without contracting marriages) and therefore are officially considered single.

In figure 2.10, migrants are grouped according to their profession and former occupation. At the time of migration, 29 percent stated they were students, while office workers made up 13 percent of Peru's migrant stock; housewives, 11 percent; and service workers, traders, and market vendors,

Pie chart data:
- Farmers, fishers, artisans, 1.3%
- Minors/underage, 3.0%
- Semiprofessionals, 5.5%
- Professionals, 9.7%
- Service workers, traders, merchants, 10.5%
- Housewives, 11.0%
- Office workers, 13.0%
- Others, 16.0%
- Students, 29.0%

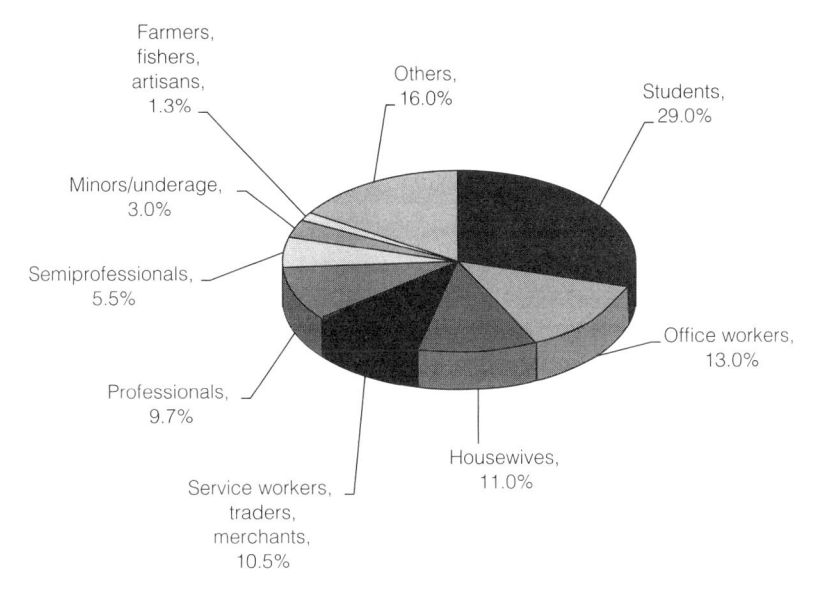

Figure 2.10. Migration from Peru by Profession and Occupation, 1994–2009
Source: INEI, IOM, and DIGEMIN 2010, 60.

10.5 percent. Professionals (mostly university graduates) constituted 9.7 percent, and semiprofessionals (technicians and the like) 5.5 percent of Peru's migrant stock. A mere 3.3 percent are minors (that is, less than 15 years old) and do therefore not have a profession. Surprisingly, only 1.3 percent stated that they were farmers, fishermen, or artisans, while 16 percent were classified as "other." The figure documents great variations in migrants' professions and occupations, affirming the picture of Peruvian migration as socially diverse. However, the broad spectrum of answers may also be a function of the many categories employed in the data collection. "Student" is a particularly wide-ranging category, which literally refers to young people enrolled in an educational program but is also used to cover other categories such as unemployment. The high number of migrants registered under this category, however, reveals that Peruvians leaving the country tend to have some form of higher education. In a similar vein, office workers and women who work at home are also categories that may gloss over other occupations and activities, but their numbers nevertheless indicate that middle-class Peruvians are clearly present in Peru's migration. If migrants registered as professionals and semiprofessionals are added, the picture of Peruvian migration becomes even clearer.

Another rather inclusive category comprises service workers, traders, and merchants. Though combining many unrelated occupations, this category establishes that many migrants belonged to Peru's urban working classes before leaving the country. By contrast, very few migrants declared that they worked in agriculture or fisheries (or as craftsmen), revealing that only a tiny fraction earned an income in nonurban occupations. However, as farming and fishing are traditionally livelihoods associated with low social status in Peru, migrants in these professions may have preferred to register under other categories.

The class composition of Peruvian migration becomes evident in figure 2.11, which shows the income groups Peruvians belonged to before migrating. In figure 2.10, more than half of those surveyed were identified as students, office workers, or professionals, indicating that the educational level of migrants is high. Figure 2.11 provides further evidence that Peruvian migration is to a large extent a middle-class project. It uses Peru's official division of the population into income quintiles that indexes the highest income group as stratum A and the lowest income group as stratum E. The figure shows that the two most migrating income groups are C (29.3 percent) and D (33.9 percent), each representing more than a quarter of the sample. Even more startling, however, is the strong presence of the better-off income groups in Peruvian migration. Over a quarter of Peru's migrants come from

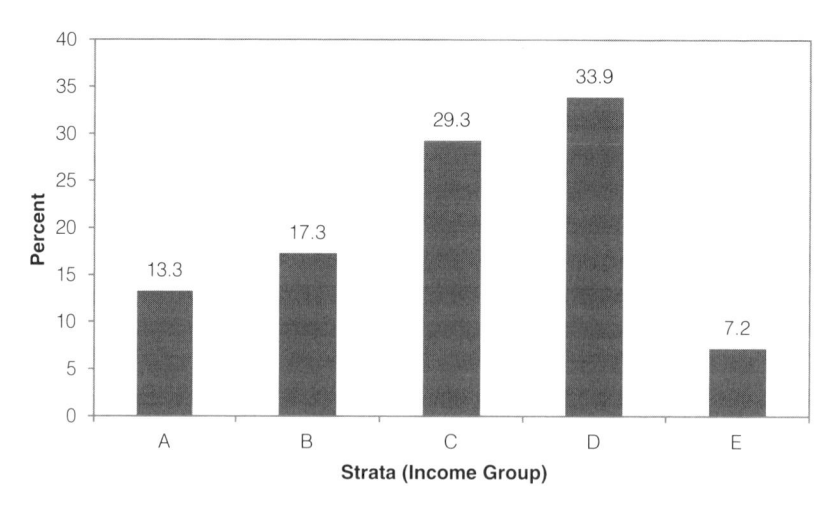

Figure 2.11. Migration from Peru by Income Group, 2006
Source: INEI and IOM 2008, 50.
Note: Stratum A is the highest income group in Peru, and stratum E is the lowest.

groups A (13.3 percent) and B (17.3 percent), and if income group C is added, we find that more than half belonged to the three highest-earning income groups. By contrast, income group E makes up only 7.2 percent of Peru's migrants. However, the numbers need to be read with caution as it can be argued that the country's two poorest income groups (D and E) together constitute 41.1 percent of all migrants. Essentially, the figure shows that migrants come from all economic strata of Peruvian society and that migration is therefore enormously diverse.

The remaining three figures in this section show migrants' geographical origins in Peru. In figure 2.12, we observe regional origins, which in Peru refers to the country's division into three geographical zones: the coast, where the capital and most of Peru's major cities (and therefore the majority of the population) are located; the highlands, which includes the Andes and most of Peru's rural population; and the jungle, the biggest of the three zones in physical extent but by far the smallest demographically. The figure is thought provoking because it shows that the bulk of Peru's migrants (70.8 percent) come from the coast, which is the most developed part of the country, whereas only 21.1 percent come from the highlands and just 8.3 percent from the jungle, the least developed part of Peru. Compared with the 2007 census (INEI 2007), which established that 54.6 percent of Peruvians lived on the coast, 32 percent in the highlands, and 13.4 percent in the jungle, the figure is even more striking as it documents that Peruvians from the coast are much more likely to migrate than other Peruvians.

Figure 2.13 adds more evidence that Peruvian migration originates in the developed part of the country. It reveals that as many as 92 percent of migrants come from urban areas and only a small fraction from rural areas (8 percent). This bias toward urban areas in the data of figure 2.13 corresponds well with the overwhelming presence of migrants from the coast in

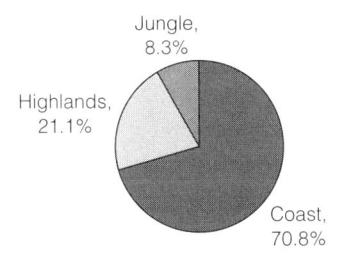

Figure 2.12. Region of Origin of Migrants from Peru, 2007
Source: INEI and IOM 2009, 22.

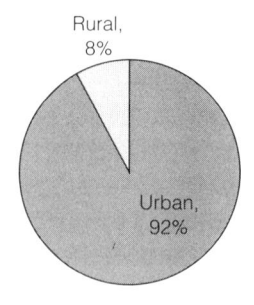

Figure 2.13. Migration from Rural or Urban Areas of Peru, 2007
Source: INEI and IOM 2010, 49.

figure 2.12. And like the findings in figure 2.12, figure 2.13 diverges from the results of the 2007 census, which concluded that 75.9 percent of the Peruvian population lives in urban areas and 24.1 percent in rural areas (INEI 2007). The data give a picture of Peruvian emigration as an endeavor pursued by Peruvians from coastal cities. However, as mentioned earlier, INEI's statistics do not provide data on migrants' previous movements within Peru, which makes it difficult to establish their place of birth and thus exact geographical origin.[4]

In figure 2.14, migrants are divided according to their place of birth using information retrieved from their identity papers. It arranges them into two groups: one made up of migrants born in the province of Lima, comprising the country's capital and its surroundings, and in the province of Callao, Lima's port, which today has merged with the capital; and the other made up of migrants from the rest of Peru. From the figure, we read that the former is slightly greater (50.6 percent) than the latter (49.4 percent). In other words, whereas the two previous figures pointed to the coast and its urban areas as the source of Peru's migration, this figure establishes that its epicenter is metropolitan Lima, birthplace of half of Peru's migrants.

From the data presented in this section, we can conclude that, even though Peruvian migration is scattered globally, the bulk of migrants are concentrated regionally in the United States, southern Europe (Italy and Spain), the Southern Cone countries (Argentina and Chile), and Japan. Moreover,

---

[4] Data on migrants' place of birth for this study are important to reconstructing their movements within Peru before they embarked on international migration. Arguably, even though some of the international migrants registered in INEI's database actually were born in Peru's rural highlands, these feel more attached to the country's urban areas where their close relatives live. As INEI's data on remittances indicate, these also constitute the main recipients of migrants' remittances.

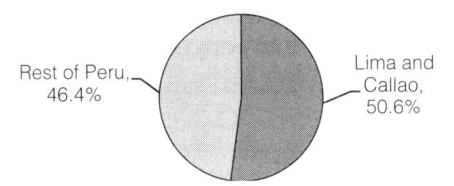

Figure 2.14. Migration from Peru by Migrants' Place of Birth, 2010
Source: INEI, IOM, and DIGEMIN 2010, 29.

within these regions, migrants tend to settle in the same cities and states, even though in the United States and particularly in Japan their settlement is scattered over many places. Another feature of Peruvian migration is its social diversity. Peruvians from all social strata and women as well as men migrate. Equally, migrants are of almost all ages. According to the figure, many migrants are single, although it is not entirely clear whether this category includes informal affinity relations. Migrants have very different occupational backgrounds, many with some form of professional training. Only a few percent admit to having worked in nonurban occupations. This seems to be related to migrants' geographical origin, which is more than 90 percent urban, with more than half coming from metropolitan Lima. Last but not least, the majority belongs to Peru's three highest income groups.

Peruvian Remittances: Concentration and Inequality

The world's remittances to developing countries amounted to $414 billion in 2010 (World Bank 2013a). The main receiving countries in the developing world are shown in figure 2.15, which puts India and China at the top. Together the two countries receive more than all the rest on the list, reflecting not merely the fact that India and China have big migrant populations but also that they are the two most populous nations in the world. Next on the list come Mexico and the Philippines, two of the best documented migration countries, receiving less than half of what India and China receive. Further down the list come Nigeria, Pakistan, Bangladesh, Vietnam, Lebanon, and Egypt. To put its remittances into comparative perspective, Peru also appears in the chart, although it receives far fewer remittances than many other countries not listed. Peru's remittances amounted to $2.788 billion in 2012 (World Bank 2013b), which is a mere drop in the ocean of the world's remittances. On a global scale, Peru's remittances therefore draw little attention,

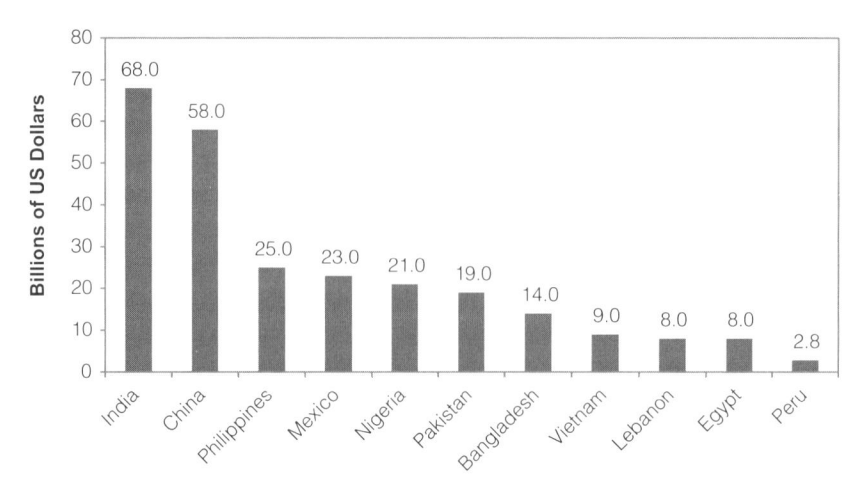

Figure 2.15. Remittances to Selected Developing Countries, 2012
Sources: World Bank 2011; World Bank 2013b.

but in Latin America they rank high. In 2010, only eight Latin American countries (Brazil, Colombia, the Dominican Republic, Ecuador, El Salvador, Guatemala, Honduras, and Mexico) received more remittances than Peru (World Bank 2011, 28).

Figure 2.16 presents world remittances as a percentage of GDP in the developing countries. In stark contrast to figure 2.15, which includes some of the largest countries in the world, figure 2.16 gives a list of countries that either have very small native populations, very large migrant populations, very small GDPs, or a combination of the three. One exception, however, is Nepal, which has a rather large population (28 million), rapidly growing emigration, but a very low GDP. For all the countries listed, remittances constituted a stunningly high percentage of GDP in 2012, ranging from Tajikistan's 48 percent, which in previous years has been even higher, to Kyrgyz Republic's 31 percent; Nepal, Moldova, and Lesotho's 25 percent; and others with remittances between 17 and 21 percent. Conversely, remittances make up only 1.4 percent of Peru's GDP, which in the first decade of the 2000s grew at an impressive rate, mainly because of the rising demand for minerals on world markets.

So where do Peru's remittances come from? In figure 2.17, the principal remittance-sending countries and their share of the remittances Peru received in 2009 are presented. It is hardly surprising that the countries listed in figure 2.17 are the same as those listed in figure 2.4 showing Peruvians'

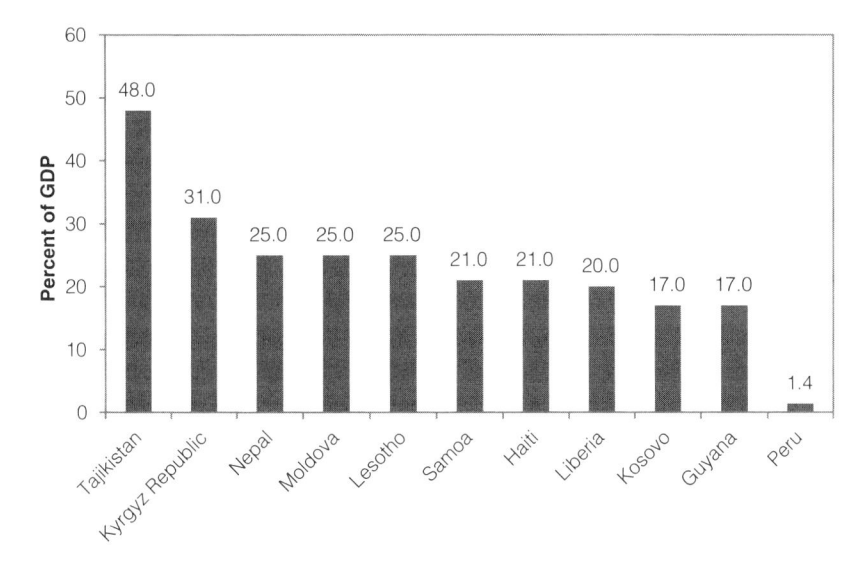

Figure 2.16. Remittances to Developing Countries as a Percentage of GDP, 2012
Source: World Bank 2013b.

principal countries of settlement. Yet there are important variations in their order and in the percentages of migrants (figure 2.4) and the remittances indicated for each country (figure 2.17). In both figures, the United States occupies a key position, as both migrant receiver (figure 2.4) and remittance

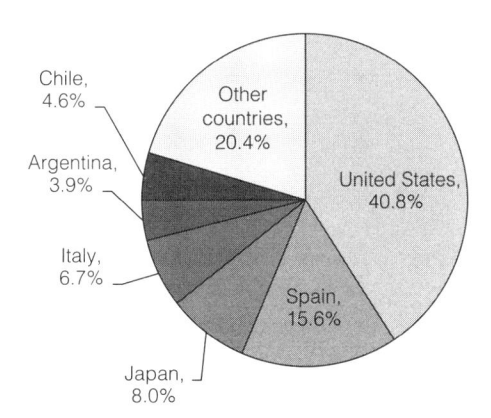

Figure 2.17. Remittances to Peru from Selected Countries, 2009
Source: INEI and IOM 2010, 74.

sender (figure 2.17). But whereas the United States receives 32.6 percent of Peru's migrants, these send home 40.8 percent of that country's remittances. A similar "positive" though smaller difference can be noted in Italy's and Spain's migrant-remittance balance. Most remarkable, however, is Japan, which receives only 4.6 percent of Peru's migrant stock but accounts for as much as 8 percent of its remittance revenues: that is a migration-remittance balance of almost 1:2. Other countries show a negative migrant-remittance balance. Argentina receives 13.5 percent of Peruvian migrants but accounts for only 3.9 percent of Peru's remittances, a negative migration-remittance balance of more than 4:1. Chile also shows a negative balance. The data in figures 2.4 and 2.17 document how migrants' choice of destination influences their capacity to remit, which to a large extent is a function of the job markets and the migrants' salaries in the receiving countries. However, other variables are also important, as the difference between Argentina and Chile shows. Work opportunities and salaries are similar in the two countries, but migrants in the latter nevertheless send home more remittances than migrants in Argentina. By the same token, the migration-remittance balance is more positive in Italy than in Spain, although the job and earning opportunities are very similar. These variations point to other aspects of the migration context influencing a migrant's remittance capacity, such as immigration policies, family structure, and the time and form of migration.

While figures 2.16 and 2.17 shed light on where Peru's remittances come from, the remaining figures in this section show how they are received and spent in Peru. Figure 2.18 presents the outcome of a national survey of 22,204 households (with a total of 95,469 individuals) conducted in 2007 that collected data on the number of migrant members of the interviewed households and the remittances they receive. The survey divides Peruvian households into three groups: (1) households with members living outside Peru, (2) households that receive remittances, and (3) households with members living outside Peru and that receive remittances. Based on the data collected, the surveys estimates that 407,600 households or 6.3 percent of all households in Peru either have members living outside the country or receive remittances from someone outside Peru, that 302,200 households have migrant members, equivalent to 4.6 percent of the sample, and that 249,700 households receive remittances, representing 3.8 percent of the sample. The figure is important because it makes the unequal distribution of remittances in Peruvian society visible: only 3.8 percent of the country's households receive money from migrants. Moreover, 4.6 percent have

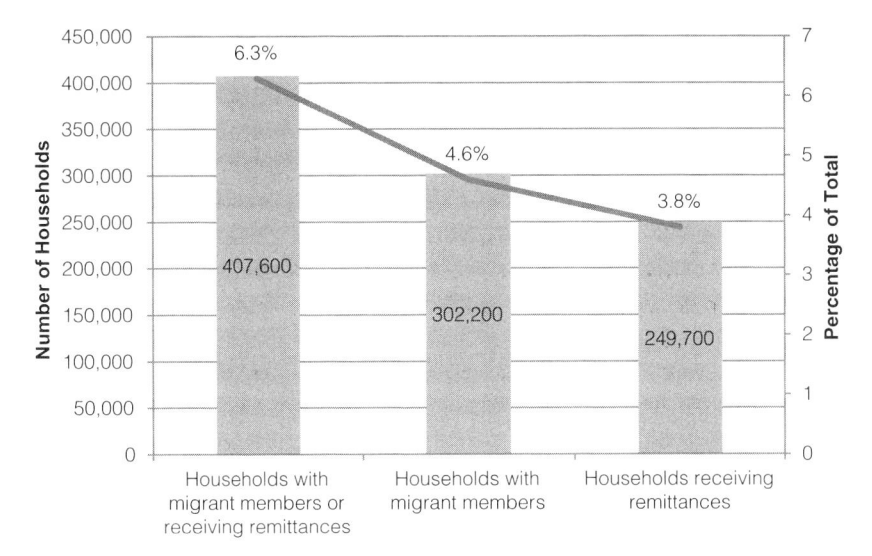

Figure 2.18. Peruvian Households Receiving Remittances and Those with Migrant Members, 2007
Source: INEI and IOM 2008, 50.

members outside Peru but do not receive remittances. Finally, the survey estimates that 407,600 or 6.3 percent of Peru's households either have migrant members or receive remittances. The figure indicates that only a tiny fraction of Peru's households receive remittances. The distribution of remittances becomes more unequal when we look into the mathematics of the figure. As the reader may have noticed, the numbers do not add up: the sum of the figures for the second (4.6 percent) and third rubrics (3.8 percent) is greater than the figure for the first rubric (6.3 percent). This lack of consistency in the figures indicates that some households receive remittances from more than one migrant and that the money Peruvian migrants send home is extremely unequally distributed. Bearing in mind that migrants constitute 8.5 percent of Peru's population and that only 3.8 percent of Peruvian households receive remittances, we can conclude that the country's migration-remittance balance is negative by a rate of more than 2:1. So far, the 2007 survey is the only consistent source of information on the distribution of remittances to households in Peru, and even though later INEI publications suggest higher numbers of households with migrants abroad (10.4 percent in contrast to 4.6 percent in the 2007 survey), they provide no new data on remittance receivers (INEI, IOM, and DIGEMIN 2010, 49).

The data in figure 2.19 are interesting because they reveal a strong gender bias in favor of women as remittance receivers. In figures 2.5, 2.6, and 2.7, we found that women have outnumbered men in Peruvian migration for nearly half a century and that they constituted 51.8 percent of Peru's migrants in 2009. Figure 2.19, however, shows that in the same year 67.7 percent of Peru's remittance recipients were women, while only 32.3 percent were men. The difference in the figures is striking, but we should be mindful that they do not correlate directly. As also demonstrated, migrating does not always imply remitting, and the same migrants may remit to several persons and households. Yet, the figures do suggest a possible tendency in Peruvian remittances: women predominate in Peruvian migration and they (and perhaps also men) tend to send their remittances to female rather than to male relatives in Peru.

Figure 2.20 reveals another intriguing aspect of Peruvian remittances: their distribution among age groups. In figure 2.8 we observed that, while most migrants are between 20 and 40 years of age, the participation of middle-aged Peruvians in migration is also common.

By contrast, Peru's migrant stock includes few children. In figure 2.20, a similar age pattern is apparent, with some variations, the most salient being that relatives older than age 65 are among the most regular remittance recipients (23 percent). Worth noting also is the fact that relatives between ages 30 and 49 (27 percent) are the age group receiving the most remittances, followed by relatives between ages 14 and 29 (26.6 percent). The 50–59 (16.4 percent) and 60–64 (7.0 percent) age groups, however, receive

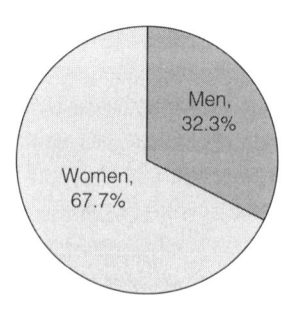

Figure 2.19. Remittance Recipients in Peru by Sex, 2009
Source: INEI and IOM 2010, 91.

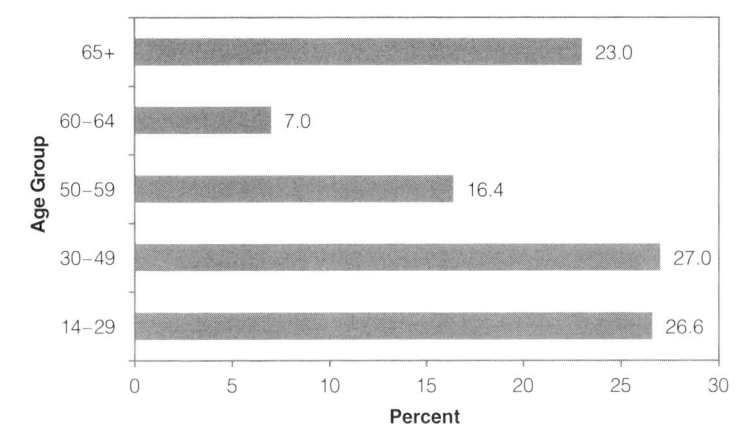

Figure 2.20. Remittance Recipients in Peru by Age, 2009
Source: INEI and IOM 2010, 85.

less. However, comparisons between figures 2.8 and 2.20 should be made with caution. The data in figure 2.8 merely document the age distribution of Peruvian migrants indicating that the majority are labor migrants. The data in figure 2.20 are more complex. They show that migrants often send money to persons of trust to distribute within the household or between several households and steward their use. Arguably, the 30–49 age group (and to some extent also the 50–59 age group) comprises spouses or other close relatives in charge of migrants' children during their absence. As the heads of migrant households, they therefore figure as the principal remittance recipients. Conversely, it is fair to assume that the 14–29 and the 65+ age groups are the direct beneficiaries of the remittances they receive.

Figure 2.21 uses the national survey of 2007 to establish the distribution of remittances among receiving households in the five income groups in Peru. Unfortunately, the chart includes figures not only for households that receive remittances but also for households with migrant members (which do not necessarily receive remittances), which makes it impossible to know the exact number of remittance receivers in each income group. Compared with figure 2.11 showing Peruvian emigration by income groups, there are few variations except for one surprising detail: the migration-remittance balance of income group E, the poorest, is "negative," while in the other cases it is either "positive" (income groups B, C, and D) or almost "even" (income group A). In fact, while income group E constitutes 20.7 percent

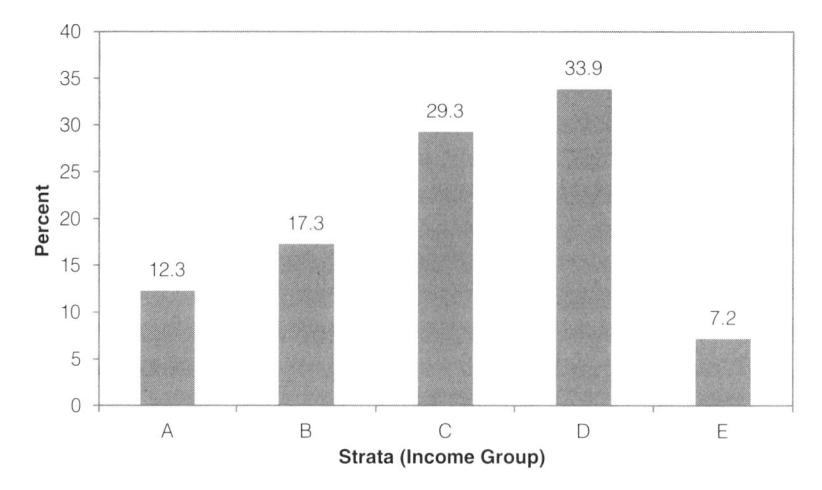

Figure 2.21. Peruvian Households Receiving Remittances and Those with Migrant Members by Income Group, 2007
Source: INEI and IOM 2008, 51.
Note: Stratum A is the highest income group and stratum E the lowest income group.

of Peruvian migrants, their remittances make up only 7.2 percent of Peru's remittances. Because the data include households with migrant members, we cannot draw final conclusions from the figure, but given the extent of the imbalance it is reasonable to assume that remittances enhance existing inequalities in Peru by favoring those with less need and failing to reach those who need them most, the poorest.

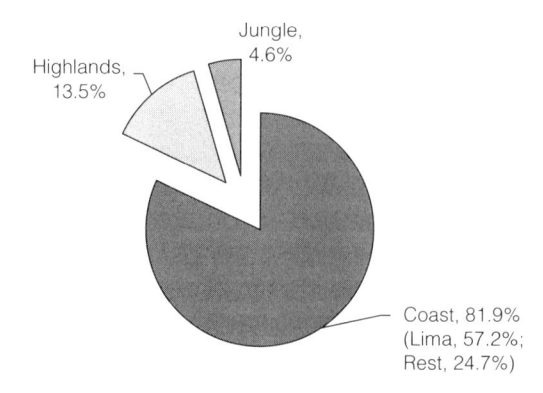

Figure 2.22. Peruvian Households Receiving Remittances by Region, 2006
Source: INEI and IOM 2008, 53.

Figure 2.12 showed the geographical origin of migrants in Peru. The theme of figure 2.22 is the distribution of remittances among Peru's geographical regions. Comparing the two figures, we learn that the coast captures 81.9 percent of Peru's remittances even though only 70.6 percent of the country's migrants come from this region. Moreover, 50.6 percent of Peru's migrant stock was born in Lima and Callao; nevertheless, 57.2 percent of its remittances end up in the two provinces. The numbers clearly point to a positive migration-remittance balance in favor of Peru's developed regions. However, 21.1 percent of Peru's migrants come from the highlands, but this region captures just 13.5 percent of its remittances. For the jungle, the migration-remittance balance is even more negative: although 8.3 percent of the country's migrants originate from the jungle region, it receives only 4.6 percent of its remittances. These remittances, then, are biased in favor of the regions that need them less.

Figure 2.23 pursues the same line of inquiry as figure 2.22 in documenting the distribution of remittances among Peru's urban and rural areas. Figure 2.13 revealed that only 8 percent of Peru's migrants have a rural background, while 92 percent were urban residents before they left the country. The data in figure 2.23 are even more biased: only 4.7 percent of Peru's remittances reach households in rural areas, whereas households in urban areas receive the remaining 95.3 percent. Again, the data suggest that remittances redistribute resources away from the underprivileged toward the privileged.

Figure 2.24 gives further detail about how remittances are distributed in Peru. It establishes how the country's regions capture remittances. The data speak for themselves: the two main recipients are Lima and Callao,

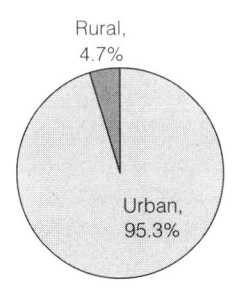

Figure 2.23. Remittance Recipients in Peru by Urban or Rural Residence, 2009

Source: INEI and IOM 2010, 92.

```
Lima         ████████████████████████ 64.4
Callao       ██ 7.2
La Libertad  ██ 6.9
Ancash       █ 4.2
Arequipa     █ 4.2
Lambayeque   █ 2.3
Junín        █ 2.1
Cusco        █ 1.9
Ica          █ 1.3
Loreto       █ 1.0
Others       █ 4.9
```

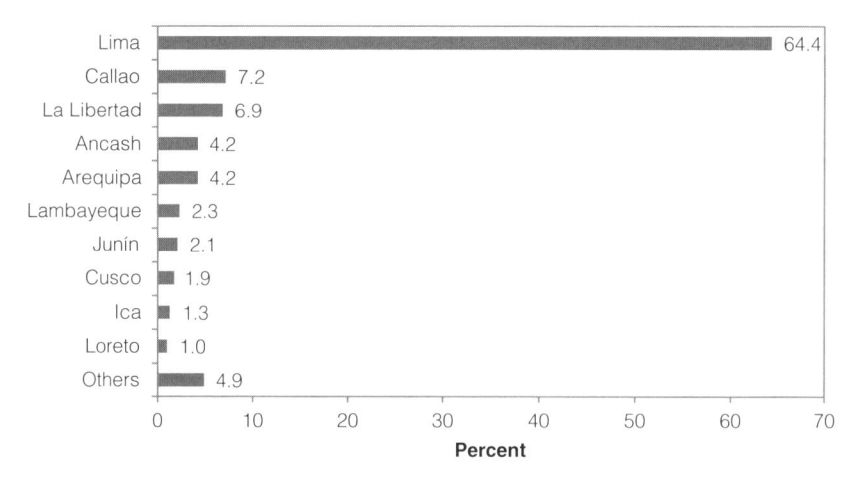

Figure 2.24. Remittance Recipients in Peru by Region, 2009
Source: INEI and IOM 2010, 98.

which together capture 71.6 percent of Peru's remittances. Other important recipients, which capture far fewer remittances than Lima and Callao, are La Libertad (6.9 percent), the location of Peru's third-largest city of Trujillo; Arequipa (4.2 percent), the region of its second-largest city, Arequipa; Ancash (4.2 percent), where Peru's largest fishing port is located; and Lambayeque (2.3 percent) on Peru's northern coast. The next on the list are Junín (2.1 percent) and Cusco (1.9 percent), both regions in the Peruvian highlands, followed by Ica, also a coastal region, and Loreto, located in the jungle.

Figure 2.25, the last figure in this section, shows how the receiving households spend their remittances. Household needs, which include food, housing, monthly bills, and electrical devices, make up 66.2 percent of spending, which is hardly surprising, but, interestingly 21.4 percent of remittances go to education. The significance of these data becomes evident when we look further into the social background of remittance recipients. Thus, in 2009, 70.5 percent of Peru's remittance recipients were studying in a private educational institution; by contrast, only 38.7 percent of nonremittance recipients could afford to take up private education (INEI, IOM, and DIGEMIN 2010, 104). Evidently, remittances make an important difference in Peruvians' capacity to finance the education of their children. The last spending items of remittances in figure 2.25 are savings and housing, and just like the "others" they take up an insignificant proportion of migrants' remittances.

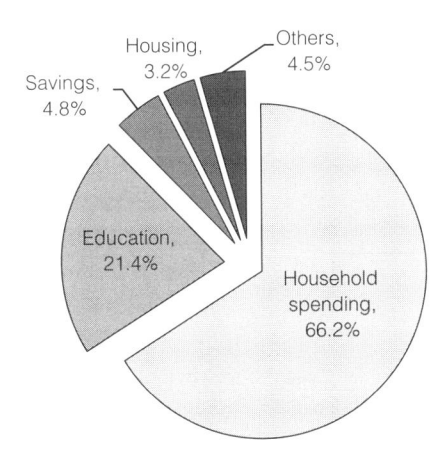

Pie chart showing:
- Household spending, 66.2%
- Education, 21.4%
- Savings, 4.8%
- Housing, 3.2%
- Others, 4.5%

Figure 2.25.   Use of Remittances by Recipients in Peru, 2009
Source: INEI and IOM 2010, 100.

Conclusion

Mexican migration is often referred to by international organizations and in the scholarly literature as a model of how remittances can foster development in migrants' home countries. Egypt, Morocco, Pakistan, and other countries have also been used as examples of remittance-driven development in the developing world. Common to these countries is the fact that migrants are predominantly males originating from rural areas who travel to the developed world to save and remit money home to their families. Peruvian migration and remittances are different from those examples. The bulk of migrants in Peru come from the country's capital and a few other cities on the coast. In addition, they are mostly women, and many have received some form of higher education. And perhaps most remarkable, the majority belong to Peru's middle class. This bias in Peruvian migration is reflected in Peru's remittances, which reach women primarily and are captured by a very small number of households, many from the country's better-off income groups. Peruvian remittances therefore enhance existing inequalities in Peru, deepening the gap between the haves and the have-nots.

However, Peru is not unique; emigration from other countries, such as Colombia (Guarnizo 2006) in Latin America or the Philippines (Asis 2008) in Asia, is also propelled by the middle classes, often represented by women, many with high educational levels. It is such migrations and the remittance flows they produce that this book's study of the Peruvian case can help elucidate. Often ignored in the remittance literature and the debate on how migration can provide leverage for development, countries such as Peru illustrate the variety of ways in which remittances can affect the lives of migrants and their relatives back home.

The aim of the following three chapters is to describe ethnographically how Peruvian migrants from rural as well as from urban areas and from the working class as well as the middle classes engage in remittance activities and how their remittance flows change family relations within migrant households and generate new forms of inequalities both between households and within migrants' home communities.

Chapter 3

Compromiso:
The Family Commitment

The bulk of the remittances circulating in the contemporary world consist of money sent by migrants to close relatives in their countries of origin. Peruvian migrants often describe such remittances as *compromiso*, a reference to the commitment they make to support their families while they are absent. The use of the term *compromiso* for this commitment evokes the notion of migration as a family rather than a personal endeavor and suggests that migrants as individuals are committed to remitting their earnings to their relatives while neglecting their own needs. Migrants make such *compromisos* for a variety of reasons: to pay back the loans they took to finance their emigration expenses, to cover their families' daily living expenses, to pay their families' monthly electricity and telephone bills, to sponsor the migration of other family members, to pay for the schooling and studies of their children, to pay the medical and hospital bills of family members who fall ill, to finance the construction of a new house, to buy domestic appliances and electronic articles, or to purchase a car. In the migration literature and policy reports, such money transfers are often seen as individual remittances (in contrast to collective remittances sent by migrant organizations) because it is assumed that migrants are acting as individual agents and that they remit out of personal interest. By evoking the Peruvian term *compromiso*, I want to elide the distinction between individual and collective remittances and emphasize that migrant remittances create relationships of exchange between individuals bound up in a network of family commitments. Moreover, by taking my analytical point of departure in the notion of *compromiso*, I underscore the importance of viewing remittances as one of many ways migrants use their money to meet the commitments made when they left Peru.

Essentially, *compromiso* means the personal commitment that Peruvians make to support families or friends at specific moments in their lives. Most commonly, people commit themselves to help close relatives by descent or marriage, but as many Peruvians are *convivientes*—that is, living together in partnerships without contracting marriages—their commitments are often made with their emotional partners. In contrast to relations of consanguinity (between parents, siblings, children, and so on) and affinity (between spouses), which involve strong and long-lasting bonds of reciprocity, *convivir* arrangements are based on temporary ties of trust and support. In the migration context, however, extramarital partnerships are also regarded as a form of *convivir*, and migrants who are married make little effort to hide such affairs, which they often call their second *compromiso*. Even though infidelity may cause tensions in many marriages, it is usually accepted as long as migrants continue to remit money to their spouses or partners in Peru.[1] *Compromiso* may also include relations based on ritual kinship known as *compadrazco* (co-godparentship), which comprise anything from the brief (but sometimes costly) commitment as the godparent of a class of graduating high school students to a lifelong commitment as the godparent of a newly baptized child.

The purpose of this chapter is to explore the relations of obligation and affection that are encompassed in migrants' *compromiso* and that impel them to remit their savings to relatives in other parts of the world. I present 10 case studies of Peruvian families with one or several members living

---

[1] In her study of Peruvian migrants in Chile, Chilean anthropologist Lorena Nuñez Carrasco (2008) points out that a second *compromiso* is based on the very idea of the first *compromiso* and that infidelity during migration is accepted only as long as migrants continue to remit money home to their marriage partners in Peru. On migrant infidelity and remittances, see also Pribilsky (2007).

outside Peru and group them into three sections that reflect different degrees of remittance activity and family involvement in the migration process. By fleshing out the concerns and exigencies in these case studies that make migrants remit and prompt other family members to emigrate, I hope to identify the circumstances in the lives of migrants and their relatives that cause remittance flows to commence, grow, peak, decrease, and eventually dry up.

These 10 case studies are representative of Peruvian migration in several respects. The migrants include five women and five men. In terms of age, the youngest migrant was 23 and the oldest 82 when I conducted the interview. As for the number of years they had lived outside Peru, the time periods range from 2 to 48 years. Geographically, the case studies cover some of Peruvians' major destinations of migration (Chile, Japan, Spain, and the United States) and include migrants from Peru's major cities and regions of emigration (Lima, Trujillo, Chimbote, and the central highlands). Their class and ethnic status also vary. Before emigrating, three migrants belonged to Peru's urban middle class, three to the country's urban lower-middle class, two to the urban working class, and two to Peru's rural indigenous communities. Migrants' class statuses are reflected in their previous income levels in Peru. While three of the migrants belonged to the country's third (and middle) income quintile, three belonged to the fourth (and next to poorest) quintile and four to the fifth (and poorest) quintile. Migrants' educational backgrounds also differ considerably. Four migrants, who also happened to be the oldest in my sample, had received fewer than 10 years of schooling, whereas two migrants had completed the mandatory schooling of 10 years up to high school (*la secundaria*) and four had received some form of supplementary education. Migrants' marriage status varies, too. While three were single and without children, four were either single or divorced with children, and three were married and had children when they left Peru. The majority of the migrants changed marriage status during their stay abroad. Six have married (and two have also had children), whereas one had separated from his wife after emigrating. In fact, only two continued to be married to the same spouse before and after migrating.

Methodologically, the case studies are based on informal interviews with migrants focused on their lives before emigrating, their migration experiences in the receiving society, their family relations after emigrating, and, of particular importance, their reasons to remit. Each case study offers a brief account of how I met the migrants and how I conducted my interviews with them and their relatives in different parts of the world. In 6 of the 10 case studies, I have followed my subjects over a period of several years, interviewing migrants and their families in both Peru and the country of settlement. This has allowed me to observe how remittance flows are initiated, how they grow, how they change direction over time, and how they eventually come to an end. In 3 of the 10 case studies, I had the opportunity to interview my subjects in only one location, and one of the case studies is based on a single interview with the migrant's wife, as I was unable to meet the man in Japan. The different approaches are reflected in the length of each case study. Whereas two of them provide descriptions of long-term remittance flows and four of them offer accounts of the ongoing negotiations that remittance senders engage in with their families, the last four are more focused on single events in migrants' remittance histories.

The Lone Wolf

This section offers four case studies of solo migrants, that is, migrants who were the only members of their households to emigrate. The four migrants represent different strata of Peru's migrant population. Two of them are women; the other two are men. Their ages range from 23 to 82, and their social as well as family statuses vary significantly. Two belonged to Peru's third income quintile before emigrating, one to the fourth quintile, and one to the fifth quintile. While one was married and another divorced at the time of migration, the other two were single.

The case studies also show geographical variations in migrant remittances. At the time of my research, the migrants were living in four different countries (Chile, Japan, Spain, and the United States), and while three of them came from Peru's northern coastal cities, one lived in Lima before emigrating. In addition, the remittances sent by the four migrants served different purposes and were aimed at different family members. One migrant felt committed to financing her younger brothers' education, the second remitted to support his two daughters in Peru, the third to pay for her sick father's medical treatment, and the fourth to pay for the daily living expenses of his wife and children.

The Devoted Commitment

Cecilia was 23 when I met her in Barcelona in 1997. We were both tenants in the apartment of a Peruvian couple (introduced in a later section) who subleased rooms to migrants, and we often spent time chatting in the sitting room on Sundays. In fact, these were the only days I ever saw Cecilia, who worked the rest of the week as a live-in caregiver for a Catalan woman in another part of the city. Unlike the other tenants, who spent their days off shopping, strolling, or visiting friends elsewhere in Barcelona, Cecilia stayed home watching television and writing letters to her family in Peru. Instead of seeking distraction from the daily work routine as a caregiver, she preferred to save her meager income and remit most of it to her relatives in Peru. During our conversations, Cecilia always talked about her family, and she repeatedly assured me that she had no wish to stay in Spain. A bird of passage on her way to a better life somewhere else, Cecilia had only one thing on her mind: to remit money home.

Cecilia was born in Otuzco in Peru's northern highlands. Her parents had migrated to Trujillo when Cecilia and her two older sisters and two younger brothers were young, and the children were raised in Esperanza, a shantytown on the outskirts of the city, where the family owned a humble house and where the children went to school. Cecilia's father worked as a truck driver and her mother sold food in a local market. After finishing school and studying to become a nurse, Cecilia found work as an assistant in a laboratory in Trujillo, but as the salary was very low, she decided to emigrate. Before leaving Peru, she agreed with her older sisters that they would all emigrate for periods of three to five years to work and send money back to their younger brothers so that they could study.

The first to emigrate in Cecilia's sibling group were Cecilia's two sisters, who traveled to Japan in 1992, a country where they had no relatives or friends but which they had been told paid their workers well. Having entered the country on tourist visas, they took work in a factory producing car parts where, according to Cecilia, they made $2,500 a month each. After three months, Cecilia's sisters overstayed their tourist visas and became unauthorized immigrants (that is, documented immigrants who have overstayed their visas). The following year they both remitted $500 monthly to their parents in Trujillo, making a substantial contribution to the family's economy. Unexpectedly, the sisters' stay in Japan was disrupted in 1993 after they were arrested and deported by the Japanese police. Rather than returning to Peru, however, Cecilia's sisters ended up in the United States. In 1997, Cecilia explained to me that her sisters "were put in on a flight to Miami with connection to Lima. But as they traveled during Christmas and the airport in Miami was very busy, they escaped the officers who were looking after them and entered the United States." "Then they went to Chicago, where they married Mexican men and now work and live," she went on. Although Cecilia's sisters managed to elude deportation to Peru in the United States, they made much less money than in Japan. As a result, the remittances they sent home were reduced to less than half of what they had been sending the previous year.

When Cecilia decided to emigrate in 1994, Japan had ended its visa waiver program for Peruvians, requiring them to apply for work and residence permits at the Japanese embassy in Lima. This change forced Cecilia to look for other destinations. Instead of following her sisters, she left for Spain, where a couple of her former classmates were working. She entered the country on a tourist visa, becoming an unauthorized immigrant after it expired. In Barcelona, she found work taking care of an elderly Catalan woman, who later helped her apply to the Spanish authorities for a work permit. She then returned to Peru, where she stayed until the Spanish embassy in Lima called and asked her to collect her work permit. Once again Cecilia traveled to Spain, which she entered this time as a legal immigrant, and in Barcelona she took up the job as the Catalan woman's caregiver. Because the work required Cecilia to live in the woman's apartment, she was able to save and remit most of her earnings. Out of a monthly salary of $1,000, she sent $600 home to her family in Trujillo and saved another $200, which left her with just $200 to cover her rent, transport, and personal expenditures. When I asked Cecilia why she did not spend more money on herself, she answered, "I am very worried about my younger brothers in Peru. I hope they can study and later find work. That's why I send almost all the money I make. My sisters in Chicago are married and have children, so they cannot help much. And I don't think they'll ever return to Peru."

Cecilia told me that even though her employer treated her well and paid her adequately, she did not feel at home in Spain. She emphasized that she missed her family. She added, "In Spain, I work to forget myself. I do not feel any need to go out. I'd rather save the money." Instead of spending her earnings in Spain, Cecilia preferred to save and remit them to her family in Peru. She also said that she felt sad because of homesickness, which periodically made her ill, causing her to lose her hair. Paradoxically, remitting alleviated Cecilia's sufferings by making her feel closer to home, but at the same time it also prevented her from seeking distractions in Spain and spending the money on herself.

When I returned to Barcelona in 2005, Peruvians told me that Cecilia had left Spain and moved to the United States, where she was living with her sisters in Chicago. This remigration from Europe to North America was part of a plan that Cecilia had made with her family: she would work in Spain and send money back to pay for her younger siblings' education in Peru. Once they had finished their studies, the plan was that Cecilia and her family in Peru would all migrate to the United States, which they regard as the most appropriate place for them to be reunited.

Cecilia's case study demonstrates the strong personal commitment many Peruvians feel to sending money back home. As is also evident in some of the other case studies in this chapter, young migrant women are viewed as an important source of remittance income in Peru, in particular when they are single, like Cecilia and her two sisters. Moreover, the case study shows that migrant women often fill this role and disregard their own needs. Thus the migration plan Cecilia made with her sisters deterred her from spending any money on herself except for such basic expenditures as rent and transport. In her own words, to emigrate means to forget oneself. But such migrant sacrifices rarely last forever. Once Cecilia had fulfilled her *compromiso* to support the studies of her younger brothers, she felt free to move on and create a new life in Chicago, where she now lives with her two sisters. Another important observation in Cecilia's case story is her conception of migration as a geographical hierarchy of countries that offer different opportunities to work and remit money home. Just as her sisters did in 1992, Cecilia had initially planned to go to Japan, where salaries are higher than in other migrant destinations. But by the time she had decided to emigrate in 1993, the country had closed its borders to Latin Americans of non-Japanese descent, and she therefore went to Spain, which offered good job opportunities but lower salaries than in Japan. As Spain was not Cecilia's preferred destination, she regarded her stay there as temporary while waiting to be reunited with her family elsewhere. After a number of years, she managed to remigrate to the United States, which both she and her sisters regard as a more promising destination than Europe.

The Tormented Commitment

I became acquainted with Julio during my stay in Washington, D.C., from 2009 to 2010. We met occasionally to take a walk and have something to eat, and I also visited Julio in his home in Virginia, where I was introduced to Soledad, his new wife. These visits opened my eyes to the predicaments the couple faced as, on the one hand, they were eager to create a new life together in the United States and, on the other hand, they were family providers committed to supporting their relatives in Peru. My friendship with Julio and his wife helped me understand why remittances are often not only an issue of concern but also a bone of contention in the lives of migrants and their families.

Julio spent the first 45 years of his life in Peru before he decided to move to the United States. He was born in Piura on Peru's northern coast, where he went to school and spent most of his childhood. As a young man he moved to Lima, where his parents had found work. After several attempts to make a living on his own, Julio got a job as a private chauffeur, first for the Korean embassy and later for an Italian businessman. In the early 1980s, he was hired by the Touring Club in Lima, Peru's major automobile association. The job provided Julio with a stable income until he was laid off during Peru's economic crisis in the late 1980s. Julio quickly found work again, this time as an administrative adviser at the United Nations headquarters in Lima, a job that paid him a very good salary compared to average earnings in Peru. The new work encouraged Julio to propose marriage to his fiancée and to enjoy a comfortable middle-class lifestyle at a time when Peru was experiencing one of its worst crises. In the following years, the couple's two daughters were born, but in the late 1990s the marriage broke up and Julio divorced his wife.

After the divorce, Julio's daughters stayed with their mother, and although Julio moved out and started a new life he continued to support them economically. In 2005, he met a former work colleague, Soledad, who had been living in the United States since her divorce in 1998 and was visiting her family in Lima. Both single, Soledad and Julio fell in love and decided to get married. Upon her return to Washington, D.C., Soledad, who had obtained US citizenship several years before, started the paperwork so that Julio could come to the United States as her spouse. The invitation opened a new chapter in Julio's life. When I interviewed him in 2010, he confessed that he "had never thought of emigrating before. I had a well-paying job and was living a very good life in Lima." Julio continued, "My boss just didn't understand. He kept on saying that I should stay and even offered me leave for one year." Nevertheless, in 2007 Julio quit his job and moved to the United States, which he entered on a temporary stay and work permit.

For Julio, the hardest part of emigrating was not giving up his job and middle-class lifestyle but leaving his daughters behind in Peru. During one of our conversations in 2009–10, he pointed out not only that he was separated from his daughters but also that he was "without a stable income and the economic means to support them." Moreover, Julio found it difficult to live up to his remittance commitment. As a newly arrived immigrant in his mid-40s, who spoke rudimentary English, he could find only low-paid, unskilled work, which hampered his ability to save and made him dependent on Soledad's economic support to remit money to Peru. But Julio also told me that he was determined to save all he made to support his daughters in Peru from the very first day he arrived in Washington. He said that, although Soledad periodically encourages him to go to community college for a year or two to improve his professional skills, he has been very insistent on finding work since he came to the United States. "I didn't come here to study," he explained. "I came here to make money so my daughters can study." He first got a job as a dishwasher in a restaurant making minimum wage, but in 2008 he was offered work as an electrician by Verizon, a big telecommunications company. His earnings from his new job allowed him to remit $800 a month to his former wife and two daughters in Lima. Julio's monthly remittance represented a considerable amount of money for a migrant who makes a living as a low-paid worker (and is more than what most Peruvian migrants can afford to remit) and was possible only because Soledad covered most of the couple's monthly living expenses.

In 2009, the economic situation in the United States deteriorated, and Julio was laid off. Fortunately, he found another job after a couple of months but was able to work and be paid only when work was available. Julio told me that he had been forced to reduce the remittances to his family to $500, which is barely enough to make ends meet for a family of three in Lima. The reduction came at a particularly unfortunate moment because Julio's former wife had stopped working and was living on his remittances along with his daughters. Julio told me that he had called his former wife and said that she needed to find some kind of job so that she could make a little money. "I am deeply concerned that my daughters now have to live on less money," he said. A few months later, Julio's remittance problems went from bad to worse when one of his sisters asked him for money for their mother to have foot surgery. When I met him again in 2010, he asked me, "What am I going to do? I have to send money to my mother, but how am I going to get it?" In fact, Julio already knew the answer. He said that he had asked Soledad for help but that rather than approving his plan to increase his remittances to Lima she had told him to reduce them to have more money to spend in the United States. To Soledad, obviously, sending money to Lima meant supporting not only Julio's two daughters but also his former wife, which she found unacceptable. Julio was therefore caught in a dilemma between creating a new life with Soledad in the United States and remitting money to his family in Peru.

When I got to know Julio in 2009, his daughters were both teenagers, and while the oldest had finished school and planned to enter college soon, the youngest was still a high school student in Lima. "I think of them every day and call them several times a week," Julio exclaimed. "My oldest daughter says all her friends are studying in university and that she feels she's wasting her time because she cannot start to study. The problem is that I don't have the money to pay for her." Instead of using his savings to pay for his oldest daughter's studies in Peru, Julio said that he had invited her to come and stay with him to study in Washington. But because Julio is not yet a US citizen and therefore has to wait several years before he can obtain the right to be reunited with his daughter, he has asked Soledad to apply for reunification in her capacity as the girl's stepmother. Although Soledad had agreed to fill out the paperwork, Julio said, "Of course, I'm happy that Soledad has invited my daughter to come, but it makes me feel more dependent on her. I want to solve my problems on my own."

Julio's remittances embody the true meaning of a *compromiso*, which is to support his family. However, Julio finds it more difficult to live up to his commitment in the United States than he had in Peru. Unlike what his relatives in Lima believe, Julio actually makes less than before he emigrated. Because of the economic crisis, he can find only hourly jobs, which means he has no stable monthly income. Julio's economic vulnerability comes to the fore in his relationship with Soledad, whose expectations of their marriage differ from his. Over the past 10 years, she has managed to bring all of her five children to the United States through family reunification, and today her *compromiso* in Peru is limited to the monthly remittance of $200 she sends to her mother in Lima. Rather than looking back to her past in Peru, Soledad is concerned with her future life as an immigrant in the United States. Moreover, she complains that Julio's monthly remittances are paying living costs not only for his daughters but also for his former wife. In a conversation with me in 2010, Julio said, "It bothers Soledad that I send all the money to my ex-wife. But that's the only way I can do it. She is the mother of my daughters and is the person responsible for taking care of them until I can bring them to the United States." Thus Julio's remittances are a constant source of negotiation and tension with all his close relatives, and only when he has redeemed the commitment to remit can he move ahead to create his own life as an immigrant.

Julio's case study shows how long-term monthly remittances become embedded in family relations and tied to migrants' sense of obligations to their close kin. His story is particularly interesting to this study because it reveals how gender shapes the remittance commitment and the dilemmas it causes. Thus the more Julio tries to live up to his obligations as provider for his daughters and former wife in Peru, the more economically dependent he becomes on Soledad in the United States. Julio's story also shows that although remittances are perceived as one of many acts of exchange between close relatives, they often become the source of conflict and contestation because they take the form of a separate, unidirectional flow of money across national borders. Thus, while Julio's children and mother in Peru regard his remittances as a way to make up for his physical absence, his wife in the United States views them as a drain on their household budget. Of course, tensions over money are likely to occur in all divorced families, but to Julio they are particularly disturbing because he makes less money than before he emigrated and because in a migration context sending remittances is the most tangible and visible way in which he can express his concern and affection for the relatives he has left behind in Peru.

Finally, Julio's case study reminds us that, whereas remittances may be resilient to economic cycles (Julio agreed to send more remittances when his sister asked for money for his mother's surgery, even though his job situation in the United States was very unstable), they are also sensitive to changes in migrants' family organization (once Julio has managed to bring his mother and daughters to the United States, he will stop remitting money to Peru). In other words, Julio's remittances are a way to make up for the hardships that the family's separation causes, and these payments then dry up as soon as the family is reunited.

The Obstinate Commitment

I have met Carmen Irma twice in Chile. In 2005, I was introduced to her by a Chilean anthropologist who was also working on Peruvian migration,[2] and when I returned to Chile in 2007, we met again. In fact, before going to Chile, I had already met Carmen Irma's mother and siblings. During a trip to Peru in 2004, I visited the family in their home in Chimbote, Peru's main fishing port on the coast north of Lima. Carmen Irma's family history struck me because it follows the dramatic rise and decline of Chimbote's fishmeal industry. In the 1960s and 1970s, when Peru was the world's leading fishing nation, the city experienced an unprecedented economic boom.

---
[2] I was introduced to Carmen Irma's family by Lorena Nuñez Carrasco, who at that time was conducting field research for her doctoral dissertation.

The bonanza attracted thousands of migrants from the Andean hinterland, but after the fishing industry collapsed in the late 1970s, Chimbote has been living in the mist of its glorious past. Occasionally, the smell of fish infuses the city's inhabitants with the hope that the fishmeal factories have started hiring again, but mostly the air is as clean (or as dirty) as in other cities in Peru, which makes people think about going elsewhere. Not surprisingly, emigration from Chimbote is high. Yet within her sibling group, Carmen Irma is the only one to have emigrated, which makes her an unusual but also solitary member of the family.

Carmen Irma was born in 1965. Her parents, who both migrated from the highlands when they were very young, met in Chimbote, where they raised Carmen Irma and her six siblings. The father first worked in a steel factory, where he saved money to buy a truck, which later served as a means to earn a living by transporting goods from the highlands to Chimbote. Carmen Irma's three brothers all left school at the age of 16 and found work in the city's fishmeal industry. When I interviewed them in 2005, they were all working in transport, and two of them had moved away from home and were living in other parts of Chimbote. One of Carmen Irma's three sisters had studied to be a secretary and another to be a teacher, while the third ran a small business. The sisters had all formed their own families, and while one was living in Chimbote not far from the family's house, the other two had moved to Trujillo and Lima. In 1995, while Carmen Irma and her oldest brother were still living at home, their father had a stroke and was hospitalized. The incident caused a major crisis in the family because their father was at risk of dying and was no longer able to maintain the family economically. In the following months, the bills for medical care started to pile up, and as Carmen Irma's three sisters and two of her brothers had their own families to take care of, she and her oldest brother, Jhony, had to shoulder the burden of looking after their parents.

In the mid-1990s, Chimbote's fishing industry was at a standstill, and the opportunities to make money were few. While Carmen Irma worked as an assistant nurse in a local hospital making $150 a month, Jhony barely made ends meet as a salesman with several part-time jobs. For several years, they had both been thinking of emigrating to send money home to cover the family's most urgent needs and, if possible, to save capital to invest in a business of their own. In fact, in the 1970s Jhony's employer had offered him a job in Panama, but because his father objected he had to decline the offer. After his father's stroke, Jhony once again considered emigrating. This time he planned to go to Spain, where he hoped to make money to repair his father's truck and take over his business transporting goods. Yet when Jhony learned that the costs of traveling to Spain were almost as high as the mechanic's bill for repairing the truck, he decided to stay at home. When I interviewed Jhony in 2003, he reasoned, "I would have to take a loan of three or four thousand dollars anyway, whether I left for Spain or stayed at home to fix the truck. So I thought, why run the risk of going away, and I decided to stay." In 2005, when I met Jhony again, he told me that he had taken a loan to repair the truck and that he was using it to transport goods from the highlands to Chimbote.[3] Although he still needed to pay back most of the loan, he felt he had done the right thing by staying put in Peru. Jhony concluded, "The last years have been very hard, and the pressure to solve our economic problems has got on my nerves. So I'd rather stay here working with the truck than go to Spain where I have no idea what's waiting for me."

Unlike Jhony, who decided to stay home, Carmen Irma stood firm on her plans to emigrate. In 1999, she borrowed $300 from a friend in Chimbote and left for Chile, where an old classmate of hers was working. She entered the country on a temporary stay permit, which she overstayed, thus becoming an unauthorized immigrant. In Santiago she found work as a live-in nanny and domestic for a Chilean family that paid her $300 a month. As soon as she had paid off her travel debts, Carmen Irma started remitting her entire salary to pay for her father's medical treatment and her mother's monthly bills. In 2005, she told me, "The first year in Chile I didn't spend anything on myself. I sent home every cent I made." Although Carmen Irma was content with her salary, she said that the family treated her very badly. She continued, "The husband made a lot of money, so they paid me well. But they didn't treat me well. When they came home late at night he woke me up and ordered me to cook. He thought that I would work for him day and night all week through." Carmen Irma also complained that the employer's wife tried to prevent her from undertaking supplementary studies to become a health worker. As Carmen Irma recalled, "The woman was always very tough with me. When I asked her permission to take some hours off every week to study, at first she said no. Later she agreed, but when I asked her for a week of vacation to do my practice, she didn't give me permission."[4]

---

[3] Jhony used his mother's house as a guarantee for a bank loan of $3,000 at a monthly interest of 6.5 percent. Making almost $300 a month as a truck driver, he hopes to pay back the loan over a period of three years.

[4] According to Carmen Irma, her employer scolded her, saying, "*Siempre haces lo que te da la gana*" (You always do whatever occurs to you) and added, "*Pero esta familia va a seguir igual con o sin ti*" (But this family will continue the same with or without you).

A year after Carmen Irma arrived in Chile, her father had another stroke. She called home, but as her father could not speak anymore, they could not communicate. Carmen Irma told me with tears in her eyes, "The only thing I could hear on the phone was my father crying." To make things worse, when her father passed away shortly afterward, Carmen Irma could not go back to assist with the funeral because her employers had gone out of town for the weekend and left her with their little son. She asked, "What could I do? I couldn't leave without their permission. And what should I have done with the boy?" To her regret, Carmen Irma never made it to her father's funeral.

Her father's death was a turning point in Carmen Irma's migrant life. The year after his funeral, she went back several times to see her mother and siblings, but rather than affirming her ties to home, the visits made her feel like a stranger in Chimbote. In 2005, she recounted, "All my brothers and sisters have their own families now. I felt that I don't belong there anymore." Even though Carmen's emotional bonds to her family remained intact, she felt estranged from her siblings, who unlike herself had established families. Moreover, after her father had passed away, the need for remittances diminished significantly, and although Carmen Irma continued to send money every month to her mother, she had also started to save part of the salary for herself. Carmen Irma's sense of having attained economic independence not only made her feel estranged from her family in Chimbote but also prompted her to stand up to her employer in Santiago, and she eventually quit her job. During her first year in Chile, her employer had sacked her several times, but she had always managed to make him change his mind and take her back.[5] Knowing that her remittances were no longer needed to pay her father's medical bills, Carmen Irma felt that she had gained the upper hand in her arguments with her employer, and when he once again threatened to fire her because of a disagreement over work, she decided to quit. Two days after the incident, the employer paid her a visit and asked her to return; but even though Carmen Irma agreed to visit his son who had been missing her, she refused to start working for the family again.[6]

---

[5] In 2005, Carmen Irma told me that during her first year in Chile, she imagined herself as two persons, one in Peru and another in Chile, to endure her employer's maltreatment. As she explained, "When I was hired my employer asked for my name. I said 'Carmen Irma' and she replied 'Well, I'll call you Irma.' So I thought, in Chile I'll be Irma but in Peru I'm still Carmen."

[6] Although Carmen Irma was living with friends at the edge of the city, her employer managed to find her. She recalled, "I was really surprised that he came looking for me. This was not a place he used to come. He even apologized and said that it was his wife who wanted to fire me, but that they would be nice to me from now on. He also said that his son was crying because he missed me. That was why I agreed to visit them again."

In 2007, Carmen received her diploma as a health assistant and found work in a private home for an elderly person suffering from Alzheimer's. Although her income was almost the same as before, she told me she felt much happier with the new job. She said that she continued to remit money home to her mother but not as regularly as before because she was now living in a rented room and had to spend part of her salary on rent and bills. Carmen Irma also explained that she was applying for legal residency and therefore not had been able to leave the country and visit her family in Peru for several years. Although Carmen Irma emphasized that she no longer missed home, she claimed that she had no future in Chile and that she wanted to go to Spain or Italy. In other words, Carmen Irma regarded Chile as a mere place to make money to remigrate. She exclaimed, "Here we are just burdened with our duties for a while."[7] During her father's illness, Carmen Irma's stay in Chile was inextricably tangled up with her remittance commitment, but after he had passed away she felt free to continue her journey to other, more promising places.

Carmen Irma's migration story helps us understand the dilemmas migrants face when emigrating to remit money home and the sacrifices such an endeavor entails. Her decision to emigrate was triggered by her father's stroke and the urgent need for medical care it caused. Unlike Jhony (who felt that the prospects of emigrating to Spain were too poor and therefore decided to stay home) and the rest of her siblings (who had already formed families in Peru and therefore never even considered emigrating), Carmen Irma responded promptly to the family's need for money and left for Chile. By choosing the closest and most affordable migration option, she was able to send money home immediately upon her arrival, and although the salaries in Chile are much lower than in other countries, she managed to remit her entire income during the first year to pay the medical bills of her sick father. However, the remittances were possible only because she accepted the maltreatment of her Chilean employers and abstained from attending her father's funeral, reminding us of the sacrifices young migrant women make to support their families. Ironically, although her father's death filled her with grief, it also released her from the burden she was shouldering in Peru and, perhaps more important, induced her to defy her employers and obtain her diploma as a health assistant in Chile.

---

[7] In Spanish, "*Acá somos encargaguidos, de paso.*"

The Platonic Commitment

During my stay in Trujillo in 2005, I visited Magda, who had invited me for lunch in her home in San Andrés, a quiet neighborhood near the city's major university. Present at the lunch were also her sons José Luís and Gastón and Gastón's daughter, Claudita. In fact, I had already acquired considerable knowledge of Magda's life through one of my students, who had rented a room in Magda's house while doing fieldwork in Trujillo in 2003. From my student's thesis, I knew that Magda's husband, Nilo, had been living as an unauthorized immigrant in Japan since the early 1990s and that the couple had been physically separated since he had left Peru.[8] I also knew that Gastón had spent a number of years in Japan before returning to Peru with Claudita. Finally, I had been told that Magda also had a daughter living in Germany. Although I tried to locate Nilo in Oyama, north of Tokyo, where he was living during my visit to Japan in 2005, I never met him. As an unauthorized immigrant, Nilo was reluctant to provide me with an address where we could meet, and being aware of his precarious situation I did not try to encourage him further. I find Magda's story compelling because it illustrates the symbolic meaning of remittances and sheds light on the many subtle ways in which migrants' commitments both affirm and reshape family relations.[9]

Until the 1990s, Nilo and Magda were relatively well off. As the co-owner of a chain of footwear shops in Trujillo, Nilo could afford to buy a house in one of the city's middle-class neighborhoods and maintain the family. Magda, however, took pride in taking care of the children and keeping the household. Although Magda did the daily shopping and cooking on her own, Nilo paid a woman to do the laundry every week. He also paid a gardener to cut the lawn and, when needed, a seamstress to sew new clothes for Magda. On Sundays Nilo invited the family to a restaurant, which allowed Magda to have the "day off" from the kitchen. Magda recalled, "It was a very nice time when we were all together. There was money enough to do what we wanted." This all changed in 1990 when the economic crisis that followed President

---

[8] I am indebted to Kristine Nielsen for helping me arrange my interview with Magda in 2005. Although I made use of her thesis (2003) to prepare for the interview I conducted with Magda, I am entirely responsible for the data presented in this book.

[9] Magda's story is also interesting because it explores the lives of those who stay behind and become dependent on the remittances their relatives send home (Ansion, Mujica, and Villacorta 2008, 2009).

Fujimori's neoliberal politics forced Nilo out of business and crippled the family's economy. Not only did Nilo and Magda have to sell their house, but Nilo and Magda's oldest son Gastón also had to interrupt his studies at the university. As there were no jobs to be found in Trujillo, Nilo and Gastón started making plans to emigrate.

The first in the family to leave Peru was Gastón. In 1991, he married a Peruvian woman of Japanese descent and traveled with her to Japan. As the spouse of a Peruvian whose grandparents had emigrated from Japan, Gastón was granted a stay and work visa in the country. In Japan, Gastón found unskilled work at a factory making almost $4,000 a month, of which he remitted $800 to his family in Trujillo. In 1992, Nilo also traveled to Japan, entering the country on a tourist visa, which he later overstayed, thus becoming an unauthorized immigrant. Just like Gastón, Nilo found work in a factory, but not at the same one as his son. For a while, they both remitted money home, but in 1995 when Gastón and his wife had a child, Claudita, he reduced his monthly remittances to $200. In 1998, Gastón divorced his wife and returned to Peru with Claudita, whom he left with Magda in Trujillo, and moved to Lima to look for work. Meanwhile, Nilo continued to make money as a factory worker, which, according to Magda, provided him with a monthly income of $2,700, of which she received $700 every month. Magda also informed me that after 13 years in Japan, Nilo remained an unauthorized immigrant, which prevented him from opening a bank account in the country and forced him to entrust a migrant friend to remit the money to her. Moreover, Magda said that Nilo's remittances were her only income and that they covered all her expenditures, including the daily groceries, house rent, monthly bills, school fees, and utilities for José Luís and Claudita and, when possible, a woman to wash the family's clothes and a gardener to cut the lawn.

During my visit, Magda was very outspoken about her marriage. Not only did she talk candidly about the remittances Nilo sent her, but she also showed me a box full of letters that she had received from her husband since he left. José Luís, who overhead our conservation, remarked, "I don't understand what's in all these letters. In my generation we don't communicate that way." But Magda assured us both that she always had plenty of things to tell when writing to Nilo and that he too informed her of even the smallest details of his daily chores in Japan in his letters. Moreover, rather than keeping the secrets of Nilo's letters to herself, Magda openly shared them with me (and apparently everybody else) as evidence not only of her devotion to him but also, what is perhaps more important, his continuous devotion to her.

The memories of her absent husband were also present in the many family photos that decorated Magda's sitting room. The photos showed Magda and Nilo as a happy couple before Nilo emigrated and Magda alone with the children after he left. They also included pictures of Nilo and Gastón in Japan and of important family events such as birthdays, the children's graduations, and Magda and Nilo's 25th anniversary, in which Gastón replaced Nilo, filling in the role of the absent husband. Magda explained that she particularly felt Nilo's absence on Sundays and at Christmas, when her husband would call at a certain hour. She never makes appointments with family or friends on Sundays, she said, because she is waiting for Nilo to call. "At Christmas he takes time to speak to all of us for some minutes, and we never give presents to each other until we all have spoken with him," she continued. "You should come back to visit us when Gastón plays Nilo's favorite song on his guitar. It's called 'When My Guitar Weeps.' Then we all start to cry."[10]

Nilo's remittances represent a visible sign of his dedication to his family and, in particular, his affection for Magda, who has been able to maintain a middle-class life in Trujillo during his long absence. And although the separation deeply affects the family, not the least Magda, she and the children are all painfully aware of the pivotal importance of Nilo's remittances for their standard of living in Peru. As Magda told me, "This is not the way it should have been. Nilo and I should have been together and enjoyed our children and grandchildren. But thanks to Nilo I'm doing well. He is a good husband." She also pointed out that many of her neighbors envy her not only because Nilo is working in Japan and makes good money, but also because he continues to be faithful to her. According to Magda, the neighbors receive less money than she does because their spouses work in Argentina, Italy, or Spain and, what is worse, they live with the constant anxiety that their husbands are having affairs with other women and therefore may stop sending money back altogether. Although Magda is better off than most of her neighbors, she too suffers because of her husband's absence. She told me that, even though Nilo sends around $100 to his parents every month for their telephone and electricity bills, his brothers and sister repeatedly reproach her for not contributing to their medical bills. She also said that tensions broke out within the family because of Nilo's absence. While Nilo routinely instructs Gastón and José Luís in their family responsibilities on the phone, the two brothers often argue over daily decision-making. The rift between the two brothers grew wider when Nilo agreed to send money to pay for

---

[10] Magda was referring to "While My Guitar Gently Weeps," a classic Beatles song.

José Luís's university tuition, leaving Gastón to cover the cost of his studies with his own savings from Japan.

Magda's case is proof that by remitting regularly male migrants can act as breadwinners for their families and thus maintain their status as the head of the household for decades. It also shows that over time remittance recipients generate a culture of honoring, memorializing, and paying respect to their absent relatives at family reunions and important holidays, thus prompting migrants to continue remitting money back home and assuring them of their future membership in their families when they return. Similarly, by sharing the sufferings that Nilo's absence is causing her with outsiders such as me, Magda reaffirms not only Nilo's position as the head of the household but also her own status as a middle-class housewife living on the remittances of her faithful husband working in Japan. More bluntly, remittances have allowed Nilo and Magda to preserve the same gender roles that they had before Nilo went to Japan. By underscoring the geographical origin of Nilo's remittances, Magda also makes an important social distinction that places her above her neighbors, who live on the money sent by their migrant spouses in countries considered less attractive as migration destinations. Remittances, in other words, are powerful means with which to claim social status and reinforce economic inequality. Yet while Nilo's remittances help Magda retain her middle-class status, they also discourage her family from adapting to the changing world that surrounds it. As Magda's children come of age, they find it increasingly difficult to follow the verbal instructions of an absent father who regularly calls them from far away but has not been back for almost 20 years. To Magda, Nilo is the bread and butter of her life, but to the rest of the family he is a remote voice from Japan who sends home 700 bucks every month.

Everybody's in the Game

The previous section provided examples of how sole migrants remit money home to their families in Peru. In this section, I show how several family members engage in the migration process and participate in remittance flows. This section provides two case studies that describe how women of a similar age but from very different social classes in Peru play a dominant role in their families' migration. The first woman, who comes from Peru's third-largest city and belonged to the country's poorest income quintile before emigrating, traveled back and forth between Peru and Chile to maintain her husband and children in Peru for several years. When she returned to Peru, her daughters took over the role as family remitters. The other woman comes from Lima and belonged to Peru's third income quintile until she left the country. She emigrated to start a new life in the United States, where she has initiated an extensive flow of remittances that involves numerous family members inside as well as outside Peru. The remittances of both women have played an important role in their household economies, but while the family of the former is still struggling to escape from poverty, the family of the latter has been able to maintain its middle-class status in Peru, suggesting that remittances have little effect on social inequality in the country.

The Unavailing Commitment

I first met Aurora and Juan in 2004 during a short stay in Trujillo, Peru's third-largest city located on its northern coast.[11] I visited the couple in their house in Esperanza, one of Trujillo's many shantytowns, and spent several hours listening to their life stories and migration experiences in Argentina and Chile. In the following years, I revisited the couple several times in Trujillo, and on a number of occasions between 2004 and 2007 I also met several of their children and sons-in-law in Santiago. My interviews with the family introduced me to the world of working-class Peruvians who use migration as a strategy to survive in an urban environment of poverty and marginalization. Unlike better-off, middle-class Peruvians, who prefer to emigrate to Japan and the United States, or Peru's lower-middle class, who have the means to go to Italy or Spain, working-class Peruvians such as Aurora and Juan, who live from day to day in the country's informal sector, view Argentina and Chile as the only opportunity to migrate and to save and remit money. The two countries are accessible by bus, which makes migration affordable for migrants who have no relatives or support network in Japan, Italy, or Spain and who lack the money to go by illegal means to the United States. Yet because salaries in Argentina and Chile are much lower than in other destinations, migration often fails to improve migrants' household economies, as Aurora's case study suggests.

When Aurora was 10 years old, she moved with her parents from her native town of Cascas in Peru's highlands to Trujillo. In 1984, at age 20,

---

[11] Chilean anthropologist Lorena Nuñez Carrasco, who was conducting field research for her doctoral dissertation on Peruvian migration in Chile in 2005, kindly introduced me to Aurora and Juan, two of her key informants.

she married Juan, who had also migrated from the Andes to Trujillo as a child. Like Aurora, Juan had 10 years of mandatory schooling. The couple moved into a humble dwelling of mud bricks and reed in Esperanza on a lot that Juan had inherited from his father. The same year they got married, Aurora found work in a fishmeal factory, while Juan was hired as a driver for a government office in Trujillo. The jobs made it possible for Aurora and Juan to provide for the five children they had in the second half of the 1980s, but in the economic crisis that occurred after President Fujimori came to power, they were both laid off in 1990 and were forced to find new ways to make a living. Aurora started a small business in the neighborhood, while Juan used his car as taxi. Even though they both struggled hard, it was difficult to make ends meet, and as their children grew older Aurora and Juan realized that the only way to survive was to emigrate.

In 1992, Juan received a letter from one of his former colleagues who had left for Spain, inviting him to come and work there. Although he wanted to go, Juan failed to raise the $3,000 he needed for the trip. When I interviewed him in 2004, he said, "At that time my only possession of importance was my car, but even if I had sold it I wouldn't have had the money to go." As Peru's economic situation deteriorated in the mid-1990s, Aurora decided to emigrate, and in 1996 she left for Argentina together with a friend.[12] The two women traveled by bus and reached Buenos Aires in three days. To finance the trip, which cost $500, Juan sold his car. As he recalled, "My sister lent Aurora the money to travel, but because she needed the money I decided to sell the car to pay the loan back. I thought that I could buy a new one with the money Aurora sent back." In Argentina, Aurora found a job as a domestic for an Argentine family making $400 a month, but after three months she gave up the job and returned to Peru to attend to Juan, who had fallen ill.

Because Aurora had used most of her earnings in Argentina on travel and Juan had spent the $350 she managed to save to buy a new car, the family's economic situation continued to be precarious. As a result, Aurora decided to emigrate again, this time to Chile. She financed the trip, which cost $250, by taking out a new loan from a private money lender in Trujillo, and in 1997 she entered Chile on a temporary travel visa that she later overstayed, thus becoming an unauthorized immigrant. Despite her illegal

---

[12] Aurora and her friend had few ideas on where to emigrate. Neighbors had told them that the demand for domestic labor in Argentina and Chile was high, but as they could not decide which of the two countries to go to they agreed to toss a coin. Aurora told me, "My friend picked up a coin and said: '*Cara* is Argentina and *sello* Chile.' So she threw the coin and it was *cara*."

status, Aurora did not have to wait long before she was offered a job as a domestic for a Chilean family that treated her well and paid her sufficiently and that helped her obtain a stay and work permit. When Aurora told me her migration story in 2003, she recalled, "It was a good job and the family was kind. They even paid for my trip back to visit my family in Trujillo. I hardly spent any money in Chile so I sent most of my salary home." Aurora remained in Chile for six years working as a domestic and caregiver for different Chilean families and making between $250 and $300 a month, of which she remitted $200 monthly to Juan and the daughters. Before she went to Chile, Juan had promised Aurora that he would use her remittances not only to cover the family's daily expenses but also to pay for the construction of a new house of solid brick. To provide proof that he was keeping his promise, Juan recorded the construction work on video and sent Aurora the tapes. During her stay in Chile, Aurora also made several trips to Trujillo to make sure that her daughters were fine and to monitor the construction of the family's new house. In 2003, Juan informed Aurora that the house was finished, and the same year she quit her job in Santiago and returned to Peru. In 2004, she told me, "During my years in Chile I was always concerned about the health of Juan and the children, and when my two oldest daughters got pregnant I went home to assist them when they gave birth. Now I want to be here to take care of my grandchildren so I don't really want to go back to work in Chile anymore."

Although Peru's economy had improved significantly during Aurora's absence and her remittances had not only helped Juan and her daughters stay afloat but also financed their new house, the family was still in desperate need of money. The high unemployment rates in Peru's impoverished shantytowns had changed little since Aurora had left for Chile in 1997, and Juan's chances of finding employment looked as gloomy as ever. He continued to drive his car as a taxi but barely made enough money to pay for the gasoline while waiting for his former colleague to invite him to Spain again. Aurora and her daughters, however, knew that the chances of emigrating at Juan's age were close to zero and that a generational shift in the family's household economy was imminent. In fact, during a trip Aurora made with her oldest daughter Rocío to Santiago in 2001, she had introduced Rocío to her Chilean employer. The introduction paved the way for Rocío to return to Chile to replace her mother as the family's remitter, but as she got pregnant the same year she had to postpone her plans to emigrate. Aurora therefore asked Rocío's partner Richard to go to Chile. Richard, whose mother had worked in Chile for several years, agreed, and the same year left for Chile accompanied by Aurora, who had promised to help him settle in Santiago. To finance the trip, Aurora borrowed $500 from a private moneylender in Trujillo. When I interviewed her in 2003, she remarked laconically, "We had to pay 30 percent interest on the loan every month. But there was no other way of doing it." To avoid paying the fee for a temporary travel visa in Peru, they traveled by illegal means for five tense and exhausting days, crossing the border first from Peru to Bolivia and then from Bolivia to Chile. Aurora recalled, "It was a very difficult trip because Richard didn't have any papers. I almost gave up but I knew we had to make it so that Richard could find work and send home money."

Aurora returned to Peru after Richard had found a job in construction. A few months later, Richard was reunited with Rocío, who had traveled to Chile to work for Aurora's former employer, leaving her two small children with their grandparents in Trujillo. When I interviewed Rocío two years later in Chile, she told me that to finance her trip Aurora had borrowed another $300 at a monthly interest rate of 30 percent. Rocío also said that although she was remitting her entire salary of $250, it took Aurora more than a year to pay back the two loans she had taken to finance the family's travel expenses to Chile and the accumulated interest of more than several thousand dollars. In other words, during her first year in Chile, Rocío's entire earnings were spent on the family's travel expenses. To make things worse, Rocío took out a loan from a private money lender in Santiago to pay for a trip she made to Trujillo to give birth to her third child, while Richard borrowed money to cover the costs of obtaining a legal stay and work permit in Chile.[13] To pay back his debt, Richard found a new job cleaning buses at Santiago's bus terminal, working the night shift and making $270 a month. But because Rocío quit her job as a domestic the same year to spend more time with their children, the couple had to struggle hard to pay back their loans and make ends meet. Rocío later found a job as cashier in a supermarket in Santiago making $175 a month. During my stay in 2005 in Chile, I visited Rocío and Richard in the room they had rented and that served as their humble home in Santiago. Rocío claimed, "Now that we have all our children with us we spent almost all our money in Chile. It's very expensive to live here with children, and I hardly have any money to send back to my

---

[13] The trip from Peru to Chile costs around $300, which covers the bus ticket, passport and visa fees, and food for three days. Migrants who already have a passport and entry permit for Chile can make the trip for as little as $100. The cost of the paperwork to obtain a work and stay permit in Chile is between $200 and $400.

parents. Nor do we save money to take with us when we go home to Peru." Rocío's and Richard's family reunification in Chile, then, has been at the cost of remitting and saving money.

On a trip to Trujillo in 2005, Aurora and Juan told me that Rocío and Richard were still in Chile with the children and that Rocío continued to remit money home, although much less than she used to. Aurora and Juan also informed me that their second daughter, Lily, had immigrated to Chile with her partner and that she had left the couple's two-year-old child with them in Trujillo. In Chile, Lily was working as a live-in domestic making $250, while her partner made somewhat less working in construction. Instead of living off the remittances from Rocío, Aurora and Juan were now relying on the money Lily was sending home. Aurora also told me that she planned to send their youngest daughter Sara to Chile to stay with Rocío and Richard. She explained, "Sara doesn't have any *compromisos* yet. If she goes to Chile she can send home almost all the money she makes." By using the term *compromiso*, Aurora was referring to the fact that Sara still was single and therefore had not committed herself to anyone other than the family,[14] which obviously made her the family's best, and perhaps also last, hope for improving their economic situation.

Two years later in Santiago, Richard told me that Rocío had traveled with their three children to visit her parents in Trujillo and that he and Rocío planned to stay in Chile for only a few more years. He also said that Lily brought back her child from Peru and that Aurora accompanied them when they went back to Santiago. Although Aurora had not planned on working in Chile anymore, she took work as a domestic for a Chilean family to pay for the cost of traveling but quit the job after three weeks. Richard remarked, "Aurora is too old to work here, and she returned to Peru because she got ill." When I asked him whether Sara had come to Chile, he replied, "Our economic situation is difficult and we don't have the money to pay for Sara's traveling." Richard added, "We don't want to live in Chile. I would like to go back to Peru and use my savings to open a supermarket in Trujillo, but we can't make that kind of money in Chile. That's why I would like to go to Italy or Japan." Rather than inviting more family members and using more money to travel between Peru and Chile, Richard prefers to save his money

---

[14] Nuñez Carrasco, who studied Peruvians in Chile, reports that married migrants often use the term *segundo compromiso* for their love affairs and partnerships with other migrants. She claims that having such extramarital affairs is accepted among migrants as long as both partners continue to remit money home and stay loyal to their families in Peru (2008, 141).

to remigrate to other, more profitable destinations, where salaries are higher than in Chile, and eventually to return to Peru to set up a business.[15]

Even though Aurora and her daughters have migrated for more than a decade, their economic situation remains much the same as in 1996. With the exception of the house they built while Aurora was in Chile and the kitchen hardware and electronic equipment that Rocío and Lily periodically bring with them when visiting Trujillo, their savings and remittances have contributed little to improving the family's fragile household economy. In fact, most of the money remitted during their many years in Chile has been used to cover daily expenses such as food, local transport, school supplies for the children, and electricity and telephone bills and, ironically, to pay back the loan they took out to travel to Argentina and Chile in the first place. To Aurora's family, migration is a way to survive in a time of high unemployment and urban poverty rather than a means to increase savings and achieve social mobility. Much like their parents, who moved from the highlands to Trujillo 50 years ago in a search of a better life, Aurora and Juan both hoped that Argentina, Chile, and Spain would offer them a way out of their economic problems. But their dreams never materialized. Unlike what Juan had imagined, the cost of traveling to Spain was too high, and, unlike what Aurora had expected, salaries in Argentina and Chile were too low to lift her family in Trujillo out of poverty. In addition, because Argentina and Chile are easily accessible by bus, Aurora and her daughters have spent a large part of their earnings on traveling back and forth to visit Trujillo. Aurora's traveling is particularly conspicuous because it has generally been prompted by her concern for her family's health and well-being, which is evidence of the predominant role of women in the transnational engagement of Peruvian migrants in Argentina and Chile. Arguably, this engagement allows migrant women to stay in close contact with their families in Peru and thus to act as breadwinners and caregivers at the same time. Yet, whereas the women's frequent traveling between Argentina, Chile, and Peru helps them maintain their links with home and strengthens their position as decision-makers in their households, the many loans they take out at high interest rates increase their economic vulnerability and reduce their ability to save. Thus, while Argentina and Chile offer affordable destinations to poor people who live

---

[15] Richard told me that one of his friends who lives in Japan has invited him to come. The friend is married to a Peruvian of Japanese descent, who has offered to adopt Richard so that he may obtain a legal work and a stay permit in Japan. Richard had also considered going to Miami, where an uncle of his is living.

in Peru's urban shantytowns and work in the countries' informal sector, the remittances the poor send home from the two countries contribute little to improving their living conditions.

The Polyphonic Commitment

I got to know Elena in 1986 at a time when she was working as an assistant for international organizations and nongovernmental organizations and enjoying a comfortable middle-class lifestyle in Lima. In the years that followed, I was also introduced to Elena's closest family members, including her husband, children, parents, uncles, aunts, siblings, nieces, and nephews. My friendship with Elena has offered me the opportunity to follow the movements of her family in and out of Peru and, of special importance to this study, the intricate chain of remittance exchanges that tie them together across national borders. When we first met in 1986, the only one to have emigrated among Elena's relatives was an uncle, who had been estranged from the rest of the family for many years. Today, Elena's relatives are dispersed across three continents.

In 1987, Elena left Peru to marry an American she had met in Peru. The decision to emigrate not only implied giving up her middle-class lifestyle in Peru but also taking her seven-year-old son out of a prestigious private school in Lima and enrolling him in the local public school in North Carolina, where the newlywed couple had planned to start their new life together. Moreover, Elena and her son had to say goodbye to the rest of their family, including Elena's parents, her two sisters and brother, several nephews and nieces, and an uncle and aunt. Although the first years in the United States were difficult, Elena and her son have fared well in the United States. Her son has received a college degree and now works in Los Angeles, and Elena has studied to become a high school and community college Spanish teacher. A few years after she came to the United States, Elena and her American husband also had a daughter, who recently received a college degree.

Elena has spent almost 25 years in the United States and is now a US citizen. However, her ties to members of her family still living in Peru remain strong. Her aging parents periodically visit her in the United States, often for long periods, but even though Elena recently tried to coax them to stay with her, they declined her offer. In 2005, Elena commented, "I once made my parents come to stay with us, but they found it too difficult to adapt. They don't speak English, and it's not easy to make new friends when you get older. Moreover, during the week when I was working and my children attended school they spent all day alone. So they started to long for home and after six months they returned to Peru." Nevertheless, Elena's parents are not alone in Peru. Her older brother Memo, his daughter and a niece, and an uncle and aunt also live in Lima.

Elena's family network outside Peru is almost as big as her network within the country. Her two sisters, Goya and Nena, immigrated to the United States with their families in 2000 and 2002. Throughout the 1990s, her sisters' husbands earned a living as white-collar workers in Lima, but they were both laid off when Peru experienced economic difficulties in 1997. Like thousands of other middle-class Peruvians, the two sisters and their families faced the difficult choice of either experiencing a dramatic decline in their standard of living or leaving the country in search of a new but unknown life as immigrants in the United States. Both families chose the latter option and traveled to the United States on tourist visas, which they overstayed after three months, thus becoming unauthorized immigrants. Unlike Elena, Goya and Nena have had a hard time getting established in the United States. According to Elena, their husbands had been able to find only low-paid, blue-collar jobs, which curbed the families' efforts to achieve social mobility and create stable lives for themselves in the United States. While Goya, her husband, and their two youngest children, who are both minors, had obtained legal residence, the couple's third child, who at that time was 25, continued to be unauthorized.

Nena and her family, however, emigrated two years after Goya and were still struggling to obtain legal residence in the United States; and although Nena's two sons wanted to get into college, the family lacked the means to support them financially. At the time of my interview with Elena, Claudia, Nena's third and oldest child, was living in Lima, where she had studied law at a private university and was working as a lawyer in a well-paid job. A final piece in the migration puzzle of Elena's family is Memo's son, Juan José. In 2005, he emigrated to join his mother in Japan, where she had been living since she divorced Memo in the late 1990s. Before migrating to Japan, Juan José had a child with a woman from whom he later separated. In 2010, Elena told me that the child was living with its mother in Chile.

Elena has been sending money back to Peru since she left the country in 1987. In 2009, she told me that for 22 years she had been remitting $80 to her parents every month to supplement the pension her father receives as a retired schoolteacher. Periodically, Elena sends money to other members of the family too, including her aunt, who lives on her own in Lima but cannot afford to pay the salary of her domestic servant. Elena also used to send smaller but regular remittances to her nieces and nephews to pay for their studies in Lima, but she stopped remitting when they graduated from college. Another part of Elena's remittances consists of the money she sends on a more irregular basis to purchase airline tickets for her parents to visit their family in the United States and to contribute to the organization of family events. Another reason for these one-off remittances, which may vary from a few hundred to more than a thousand dollars, may be to pay the medical and hospital bills of family members who fall ill, as happened in 2009 when one of Elena's uncles contracted cancer. Finally, Elena remits smaller amounts of money to individual family members at Christmas or on their birthdays. In contrast to the regular monthly and irregular one-off remittances, which Elena described as true commitments, she said that these contributions were meant to *compartir*, that is, to share. As she explained, "I've made a commitment [*compromiso*] to support my parents and I sometimes send money home to support my family when someone falls ill or they are in urgent need, but I may also send money back to, let's say, my mother, niece, or brother, which they can spend on themselves. In this way I share [*yo comparto*] my money with them."

In 2010, Elena told me that her two sisters also remitted money to Peru. Just like Elena, Goya sends monthly remittances to her parents and smaller amounts to other relatives as well. According to Elena, she and Goya pool most of the remittances they send in a single money flow, which allows them to save the fees for wiring money separately and to exchange information about how it is used. At the end of each month, Goya deposits the money in a bank account she shares with Elena and sends it directly to their relatives in Peru. Although Elena and Goya rarely remit the same amount of money, the recipients do not know exactly how much each of the two sisters has sent and precisely what needs the money is intended to satisfy until they receive notifications from Elena or Goya by telephone. One of the recipients is their brother Memo, who lives with his daughter in Goya and her husband's apartment in Lima. To pay the rent, Memo wires $1,000 every month to Goya's personal bank account in Florida. Meanwhile, Elena and Goya send Memo money to supplement his income in Peru and to finance his daughter's studies. In other words, money circulates back and forth between the three siblings in a series of exchange acts that makes them senders and receivers at one and the same time. Yet, according to Elena, they are all perfectly aware that the sums Goya and Memo send to and receive from each other make up two distinct acts of exchange. While Goya (and Elena) sends money to Memo to cover the cost of his daughter's studies, Memo sends money to

Goya to pay his rent. As Elena pointed out, "The money we send to Memo is not for him but for his daughter. He makes his own money to pay the rent. Of course, we do not know how he makes this money. But he knows that it's very different money." The use of the term *different money* is a key trope in Elena's account of her remittances, revealing that the continuous flow of money relies on a mutual agreement between sender and recipient on how it is classified, managed, and eventually used.[16]

Nena, Elena's second sister, sends monthly remittances to her parents, too. Although Nena used to send money to her daughter as well, she stopped remitting when Claudia graduated as a lawyer from one of Lima's universities in 2005 and began to make her own money. In fact, Claudia's graduation not only released Nena from her commitment to support her daughter but also triggered a major change in the remittance flow that keeps Elena's family afloat. In 2009, Nena's husband, who had been the family's breadwinner since they had arrived in the United States, lost his job. To help her parents pay their bills, Claudia has started to send them monthly remittances, which makes Nena and her husband remittance receivers as well as remittance senders. Furthermore, after Claudia graduated and began to make her own money, Nena has entrusted her daughter with the role of remittance manager. Instead of remitting her contributions directly to her parents, brother, aunt, and other family members, Nena now sends the money to Claudia, who then distributes it among her relatives and monitors how they spend it. This reorganization of the remittance flow pays off in two ways. First, by pooling all the money into a single remittance, Nena saves the fees it would cost to send several separate remittances. Second, by using her daughter as an intermediary, Nena feels more certain that the money ends up in the hands of the right persons and that it is spent the right way. Thus, every month she and her two sisters remit a total of $150 to their aunt, who lives by herself in Lima, to pay the domestic who works for her. However, instead of remitting the money directly to the aunt, as they used to, or to the domestic, who happens to be a remote relative of the family, Nena sends the three sisters' contributions to Claudia, who then pays the domestic her monthly salary. Thus by assuming the role as both remittance

---

[16] Research from other parts of the world also provides evidence that remittances are classified according to their destination or intended use. In a study of the impact of remittances in Nepal, Ann Vogel and Kim Korinek examine the use of what they label "special monies"; that is, remittances in foreign currencies are associated with more value than domestic transfers and remittances from India, and are spent exclusively on education (2012, 71).

sender (Claudia sends money to her parents and brothers in California) and remittance distributor (Claudia relays her mother's and aunts' remittances to their relatives in Lima), Claudia serves not only as a remittance manager in Elena's family but also as a facilitator of communication between Elena and her sisters in the United States and the rest of their family in Peru.

Another family member who participates in the remittance flow of Elena's family is Memo's son Juan José. For almost 10 years, Juan José and his mother (Memo's former wife) have lived and worked as unskilled factory workers in Japan, remitting money monthly to Memo in Peru and to Juan José's former wife in Chile. Just like Elena and her two sisters, Juan José has made a *compromiso* to provide for his family, but, as Elena pointed out to me, unlike his three aunts in the United States, his commitment involves close relatives in two countries, Peru and Chile. On the one hand, Juan José and his mother send monthly remittances to Memo in Lima to pay the school fees of Juan José's sister, who is 17 and studies in Lima. To ensure that the remittances have arrived all right, Juan José regularly calls his sister, who also updates him on Memo's use of the money. On the other hand, Juan José sends money every month to his three-year-old daughter, who lives with her mother in Chile. But in contrast to his sister's monthly reports on Memo's use of the remittances in Lima, Juan José's former partner provides him with little if any information on her use of the remittances he sends to Chile. As Elena pointed out to me, "It's a long way to travel to Chile from Japan just to know that your money has ended up in the right hands."

Elena's family history makes it possible to view the remittance flow from the perspective of different family members and sheds light on the tensions and conflicts that prompt senders and receivers to shift roles in the remittance flows, causing them to reverse direction or change course. By creating a picture of remittances as a web of social relations in which money flows not only from migrants to nonmigrants but also from nonmigrants to migrants (reverse remittances) and sometimes in several directions between a group of migrants and nonmigrants (multiple remittances), Elena's case questions the analytical value of the term *remittance* in understanding the social and moral meaning of transnational money flows. It also challenges conventional ideas of remittances as a simple money transfer between a sending migrant and a receiving nonmigrant by showing that all the migrant's family members participate in the flow by sending, relaying, managing, or receiving money, and that remittances therefore carry the fingerprints of not just two but many individuals. Finally, the ethnographic insights discussed here suggest that, although money does not come tagged with instructions, remittances are always followed by a call from the sender to the receiver (whether by phone, Skype, or other means) to specify the proper recipient and what need the remittances are intended to satisfy. More bluntly, my data reveal that remittances reinforce existing bonds not only of trust and affection but also of power and control. The remitters want to know, first, who received the money and, second, how it was spent. Although the receivers at the other end of the flow may be hesitant to provide all the requested information, they are painfully aware that the fuel that keeps money flowing is accountability and the trust it entails. Obviously, in Elena's family such accountability and trust thrive best among members of the same sex. Thus, Claudia receives and relays the remittances that Elena and Nena send to Memo and their aunt; similarly, Elena and Nena send their monthly contributions to their parents in Lima to Claudia, who then forwards them to her grandparents. As a remittance manager, then, Claudia facilitates the family's money flow across gender and generational boundaries. Her cousin Juan José, by contrast, provides proof that male migrants often have difficulties in gaining information on the use of the remittances they send home.

The remittance flow of Elena's family not only spans several continents and involves a large number of people but also blurs the boundaries between senders and receivers. While most studies of remittances present them as unilateral flows of money from a migrant (the sender) to his or her household in the home country (the receiver), this case study documents how remittances can be part of a chain of relations of exchange between many family members related by both consanguineous and affinal ties. Elena's family also provides a case in point for a remittance flow that extends over three generations and therefore lasts for several decades. Moreover, it shows how gender shapes the webs that connect remittance senders and recipients and how these webs are enacted and reinforced through the remittance flows. Finally, it suggests that remittance senders and receivers are tied together in relations not only of concern and affection but also of accountability and supervision, and that the money that circulates in the remittance flows makes up a critical means of communication and exchange among family members in such disparate places as Chile, Japan, Peru, and the United States.

Mission Accomplished

The first two sections of this chapter showed how remittance flows not only grow in size but also become more complex as more family members engage in the migration process. By contrast, this section demonstrates what happens when migrants stop remitting. The four migrants presented in this section originate from very different social and regional backgrounds in Peru. While two migrants, a woman and a man, come from the cities of Lima and Trujillo, the other two, both males, spent most of their lives in rural communities before emigrating. Two of the four migrants belonged to Peru's fourth income quintile (the next to poorest) and the other two to the country's fifth income quintile (the poorest). Their remittance commitments also vary. One migrant engaged in labor migration to the United States with the specific aim of remitting money to his wife and saving capital for his return. The other three left Peru because they wanted to start a new life abroad. Whereas two of them remitted money home on a regular basis for a longer period, the third made only one substantial remittance in his entire life. Eventually, they all stopped remitting: one because she obtained family reunification with her close relatives, another because he reached the age of retirement, the third because he lost contact with his relatives in Peru, and the last because he severed his ties with his wife and children.

The Weary Commitment

While conducting field research in Barcelona in 1997, I rented a room in Vanesa and Telmo's apartment for two months. We quickly became friends, and I spent many hours in their company, either at the kitchen table in the apartment or in the city running errands or shopping. The couple paid their rent by subleasing most of the apartment to other Peruvians, and I thus came to know a large number of migrants during my stay. Moreover, as Vanesa and Telmo's telephone was located in the room I rented, I was frequently a circumstantial witness to the calls they received from Peru (see Lindley 2009). These often took place after midnight because of the time difference of six hours; and although it was difficult to actually hear the voice of the person on the other end of the phone, Vanesa and Telmo's responses clearly indicated that it was always someone asking for money. I soon learned that these calls came from families in Peru who had taken out loans to make ends meet and who were asking Vanesa and Telmo for money to pay overdue (and exorbitant) interest rates. Although the couple separated and moved out of their apartment shortly after I left Barcelona, I managed to locate and interview Vanesa when I returned in 2004.

Vanesa's parents are both rural-urban migrants from Peru's northern highlands who have struggled hard to provide for their six children and offer them an education. Before emigrating, Vanesa worked as a secretary in Trujillo, Peru's third-largest city on the north coast of the country, where she had spent her childhood and gone to school. When she lost her job in 1991, she decided to go to Spain, where a sister of her boyfriend, Telmo, was living. She arrived at a time when Peruvian migration to southern Europe was starting to gain momentum, and the borders of the European Union were still open to Latin Americans. She entered Spain on a tourist visa, which she overstayed three months later. Vanesa remained unauthorized until she was granted legal residency by the amnesty issued by the Spanish government in 1992. Upon her arrival, Vanesa quickly found a job as a domestic worker in Barcelona, where she rented a room with Telmo's sister. In 1992, Telmo followed her, and together they rented a flat in central Barcelona and sublet some of the rooms to other Peruvians. While Vanesa continued to work as a domestic, Telmo found work in a factory.

During the 1990s, Vanesa and Telmo invited several of their relatives in Peru to come to Spain. The first to travel was Vanesa's sister Julia, who came to Barcelona in 1995. Like most other Peruvian women, she found job as a domestic for a Spanish family. The next to be invited to Spain was Nely, a cousin of Vanesa's, who also came in 1995. Like Julia, she entered the country by illegal means. A couple of weeks after her arrival she was introduced to a family that agreed to apply for one of the annual work permits that the Spanish government issues for Latin Americans to take work as domestics. In the late 1990s, Telmo managed to persuade his Spanish employer to file the papers required to hire yet another of Vanesa's sisters in Peru, who was waiting to come to Spain to work. In 2000, the employer's application was approved, and the same year the sister arrived in Spain and entered the country on a temporary work permit. For the first few years, Telmo helped bring Vanesa's relatives to Spain, but in the late 1990s he increasingly felt that her family was becoming a burden for them. As he explained in 1997, "I want to save money to buy my own flat one day. Where we live now, the house is full of relatives arriving from Peru. And I'm always afraid that my employer feels that I'm exploiting him too much." When I revisited Vanesa in 2004, she told me that she and Telmo had broken up four years earlier and that she was now living with their six-year-old son and her mother, who had come to Spain in 2003 to be reunited with Vanesa. Two more sisters had also arrived in Spain since my last field visit to Barcelona and had gone to work as domestics. The last remaining members of Vanesa's family in Peru are her two younger brothers. In 2005, Vanesa told me that she hopes they will come to Spain once her mother has been granted Spanish citizenship and has thus obtained the right to apply for family reunification with her sons.

Helping relatives come to Spain had not been Vanesa and Telmo's only commitments in Peru. Throughout the 1990s, they both remitted $200 to their mothers every month, and from time to time they sent money to other relatives as well. Both Vanesa and Telmo have painstakingly told me how remote family members repeatedly ask for money to pay telephone and electricity bills and to meet urgent needs such as interest on loans and payments for school uniforms and supplies.[17] Other relatives have also requested economic help, although on a more irregular basis. Thus Vanesa remembered how once an uncle and at another time an aunt called her to ask them to send money because someone in their families had fallen ill or had had an accident. She also recalled that the parents of one of her godchildren in Trujillo called several times because they needed money to pay for one of their children's education. She commented that "they don't understand that although we are paid in euros, the cost of living is much higher here. The first times I visited Peru, I brought money to give to my cousins, nephews and nieces, but now they expect that I will continue to send them money when I'm in Spain." She claimed that she knows all too well that when the telephone rings at 2 a.m., it is a relative from Peru calling to ask for money. "Sometimes when I don't have any money, I don't answer," she continued. Rather than send all her savings to Peru, Vanesa said she felt that it was time for her to think about her own and her son's future. "It's now up to my sisters here in Spain to do their part," she said. "The only family members in Peru are my two younger brothers, and once they come to Spain I don't have to send money to Peru anymore."

During my stay in Vanesa's and Telmo's apartment, I witnessed the sacrifice they were making to remit to Peru and bring relatives to Spain and the tensions it was causing between them. While Telmo preferred to invest their hard-earned money in their future in Spain, Vanesa continued to feel committed to use it for her family members in Peru. When I returned to Barcelona in 2004, I found Vanesa was living by herself with their son. I also discovered that Vanesa and Telmo had both brought their mothers and several other

---

[17] By offering Vanesa and Telmo prepayment of my monthly rent, I also learned that I could help them raise the money their relatives were requesting. In this way, I not only engaged in a relationship of mutual trust and support with Vanesa and Telmo but also became an agent in the flow of remittances I was studying.

relatives to Spain. In other words, they had both lived up to their individual family commitments in Peru, but at the cost of their own family life in Spain. Moreover, Vanesa told me that she had become weary of supporting her relatives in Trujillo and that she would rather save her earnings for herself and her son in Spain. Just as Telmo seven years earlier had complained that Vanesa's *compromiso* had become a burden for their marriage, she too was now dreaming of a life free from the need to send remittances back home.

My case study of Vanesa's migration experience is evidence of the dilemmas migrants face when balancing their commitments to those they left behind in their country of origin and their struggle to construct new lives in the receiving society. Unlike the marriage problems of Julio and Soledad that were caused by disagreements over whether Julio should have used his earnings to support his daughters and former wife in Peru, Vanesa and Telmo both felt committed to supporting their relatives back home. Their disagreement was not a question of whether they felt committed to remit or not, but the price of that commitment. Loyalty to consanguineous and affinal relatives is a well-known source of conflict in all families, but such conjugal tensions are particularly prevalent in migrant households because they invest so many resources in helping the family members they have left behind and because most marriage partners feel more committed to supporting their own relatives than those of their spouses. The case study also sheds light on the tension between remitting money back to the sending country and bringing newcomers to the receiving country. When emigrating, most Peruvians believe that their migration is temporary. They think that a few years of hard work abroad will satisfy their family's need for remittances and allow them to save enough money to construct a new house, start a business, or pay for the education of their children in Peru. Contrary to their expectations, their stay often lasts much longer, which prompts many to look for ways to reunite with their families in the receiving country. As the formal procedure for obtaining family reunification in most countries takes many years, migrants often find themselves in a situation similar to Vanesa and Telmo, who have remitted money to maintain relatives in Peru for more than 15 years and at the same time struggled to bring them to Spain. Rather than using their earnings to achieve social mobility in the receiving society or to save capital to invest in their home country, they continue to remit most of their money to close as well as remote family members, who view them as an infinite source of support. The only way Vanesa and Telmo could redeem their *compromiso* was to bring them all to Spain.

The Redeemed Commitment

I got to know Emilio when I was living in Washington, D.C., in 2009 and 2010. He spent every weekday at a daycare center for elderly Latinos located close to my apartment, and I made it a habit to pass by occasionally and chat with him. During our short but frequent conversations, Emilio introduced me to his eventful and exciting life as an immigrant in the United States and his moving but sad experience as a remittance sender to his family in Peru. I have never met any of Emilio's relatives in Lima or Washington, D.C., and am therefore unable to present their interpretation of his role as a family provider. Although it is likely that they would offer a different version of Emilio's situation, his narrative is important because it highlights the moral predicaments that drive migrants to remit money for an entire lifetime.

Emilio has spent most of his 83 years in the United States. He was born in La Victoria, a working-class neighborhood in Lima, and raised in a family of two children; his father worked as a carpenter and his mother as a housewife. Emilio's only sibling, an older sister, is the child of his mother's previous marriage with a man from Huancayo, a provincial city in Peru's central highlands. After Emilio finished school, his father taught him carpentry, which became his profession for the rest of his life. In 1953, Emilio got married, and in the following years he and his wife had five children in their modest home in La Victoria. Although Peru experienced an economic bonanza in the 1950s, Emilio had to work hard to maintain his family, and in 1960 the marriage broke up and Emilio divorced his wife.

In 1962, Emilio's sister invited him to come to the United States, where she was making a living as a domestic for an American family in Washington, D.C. The sister had worked for the same family when they lived in Peru and traveled with them when they returned to the United States in 1952. In 1955, Emilio's sister quit her job, which she found unrewarding, and found work as a waitress in a restaurant in Washington. The same year she was granted permanent residency in the United States, which also gave her the right to be reunited with her mother and two children, who were living in Peru. In 1960, Emilio's sister, mother, and nieces all became US citizens, and two years later it was Emilio's turn to emigrate. When I interviewed him in 2010, Emilio recalled that he had just gotten a divorce and "thought it was a good idea to try something new. I was always very close to my mother," he said, "and as both she and my sister were living in the United States, I wanted to visit them and maybe stay there. I also thought that it could a good opportunity to offer my children a better life."

When Emilio arrived in the United States, he first stayed at his sister's place but moved out after a couple of months and rented a room for himself. Emilio soon found work first as a waiter in a restaurant and later as a carpenter in a construction company, and for almost 40 years he continued working in both jobs. In the mid-1960s, he became a US citizen, which allowed him to invite his five children to come to the United States through the family reunification program. They all accepted his invitation and came to Washington, D.C., in the early 1980s. Although Emilio felt happy that his children made use of the opportunities he offered them, their reunion did not turn out the way he had expected. One of his two daughters was killed in a gun fight in Los Angeles, where she was living with her Hispanic boyfriend, a few years after she arrived in the United States. The rest of Emilio's children returned to Peru in the late 1980s. Emilio claimed that his children left because they were not used to hard work. "Their mother had spoiled them," he said. "They returned to Peru because they didn't like the way you have to work to make your own money in the United States." Upon their return, the four children all married and established families in Lima, where they were living at the time I interviewed Emilio.

From the time he left Peru in 1962 until he retired in 2002, Emilio remitted $200 every month to his family in Peru. Initially, he assumed that his former wife was spending the money on their children, but after they grew up he had little idea how the money was used. All he knew was that someone in the family collected the money he remitted. "I gave up long ago asking how the money was being spent, but I felt the obligation to continue sending money," he said. The only break in the remittance flow occurred during the years when Emilio's children stayed with him in the United States. When Emilio retired in 2002, he traveled to Lima to inform his children that he could no longer afford to send them money and that he would therefore stop remitting. To his surprise, the children became upset and insisted that he should not just continue sending money but increase the monthly amount. The 2002 visit was Emilio's last trip to Peru, and he has had no contact with his children and grandchildren since he returned to the United States. In 2010, at the age of 83, Emilio claimed that he no longer expects to go back to Peru and that he wants to be buried next to his mother's tomb in the same cemetery in Washington, D.C., where she lies. He felt that he had done what he could to support his children since he emigrated in 1962. His remittances are evidence of this commitment. In Emilio's own words, "I have lived up to my obligations (*yo he cumplido*). That's all I can do."

Emilio's lifelong remittance flow embodies the quintessence of a *compromiso*. For 40 years, the $200 was a monthly signal from Emilio to his children that he had not forgotten them and that he continued to identify as their father, although they were all living thousands of miles apart. The children's response to his decision to stop remitting when he retired at the age of 75 (and when his four children were between ages 45 and 52) is an example of the instrumental power of children who receive remittances from their parents. Their breakup of the relationship with their father still upsets him, and he continuously referred to it with bitterness in our conversations in 2010. Yet, eight years after Emilio stopped remitting, he has come to terms with the fact that he may never see his children again and that he will end his days in Washington and not in Lima, where they live. To Emilio, 40 years of remitting has redeemed him from all his failings as a migrant father.

The Repentant Commitment

During my stay in Los Angeles in 1998, I spent numerous afternoons with Rómulo in his workshop in Hollywood. He always took time to talk with me extensively about his life in the United States. I was especially intrigued by the bearing that Rómulo's remittance experience had on his narrative. All life stories are biased by the narrator's current view of the past (Ochs and Copps 1996). This bias is particularly evident in migrants' life stories, which tend to focus on experiences related to their decision to emigrate. In 1998, Rómulo pictured his life in two parts: one before emigrating, which he portrayed as hotheaded and eventful, and another after emigrating, which he described as agonizing and remorseful. While Rómulo recounted the first part in the past, he narrated the second in the present, thus attributing importance to the hardships he had suffered after arriving in the United States. In Rómulo's life story, these sufferings are closely associated with his decision to remit all his savings when his brother in Lima contracted cancer.

Rómulo was born and raised in Cora Cora, a village in the province of Paricocha located in the department (region) of Ayacucho, in 1940. At the age of 18, he moved to Lima, where many people close to his age from Cora Cora were living. They helped him get established, and after a couple of years he had saved enough money to rent a printing workshop in downtown Lima. In the following years, Rómulo received several offers to emigrate. In 1961, a cousin who was living in Los Angeles invited him to come to the United States, but Rómulo declined the offer. And in 1969, his former girlfriend from Cora Cora, who was working as a domestic in Boston, tried to persuade him to go, but also in vain. When I met Rómulo in Los Angeles in 1998, he said that going to the United States just did not interest him then. "I was having a nice time in Peru," he said. "To tell you the truth, I was a womanizer in those days. I had girlfriends everywhere, and I even had three children who were living in Cora Cora. Why should I leave?"

In 1982, Rómulo's life took a dramatic turn. At the age of 42, he fell ill and was hospitalized, and during his recovery he started to reflect on his way of life and to rethink his plans for the future. As he explained in 1998, "I had hepatitis and spent much time wondering about my life. I realized that I had to choose one among all the women I had been chasing." He then decided to ask his girlfriend from Cora Cora to marry him and to invite him to come to Los Angeles, where she was working as a domestic.[18] The woman, who had migrated to the United States in the late 1960s and who had been granted US citizenship in the 1970s, accepted Rómulo's proposal and traveled to Peru to marry him. Two months later, Rómulo entered the United States on a temporary resident visa, which he had been granted as the newly wedded spouse of an American citizen.

When I interviewed Rómulo, he recalled the years after he arrived in Los Angeles as extremely tough. His first job was parking cars at a big mall, but at age 42 he was too slow to compete with the other car parkers. Rómulo recounted that he "had to run in order to get the cars. But the other guys were much younger than me. They were 20 or 25 years and I was 42. They were faster than me, so I almost didn't make any money." Then he got a job in a factory, but only by telling the employer that he was 10 years younger. "It's hard to emigrate when you're 42," he said. "Nobody wants to employ someone at my age. They all want young people. They run faster and work harder." Two years later, he got a job at a printing workshop owned by a Spaniard, but although Rómulo was happy to work in the same profession he had had before he migrated, he felt exploited and badly treated by his employer. After a couple of months in the new job, he was ready to give up and return to Peru. "One day I sat down and wanted to cry," he confessed. "I wanted to give up everything. But then I began to believe in God, and while I was praying I felt that someone placed his hand on my left shoulder,

---

[18] Rómulo told me that his girlfriend went to Cora Cora every second year for the village's annual fiesta, always in even years. In 1982, he traveled to Cora Cora to search for her and found her. Rómulo explained, "When I arrived in the village, I followed the procession. And imagine what happened? I looked into my girlfriend's house, and there she was!"

and I heard him saying that I shouldn't give up." Rómulo continued to work for the Spaniard, and after short time he had saved $500, which he used to buy his own printing machine and start his own business.

To Rómulo, the possibility of working on his own represented a turning point in his life as an immigrant. As he recounted, "The truth is that the 500 dollars wasn't enough. But the American who sold me the machine didn't count the money right. And you know, after paying I had just enough money to pay someone to transport the machine to my home. He only helped me to get the machine down from the truck but then I had to carry it myself from the street to my garage. Today, I don't know how I managed to carry it by myself, but I did it." Six months later, however, the local authorities ordered him to close the workshop in his garage. Rómulo therefore rented a small shop in Hollywood and moved the printing machine again. At the beginning, the business went fine, enabling Rómulo to save $12,000, which he decided to use to help his aging parents in Peru. "I never had so much money in my hands. I always wanted to help my parents, so I decided to buy them a house in Lima," Rómulo told me. Unfortunately one of his brothers contracted cancer the same year, and instead of buying a house for his parents, Rómulo decided to send all his savings to Lima to pay for his brother's medicines and hospital bills. Shortly after Rómulo had sent the money, his brother passed away. Rómulo remarked bitterly, "My brother died, and I couldn't do anything to save him."

Although Rómulo sometimes thinks about returning to Peru, he hesitates to go back because of his family in the United States. In 1995, he invited his three children, who were born in Peru, to come to the United States through family reunification. Two of them have married North Americans and are living on the East Coast, while the third lives with Rómulo and his wife in Los Angeles. He also has relatives in Ohio and Texas, which makes him feel as much at home in the United States as in Peru. As he explained in 1998, "When I came to the United States, I was too old to start a new life. Of course, I could have gone before when I was young. But I didn't do it. Now most of my family lives in the United States, so returning to Peru is difficult. My wife travels almost every year for the fiesta in Cora Cora. But I have only been back once in the last 15 years, when my father died in 1996."

Rómulo's life first as a rural-urban and later as an international migrant has been both adventurous and erratic. Until he was 42, Rómulo enjoyed the life of a bachelor in Lima, but as a migrant, he found himself in an entirely new role as the provider not only for his family in the United States but also for his relatives in Peru. His story is noteworthy because it shows how important a single remittance can be in a migrant's life and exemplifies the role remittances play in migrants' sense of themselves as a morally good or morally bad person. Although Rómulo toiled hard to establish a business in Los Angeles, he never accomplished what he felt was the most important commitment in his life: to buy a house for his parents in Lima. His remorseful narrative illustrates the meaning that remittances have for migrants' sense of morality and responsibility, even in situations when they fail to live up to their *compromisos*.

The Broken Commitment

I met Bernardo on a sunny spring day in 1998. At that time he was 38 and working as a shepherd in the California desert. One of his former work mates accompanied me on the two-hour trip from Bakersfield to the small trailer where Bernardo was staying with two other Peruvian herders. After we had been introduced, Bernardo offered me a tour of the area and showed me how he lived and worked. Later I invited them all to California City, the nearest town, where we spent the rest of day eating, drinking, and playing billiards and where the three herders told me about their migration experiences. During a previous period of fieldwork in the herders' home communities in Peru's central highlands, the villagers had provided me with extensive second-hand information on the lives of their relatives working as shepherds in the United States, but visiting them *in situ* was a very different experience. In particular, I was stunned by the wretched living conditions they had to endure and the physical seclusion that prevented them from communicating with their relatives in Peru during most of their stay in the United States. Notwithstanding these hurdles, Bernardo and his colleagues asserted that they appreciated the work because it allowed them to remit and save money.

Bernardo was born in Corpacancha, a former hacienda and later peasant cooperative in Peru's central highlands. In the early 1970s, two of Bernardo's brothers went on three-year contracts to work as shepherds in the western United States. The contracts were brokered by the Western Range Association (WRA), an organization that hired shepherds in Peru and other countries to work for sheep ranchers in the United States. In 1979 at the age of 17, Bernardo joined his brothers and traveled to the United States. His first work contract was on a ranch in Oregon, where the dense woods made sheepherding and the life of a shepherd particularly hard. When I met Bernardo in 1998, he told me that he suffered a lot because he had to sleep in a tent while living in the mountains even when it got cold and snowed. He also said that transport was difficult and that the ranch owner, who was of Basque origin, did little to make life easier for his employees.

In 1983, Bernardo left on his second contract, which sent him to California to work for an American rancher, who turned out to be friendlier than the Basque. Upon his return to Peru in 1986, Bernardo spent his savings on a van, which he used to transport villagers between their rural communities and Huancayo, the major city in Bernardo's home region. The van provided Bernardo with a steady income for some years, but in the late 1980s Peru's political crisis and battered economy made transportation an unprofitable business. Furthermore, in 1990 Bernardo got married and, as he had spent the savings of his first two work contracts in the United States on maintaining the van, he decided to apply for yet another contract. In 1991, the WRA accepted his request, and the same year Bernardo went to work for another ranch owner in California.

In 1994, he returned to Peru but left again in 1996 on his fourth contract to work for the same employer. During Bernardo's absence, his wife and their three children lived off his monthly remittances. Of his monthly income of $700, Bernardo said that he was able to send $300 back to his wife and put another $300 away into savings. Asked how he managed to make ends meet on the remaining $100, he replied, "Look, where I work there is nowhere to spend your money. My employer provides all the food we need and I don't pay for accommodation, so I save almost all my earnings."

In 1998, Bernardo also claimed that he was planning to return to Huancayo for good to set up a new business when his contract expired the following year. "I have worked in the United States for almost 20 years and it's time to return," he said. "My children are getting older and I want to spend more time with them. During my contract I have saved enough money to start a business in Huancayo." However, when I visited Huancayo in 2000, Bernardo was still in the United States. Relatives of his told me that instead of returning he had become an unauthorized immigrant and that he had stopped remitting money to his wife in Peru. They also said that Bernardo planned to marry a Mexican woman and that because she is a legal resident in the United States, he hopes to apply for a stay and work permit and in this way become a legal resident. Rather than fulfilling his *compromiso* to his wife and children, returning to Peru, and setting up a business in Huancayo, Bernardo had decided to create a new life for himself in the United States. Arguably, the many years of hard work and solitude had estranged him from his family and induced him to break his *compromiso* to remit and to return.

Bringing It Home

This chapter has shown how remittance flows evolve in response to migrants' role in the household economy and the needs of individual family members. More specifically, it examines how these two factors mold migrants' concerns for other family members and shape their commitments to remit at three stages in the migration process: (1) when only one member of the household migrates and remits, (2) when several members migrate and remit, and (3) when migration and remittances come to a stop. The four migrants in the first section, "The Lone Wolf," were all solo migrants; that is, migrants with no other family members in their new country of residence. The purpose of their migration was either to sustain their families in Peru, to cover major or exceptional expenditures in their household economies, or to finance the migration of other family members. The second section, "Everybody's in the Game," explored what happens to remittance flows when several family members emigrate. The two case studies, which are the most comprehensive in my sample, discussed how remittance flows penetrate the entire household economy over time and restructure gender and generational relations in migrants' families. The last section, "Mission Accomplished," examined four cases of migrants who have either been reunited with their families, have severed their ties to them, or have simply lost contact with them. The aim of this section was to examine what makes migrants stop remitting and to investigate how migrants and their families reorganize when the remittance flows dry up.

The 10 case studies convey two different but complementary tales. They can be read as a collage of unique stories of the concerns and needs that prompt Peruvian migrants to remit. The ethnographic insights of these stories challenge the conventional wisdom of remittances in several ways. While the migration literature often makes an analytical distinction between individual and collective remittances, my material suggests that, although migrants sometimes pool their money in a single remittance to save the bank fees, they regard this approach as a collection of individual remittances rather than as a single collective remittance. These stories also show that after remitting migrants usually make phone calls to instruct their relatives in the use of the money they have sent and that this communication is highly gendered and shaped by the sender's and the receiver's opposed positions in the remittance flow. While migrants' major concern is to know that the money arrived in the right hands and will be spent as agreed, such information is often difficult to obtain either because the receiver is reluctant to provide it or because the remittance has become part of other money flows. In a similar vein, these stories reveal that because migrants view women as more responsible than men and therefore have more trust in them, they often ask their female relatives to act as financial stewards of their remittances. This insight helps us understand why women often appear as the principal recipients of migrants' remittances in migration surveys and statistics, which rarely make a distinction between remittance recipients and remittance beneficiaries.

Another important insight is that in some remittance flows, money circulates in several directions at the same time, proof that the border between remittance senders and recipients is blurred and that remittances are sums of money that flow not only from the developed world to the developing world but also in the opposite direction. The vicissitudes of remittance flows also remind us that remittances are acts of exchange between family members and therefore should be seen as transactions in an ongoing process of negotiation between senders and recipients. It is often argued that remittances are more resilient to economic uncertainty than other forms of investment because in times of hardship migrants feel even more committed to supporting their relatives. My own data, however, suggest that migrants' commitments also encourage them to finance the migration of their families and thus to reunite with them in the receiving country. Family remittances, then, last only as long as migrants and their relatives are separated. Finally, several of the case studies shed light on the many sacrifices that migrants make to remit money home. While some submit themselves to the abuse of their employers for long periods of time, others become indebted for years to pay travel costs, refrain from traveling to important family events, or break up their marriages and sever their ties with the very same relatives for whom they made all the sacrifices to help in the first place.

My case studies can also be read as an illustration of the power relations and structural constraints that shape Peruvian migration. From this perspective, they make up a continuum of different degrees of migration engagement and remittance activities in migrant families that come from different social strata and regions in Peru and that have migrated to different countries in the world. Although economic studies show that remittances make a significant contribution to reducing the poverty rates of migrants' countries of origin, my data show that economic inequality often remains unchanged in their home regions. My study reveals that because migrants from the country's poorest households often spend more money on traveling than they save and remit home, migration rarely improves their families' living standards.

It also shows that in times of economic crisis middle-class families prefer to use migrant remittances to sustain their levels of consumption and thus avoid downward mobility.

In a country like Peru, where the vast majority of emigrants come from the urban middle and lower-middle classes, the relative deprivation of the poorest sectors of the population is especially notable. Another peculiarity of these stories is the dominant role of women in both the migration process and the flows of remittances. My research clearly shows that male migrants remit with the same dedication as female migrants. Nonetheless, in many of the countries receiving Peruvian migrants, the labor market offers better opportunities for women than for men. Indeed, except for Japan, where Peruvians primarily take up factory work and where for a number of years male labor has been in greater demand than female labor, women occupy a dominant position in Peruvian migration. This difference in gender relations is enhanced by Peruvian women's conventional role as caregivers of the elderly and children and their strong sense of family commitment. A final observation of importance is the regional imbalance in Peru's remittance economy. Even though migration from the country's rural communities has been growing in the past decade, as I shall demonstrate in the following chapter, the impact of Peru's remittances is felt primarily in its major cities. As migrant remittances in an urban context are overwhelmingly spent on domestic consumption, it is therefore unlikely that migrants will make any significant investments in Peru upon their return.

Chapter 4

Voluntad:
The Community Commitment

In the previous chapter, I discussed the importance of the remittances that migrants send to their families in Peru. In this chapter, I follow the remittances that migrants send home to their communities, which are known as acts of *voluntad*. Many Peruvians are members of hometown associations, religious associations, or cultural institutions that provide services and make contributions to their villages of origin or donate money (or goods) to people in Peru who are in need. Sometimes migrants remit the money they raise in such collections individually, but mostly they pool it and either send it collectively or bring it with them when they travel to Peru.

In the migration literature, such acts of *voluntad* are often described as collective remittances, in contrast to money sent as *compromiso*, which are individual remittances (Altamirano 2010, 60–66; Boccagni 2010; Delgado Wise and Márquez Covarrubias 2008; Lacroix 2013; Orozco 2005). This is regrettable because the use of the terms *individual* and *collective remittances* blurs two important analytical distinctions in the study of migration. The first usage concerns the different commitments that prompt people to remit money. Here, migration scholars need to distinguish the money migrants send home to their families from the money they donate to institutions and organizations in their country of origin. The second usage concerns the way migrants remit money home by sending it either individually or collectively. To maintain these two distinctions and avoid confusing the *purpose* of remitting money with the *way* it is remitted, I center the analysis of this chapter on the commitment that drives migrants to contribute and make donations to their home communities, rather than on the specific way they transfer, wire, or transport these contributions and donations from their places of residence to their places of origin in Peru. Consequently, just as in the previous chapter I examined migrant remittances to close relatives through the lens of *compromiso*, in this chapter I explore migrant remittances as they take place through acts of *voluntad*. As in my examination of *compromiso*, I study *voluntad* as the outcome of the commitments migrants have made to their home communities. Yet, as I shall show, unlike *compromiso*, which obliges migrants to support a narrow group of relatives for a long period of time, *voluntad* implies an optional commitment to a broad range of community members often in the form of a single act of altruism or charity.

In Peru and other Latin American countries, *voluntad*, which literally means "social volition," indicates a commitment that is prompted by altruism and that signals people's readiness to serve the wider community. Usually, *voluntad* takes the form of money donations (or donations of goods), voluntary work, or political lobbying to assist one's native village in Peru or of such support to an institution (a neighborhood organization, a religious congregation, a professional association, a political grouping, a soccer team, or a leisure club, for example) in their region of origin in Peru or simply to their fellow Peruvians. Unlike *compromiso*, which in the migration context is synonymous with a commitment to remit money on a regular basis over a long period of time, *voluntad* indicates a commitment triggered by migrants' spontaneous desire to "do something" for their home region or country. Commitments in the form of *voluntad* are therefore rarely long term, and their symbolic value is often considered more important than their material value, even though this is often huge, as I shall demonstrate below. The nature and magnitude of *voluntad* can vary considerably. The term can refer to anything from contributing annually to the home community in Peru, to making small monthly donations to religious organizations that look after the orphans and homeless of Lima, to donating money (sometimes in significant amounts) to help with natural disasters or other emergencies, to giving development aid for specific projects, to sponsoring a once-in-a-lifetime religious fiesta in a remote village that costs many thousands of dollars and entails huge personal and financial sacrifices for the people involved. Yet, whether *voluntad* implies a donation to help migrants' fellow countrymen, a fee for development in their region of origin, or the sponsoring of a fiesta to celebrate the patron saint of their home village, it has the same motivation: to support the communities that the migrants belonged to before emigrating, whether economically or otherwise.

Voluntad embodies the spirit of the gift, and migrants' contributions, services, and donations therefore receive much attention from relatives, friends, neighbors, and fellow villagers, who read them as a sign of the giver's *fieldad* (loyalty or devotion) to their communities in Peru. Migrants' contributions and donations also rank high on the agendas of nongovernmental organizations (NGOs), government institutions, and international organizations in whose eyes Peruvians living abroad are economically privileged and morally obliged to share some of their wealth with their fellow Peruvians. Hence, migrants are careful in selecting the moment or occasion of the donations and services they offer and, perhaps more important, in calculating their size. By meeting or, even better, exceeding the receivers' expectations, migrants hope not only to gain their gratitude and respect but also to affirm their own status as successful "children" of their home communities and build up social capital among other migrants. *Voluntad*, then, is a Janus-faced relationship of exchange with people in Peru that allows migrants both to demonstrate their readiness to help their compatriots in Peru and to bring their own influence to bear in their home communities.

The chapter examines the commitments of rural migrants, who make up only a small fraction of Peru's total emigration but nevertheless are much more likely to engage in *voluntad* than other migrants. This section is structured around three case studies of Andean rural districts that have experienced extensive international migration in past decades. The case studies offer a brief introduction to the districts' community and migration history and a discussion of the contributions migrants make to their home communities. These contributions take different forms in the three cases: in the first, as a *fee* to improve community services; in the second, as a form of *sponsorship* to celebrate the village's patron saint; and in the third, as a *donation* to renovate a church and construct a computer center. As in the previous chapter, the case studies illustrate different degrees of migration intensity and migrant engagement and shed light on how flows of money, goods, and services begin, gain momentum, and dry up.

The data in this chapter were collected by various means. I have conducted long-term fieldwork in the two rural districts that make up the first case study since 1983 and have visited the district that makes up the second case study regularly since 1985. My research in the rural district that makes up the third case study has been less extensive and is based on somewhat shorter visits in 2005. My study is the outcome of multisited fieldwork that includes several trips to the United States, where I visited migrant communities from all four districts on several occasions between 2004 and 2008. The case studies are based on informal interviews with migrant leaders and individual migrants in Italy and the United States and are focused on such questions as migrant networks, migrant organizations, communication between migrants and village leaders, remittance flows, and participation in public events and fiestas in the districts. I also participated in migrant reunions, fiestas, and meetings in Peru as well as in Italy and the United States, which has helped me understand the importance of the different contextual settings in which migrants engage in *voluntad* commitments, donate and remit money, and interact with their communities in both Peru and the receiving society.

Rural *Voluntad*

Recent studies by Andean scholars demonstrate that highland communities in Bolivia, Ecuador, and Peru are undergoing important changes, leading to the increasing commercialization of agricultural production and to more modern lifestyles, as well as consumerism, international tourism, and social conflicts (Colloredo-Mansfeld 1999; Goldstein 2004; Kyle 2000; Meisch 2002; Travick 2003). Andean scholars have also shown that migration and globalization are radically transforming the communal life of Andean society, causing not merely a growing rift between rich and poor but also new forms of differentiation along gender, generational, and ethnic lines. One of the most important forces for change is migration from Peru's rural areas to its major cities and transnational migration to other countries in the world (Altamirano 2010; Paerregaard 1997, 2008a; Miles 2004; Pribilsky 2007). In this massive exodus, migrants play a critical role in their home communities as the main agents of external influence as well as the focus for internal tensions and divisions between those who are linked to networks facilitating migration and those who are not (Berg 2008).

The chapter contributes to the growing body of literature on changes in Andean communities by comparing the social and cultural meaning of migrants' remittances and engagement in four rural districts. Its aim is to explore the following aspects: first, how migrants create networks and establish communities in the receiving society; second, how migrants spend their earnings and engage in activities in their villages of origin; and third, how this engagement affects relations of inequality and power between the villages and the migrants. The four districts are Usibamba, Chaquicocha, Cabanaconde, and Bolognesi, located respectively in Peru's central, southern, and northern highlands. They are approximately the same size (populations between 2,000 and 4,000) and have all experienced significant changes in past decades caused by land reforms, political violence, international tourism, and out-migration. Nevertheless, the migration histories of the four districts are quite different. In Usibamba and Chaquicocha, rural-urban migrants have settled mainly in provincial towns and cities in the Peruvian highlands, whereas international migrants have been traveling to the United States on temporary job contracts to work as shepherds for the past four decades. In the two other districts, rural-urban migration to Lima and other cities in Peru dates back to the first half of the twentieth century, and immigration to the United States is more than 30 years old. Yet while immigration to the United States from Cabanaconde is almost entirely undocumented, immigration to the United States from Bolognesi is predominantly legal.

Since these differences in the migration histories of the four districts—ongoing circular labor migration in Usibamba and Chaquicocha, permanent undocumented migration in Cabanaconde, and permanent documented migration in Bolognesi—are reflected in migrants' engagement in their villages of origin, I use them as an organizing principle for the section. Another guideline in structuring the section is the kind of *voluntad* that migrants offer their home villages and the contributions and activities that it includes. Whereas in the first two districts, *voluntad* takes the form of a *fee* that migrants pay to ensure continuous membership in the community, in the third districts it refers to migrants' *sponsorship* of the annual celebration of its patron saint. By contrast, in the fourth district *voluntad* consists of the collective *donations* that migrants make to development projects and the construction of a new church. I develop my analysis of *voluntad* by first reviewing the community histories of Usibamba, Chaquicocha, Cabanaconde, and Bolognesi, and then examining how rural-urban and transnational migration is organized in the four districts before finally discussing how migrants contribute to their development.

The Fee

Over the past 30 years, labor migration to the United States has provided the population of Alto Cunas and other pastoral areas of Peru's central highland with an important source of income. Traditionally, the main economic activities in this region, situated between 3,600 and 4,000 meters above sea level and at a distance of 40 kilometers from the city of Huancayo, are agriculture combined with stockbreeding. Although agricultural production is primarily for local consumption, pastoral products such as meat, milk, cheese, furs, and wool are sold in weekly markets either in the villages or regionally in Huancayo, Jauja, and other cities. This trade, which provides the villagers with an important source of income and links them to the national economy, is spurred by the region's close location to Lima and a fairly well-developed transportation system. Other important economic activities include temporary salaried work in the mining industry. Until the land reform implemented by the military government of President Velasco in 1969, the population also found employment in the haciendas and big estates specializing in stockbreeding, the main commercial activity of the hacienda economy in the central highlands for centuries. When the wool trade was booming on the world market and the sheep-ranching industry prospered at the beginning of the twentieth century (Manrique 1987, 254–61), the ranchers began to encroach on the highland pastures, causing great tensions between the mestizo-owned haciendas and the Indian communities (Smith 1989, 67–96). The conflicts deteriorated after the American mining company, Cerro de Pasco Corporation, bought vast areas of pastureland in the central highlands from a Peruvian sheep-ranching company in 1924 and engaged in stockbreeding on a large scale (Mallon 1983, 214–43). In the aftermath, the region witnessed numerous land invasions by peasant communities claiming back land that had been encroached upon by neighboring haciendas and mining companies (Caycho 1977, 26–28; Vilcapoma 1984, 112–33).

However, it was not until Peru's military leaders expropriated the large estates and the foreign-owned mining companies at the beginning of the 1970s that the hacienda system lost its dominating influence in the region (Roberts and Samaniego 1978). To spur economic development in the country's rural society, the government introduced a cooperative model that integrated the former haciendas and the peasant communities into cooperatives called SAIS (Sociedad agrícola de interés social). The cooperatives were formally owned by former hacienda workers, who were paid a monthly salary and ensured such rights as health care, schooling, and housing. The neighboring peasant communities were also associated with the SAIS and had the right to receive part of the profits of the cooperatives and to enjoy the same privileges as their workers (Caycho 1977). Thus, in 1972 the district of Usibamba (population: 3,618) became an associated member of the SAIS

Túpac Amaru, one of the largest cooperatives established in the region, together with 15 other peasant communities in the region. In the following year, the neighboring district of Chaquicocha (population: 3,634) joined the SAIS Heroínas de Toledo, a much smaller cooperative with only two associated peasant communities. Subsequently, first Usibamba (in 1972) and then Chaquicocha (in 1980) implemented a so-called *reestructuración de tierras* (restructuring of the land), an official term used for the expropriation of privately owned land and its redistribution in equal shares among the village households. The shares amount to 5.5 hectares, which the household can keep as long as its members are able-bodied. When the head of the household retires, the community receives half the share, and when he or she dies, the community receives the other half.

The villagers in Usibamba and Chaquicocha also created their own cooperatives, formally known as *comunidad campesinas* (peasant communities), which became the official owners of village land after the "restructuring." Village households that received land were granted membership (*comunero*) in the peasant communities on the condition that the household leaders live permanently in the villages and participate in the community general assemblies (*asamblea general*) and community work days (*faena*) (Paerregaard 1987, 80–84). Failure to comply with these requirements could lead to expulsion from the community (*descalificación*) and the seizure of the land the household had been granted the right to use. Moreover, with the support of a German aid organization, Usibamba and Chaquicocha established a communal company (*empresa comunal*) that was made responsible for the commercialization of the community's herd of more than 2,000 cattle and the management of its grocery store, truck, tractors, and agricultural machines. Households enjoying the status of *comuneros* automatically became members of the cooperatives too, with the right to receive a share of its annual profits and to benefit from services such as shopping in its store and leasing its tractors and agricultural machines (Paerregaard 1987, 73–79). The idea of reform was to include everybody in the peasant communities and the communal companies, but a small group of villagers who make a livelihood from trade and other nonagricultural activities were denied membership. Even though these households were granted a small lot on which to construct a house and put up a shop or workshop, they have neither a right to the land nor the right to attend and vote in community assemblies. As a result, the restructuring of the land created a division between the majority, who had status as *comuneros*, and a minority, whose status as *no comuneros* restricts them from cultivating the land and making their voice heard in village affairs (Nuitjen and Lorenzo 2009).

When Peru's military government stepped down in 1980, it left a political vacuum that was soon filled by the Maoist rebel group Shining Path. In the early 1980s, the rebels gained ground in the Ayacucho region in southern Peru, and in the mid-1980s they extended their activities into the central highlands. Upon entering an area, Shining Path severed the villagers' ties with the regional market and government institutions, dissolved their community organizations, and introduced a social order in accordance with the revolutionary slogans of Marx and Mao (Paerregaard 2002a). Initially, Shining Path received the support of many villagers, who felt deceived by the promises of the newly elected democratic government, but as the rebels started to recruit members by force and punish villagers who refused to feed and house them, the support rapidly diminished. Shining Path was finally defeated after the Peruvian army entered the Alto Cunas area in the late 1980s, encouraging the villagers to form local militias known as *rondas campesinas* to offer the rebels fierce resistance. Although it was the Peruvian army that introduced the idea of forming *rondas campesinas* in the Alto Cunas area to gain peasant support in the fight against Shining Path, the *rondas* soon took the form of a genuine peasant movement that expanded from northern Peru to almost every part of the Peruvian Andes.

The aim of the land reform introduced in the 1970s was to dissolve the haciendas, nationalize the mining companies, and form agrarian cooperatives and peasant communities in the highlands. However, the reform also had unforeseen consequences, which triggered a labor migration from the peasant communities to the United States that has lasted four decades. Throughout the twentieth century, the American-owned Cerro de Pasco Mining Corporation bought land from neighboring haciendas, and at the time of the reform it owned large flocks of sheep in the central highlands. In 1972, the company's properties in Peru were expropriated, and when its employees returned to the United States they acted as brokers between the Peruvian shepherds they had worked with before the land reform and American sheep ranchers of California, Colorado, Idaho, Montana, Nevada, Oregon, Utah, and Wyoming.[1] Until the mid-twentieth century, the ranchers contracted mostly with Basque shepherds, but as the Spanish economy started to prosper in the 1970s these shepherds lost interest in working in the United States. Subsequently, the ranch owners began recruiting Mexicans

---

[1] Pericles León reports that the first Peruvian shepherds arrived in the United States in 1969 (2001).

and Chileans and later Peruvians, who were seeking new work opportunities in the wake of the land reform in Peru.[2] In a few years, Peruvians exceeded Mexicans, Chileans, and Basques in numbers, and today migrants from the former haciendas and peasant communities in Peru's central highlands make up the chief source of cheap labor for American sheep ranchers.[3] Most of the shepherds are recruited through an association called the Western Range Association (WRA) based in Sacramento, California. An engineer who worked in the American mining company before the land reform and who moved to Lima after the expropriation acted as a contracting agent for WRA for several decades (León 2001, 147).[4] In the early 1990s, the man retired and was replaced by his son, who is now responsible for the recruitment.[5] According to data collected by the engineer and his son, more than 3,000 Peruvians have worked on American sheep ranches on H-2A visas in the past 30 years, and currently almost 2,000 Peruvians are working for the WRA.[6] In Usibamba almost 10 percent of the male population and in Chaquicocha more than 15 percent of the male population are currently working in the United States. The number is even higher when shepherds who lived outside the villages or were working in Peru's jungle or mines before going to the United States are included. Many of these shepherds are second-generation rural-urban migrants born in Huancayo, Lima, and other Peruvian cities who worked as schoolteachers, factory workers, or

---

[2] Since 1965, changes in immigration policies have made it more difficult for Latin Americans and other migrants from developing countries to enter the United States. However, as US immigration legislation allows the import of foreign labor to take jobs American workers are unwilling to do, Mexicans, Chileans, and Peruvians recruited as shepherds meet with few legal obstacles. Although immigration has become a growing concern with the American public and an issue pursued by many politicians to win votes, agribusinesses continue to import foreign labor on H-2A visas.

[3] Peruvians in California report that the WRA also tried to import shepherds from Mongolia but stopped recruiting because of language difficulties.

[4] During my interview with the engineer, he told me that the first shepherds he sent to the United States came from the Corpacancha hacienda (northwest of Huancayo) in Peru's Junín department (region), where he had worked as an administrator up until the land reform in 1969 (after 1970, Corpacancha became part the SAIS Pachacútec cooperative).

[5] Before recruiting new shepherds, the engineer submits them to a medical examination. He also conducts personal interviews with them, interrogating them about sheep breeding techniques (grazing, shearing, calving, diseases, and the like) and their families and communities of origin.

[6] The engineer in Lima who is responsible for the recruitment of new shepherds to the WRA claims that over the past 30 years, 3,800 shepherds have passed through his office. While approximately 1,000 have returned to Peru, almost 2,000 are currently working on contracts in the United States. More than 800 have overstayed their H-2A visas, however, and have either settled in the United States (as legal or unauthorized residents) or returned to Peru on their own account. Two other organizations are reported to be recruiting Peruvian shepherds in the United States.

businessmen before immigrating to the United States. Some shepherds have even studied at universities in Peru, and a few hold academic degrees.

Although labor migration to the United States offers the shepherds an important opportunity to earn in dollars, it also requires huge personal sacrifices. Even though several shepherds often work on the same ranch, they spend long periods in solitude and isolation while grazing the sheep in the desert or mountains of the western United States.[7] The shepherds are usually responsible for overseeing and attending to 2,000 to 3,000 sheep, but as some ranchers have more than 30,000 sheep, the distance between these shepherds is often great. The employer provides the shepherds with shelter, food, vehicles to transport water for the animals, and a small TV operated by batteries, which is their only access to information and news from the outside world. Periodically, the *campero*—the foreman or ranch owner—comes by to inspect the sheep and deliver food, and only on rare occasions do the shepherds get together or go to town. The H-2A visa permits the shepherds only to herd sheep, but some report that they are ordered to ranch cows, construct fences, and do agricultural work as well. In addition, many sleep in small camping cars or in tents despite the harsh climate of the mountains and deserts, where temperatures fluctuate between 30 degrees centigrade below and 40 above zero. The shepherds also say that they live off canned food most of the time and that the water they drink is dirty. Similarly, some catch dangerous diseases such as valley fever, which is caused by the dust that blows in the desert and the insecticides the ranchers use; and they may be injured using tools or driving vehicles without a proper license or instruction.

---

[7] Shepherding in the western United States follows a three-stage annual work cycle. From December to March, the shepherds are brought down to the ranch, where they have the opportunity to meet other migrants. It is also a demanding time, with hard physical work. Although the principal activity in this period is the lambing, many ranchers order the shepherds to do the fencing as well, a job that often causes serious back pains. In April, the shepherds take the sheep to the pastures for grazing, and after another two months they continue pasturing the sheep in the mountains until it is lambing time again. The work cycle differs according to geographical location and individual ranch owners. Some shepherds explain that they pass most of the year on the ranches doing all sorts of work, while others report that they spend all spring, summer, and fall in the desert, woods, and mountains, often incommunicado for weeks or months on end. Yet others work as *camperos*, who deliver food and goods to employees who work outside the ranch. In California, the shepherds are often sent up to the mountains in the northern part of the state from April to December because the pastures are greener there than in the south in the summer and fall. In Idaho, Montana, Oregon, and Wyoming, however, where the pastures are more plentiful but also more remote, the shepherds sometimes spend part of the year in tents isolated from the outside world because of snowfalls.

To make things worse, shepherds report that they are sometimes denied medical treatment when they fall ill or have accidents and that the employers meet their complaints about working conditions with threats of physical violence (Paerregaard 2011a). While *gringo* employers are said to be demanding but fair, employers of Basque origin are known to be harsh[8] and particularly feared because of their bad temper and rough language.[9] Claims have also been made that shepherds are beaten up, disappear, or even perish under circumstances that have not been officially investigated.[10] Similarly, some deplore the fact that it is extremely difficult to document or obtain access to data on these incidents as many shepherds are afraid to contact the authorities, and the health, labor, and immigration authorities in the United States do little to supervise or control American ranchers' use of foreign labor. Many employers reportedly prefer to hush up work accidents, cases of illness, negligence in providing medical attention, or excesses committed by their foremen, and some simply say that the shepherds who have been injured or have perished committed suicide or escaped.

Despite the hardships, a growing number of shepherds return to work on a second, third, fourth, or fifth contract, and when they finally decide to settle in Peru again, many feel estranged from their wives and children, who may no longer recognize them. Moreover, as these former shepherds rarely talk about the sufferings they have been through, younger villagers continue to consider US immigration an attractive alternative to traditional livelihoods in Usibamba and Chaquicocha. Indeed, many wait for years to gain their first contract, and as the WRA and the sheep ranchers often ask their employees to suggest new shepherds and migrants prefer to recommend their own relatives, entering the recruiting networks is difficult. During my fieldwork in Usibamba in the 1980s, several villagers told me that they wanted to go to the United States to work but that they had no family members to recommend them. In 1997, when I asked a young man in Usibamba whether he had plans to go to the United States, he replied, "Sure I want to

---

[8] Today, the owners of some of the largest sheep ranches are Basques or descendants of Basque immigrants who came to the United States as shepherds themselves.

[9] Peruvian shepherds and Basque ranch owners generally have few difficulties communicating in Spanish. However, many Peruvians resent the ease with which the Basques swear and curse, a habit they find insulting and frightening.

[10] In 1996, the Peruvian magazine *Caretas* reported that seven shepherds had perished in California (June 20, no. 1419, 1996). That same year, the Lima daily *La República* reported the news of the death of shepherd Apolinario Quiñones (August 16, *Local*, 11, 1996). Similarly, the weekly *Perú de los 90* in Los Angeles claimed that approximately 30 shepherds had died between 1985 and 1995 (December 1995).

go, but I have no one in the family there to call upon me" (see Paerregaard 2012a and Krögel 2010).

Just as young recruits rely on older shepherds to recommend them, so too do the latter need their employers' approval to renew their work contracts. Migrants therefore do their utmost to stay on good terms with their employers and, most of all, not upset them by complaining about working conditions, quitting their jobs, or returning to Peru before the contract expires. By inspiring the confidence of their foremen and gaining the trust of the ranchers, some shepherds even hope that they will be offered a permanent work contract, which saves both the shepherds from having to visit the WRA's agent in Lima and their employers from having to contact the WRA. In Usibamba and Chaquicocha, a permanent work contract is viewed as a sign of status because it ensures the shepherds a steady income in dollars in the future and allows them to act as brokers between the new recruits and the American ranchers. During my stay in Usibamba and Chaquicocha in the late 1990s, several return migrants proudly asserted that they were using the public telephones in their villages to call their American employers to ask for new contracts and suggest new recruits. One villager, who had worked for an American rancher called Mike on several contracts, told me, "I called Mike the other day to ask for another contract. He invited me to come to work for him again and said that I should pass his regards to my wife." The villager's remark underscores the significance a personal friendship with an American employer may have for the shepherds.

The shepherds' efforts to befriend their American employers are encouraged by their relatives in Peru, who expect them to broker a work contract in the United States for younger family members (Paerregaard 2002b). Shepherds who have been gone for longer periods or who are reaching the age of retirement come under particularly strong pressure to help their sons, brothers, cousins, or brothers-in-law obtain a contract. The latter are expected to accept such offers and in this way make use of the opportunity to earn in dollars. In 1998, when I visited Bakersfield, California, a shepherd told me that he went on his first contract on his brother's recommendation. At that time, most of his brothers and brothers-in-law were already working in the United States. The man recalled that his family in Peru encouraged him to go by arguing, "If they can do it, you can too! Think of what they are doing for you so you can go too!" The shepherds' migration, then, is based on ties of mutual trust between employers and employees, spurring not only the latter to return again and again but also their younger relatives to take up work in the United States. More important, the ranchers use these bonds to discipline the shepherds to endure the harsh working conditions in the mountains and the desert and to deter them from running away.[11]

The contract that the shepherds sign with the WRA lasts for three years and guarantees them a monthly salary of $600–$800.[12] As the employers cover the shepherds' travel expenses between Peru and the United States and most of their costs during their stay, the contract enables these migrants to remit a substantial amount of their earnings to their families in Peru. Most shepherds send a monthly amount of $300 to their wives, who use the money to buy food, clothes, and medicines and pay school expenses for the children; and because the shepherds have only a few personal needs and rarely go to town during their stay, many save as much as $300 a month. A three-year contract can therefore yield almost $10,000 in savings. Indeed, single shepherds who remit little or no money during their stay in the United States may save as much as $18,000. Upon their return, some spend their savings in their home villages on land, cattle, or tractors, which they rent to other villagers;[13] others may use their US earnings to construct a new house (either of bricks or concrete) in their home village or to start up a business in the area. Yet others buy a lot, construct a house, and settle in Huancayo or Lima, or they may purchase a used pickup truck or van and make a living transporting passengers back and forth between Huancayo and the Alto Cunas villages.[14] In effect, the number of vehicles offering such transportation has more than tripled in Usibamba and Chaquicocha in the past 20 years. Finally, some shepherds set up a small grocery store or a workshop in the city and make an income out of commerce or small industries.

The *reestructuración de tierras* in 1972 and 1980 in Usibamba and Chaquicocha aimed to reduce migration to Peru's cities by depriving villagers who reside for more than a year outside the village of their status as *comuneros* and their right to land (Paerregaard 1987, 85).[15] Yet, as labor migration

---

[11] The conflicting relation between not only shepherds and their employers but also between the shepherds themselves is reminiscent of the tensions other scholars report that exist within the migrant communities (Mahler 1995; Menjivar 2000).

[12] Ten dollars are withheld for the health insurance, while the WRA charges $15 as a general fee.

[13] In Usibamba, there are currently six former shepherds who make their living by renting out the tractors they bought after returning from the United States. Another popular way of investing savings is to buy pickup trucks and vans to transport local villagers to Huancayo, or to buy cattle, particularly milk cows.

[14] One of the most prominent ways in which migrants gain prestige upon their return to Usibamba or Chaquicocha is by constructing a new house of *material noble*, that is, concrete or bricks.

[15] In a study of migration and communal labor in a Mexican community, Tad Mutersbaugh found that when migrants obtain jobs in the United States, the village authorities allow them to sustain "quasi-permanent" membership by paying fines, much like in Usibamba (Mutersbaugh 2002, 489).

to work on the sheep ranches in the United States gained momentum in the 1980s, Usibamba and Chaquicocha extended the restriction on the *comuneros*' absence from one to three years. At the same time, the two communities started to charge annual fees ($200 in Usibamba and $300 in Chaquicocha) to villagers who go abroad and earn their salary in dollars on more than one contract. Today, *comuneros* are allowed to reside for several periods of three years each outside the districts (in Usibamba two and in Chaquicocha three) if they apply for permission before leaving and pay the required fee to the community for each period they are gone.[16]

The absence fees and restrictions were introduced to discourage villagers from migrating and to reduce the gap between rich and poor that migration creates, but even though it has become more difficult to accumulate wealth, new forms of inequality have emerged in the villages. Before the *reestructuración de tierras*, the villagers were divided into small and large landowners. Now the dividing line runs between those who are part of the networks recruiting villagers to work in the United States and those who are not part of these networks. In addition, a division has emerged between two groups of US migrants: those who pay their fees during their absence and return after three contracts, thus living up to their duties as *comuneros*; and those who are absent for more than three contracts and consequently lose their status as *comuneros* and their rights to land in the villages. This division is reflected in the way return migrants spend their earnings in dollars. Many returnees who have been absent for fewer than three contracts resume their former lives as *comuneros* and invest their migration capital in cattle or tractors. By contrast, villagers who have spent more than three contracts in the United States and have therefore saved more than those who return after three contracts often use their money outside their villages to establish a business, buy vehicles, or construct a new house. Indeed, in recent years migration has generated yet another dividing line in Usibamba and Chaquicocha as a growing number of shepherds have given up the idea of

---

[16] Leah VanWey, Catherine Tucker, and Eileen McConnell report similar regulations in Mexican communities that have experienced large-scale labor migration to the United States. They report that migrants from the community of San Matías have to return every one or three years to carry out their services or find someone close to carry out their responsibilities. Otherwise, they risk loss of membership rights (2005, 94). In some communities in Mexico, the authorities even levy fees on remittances when migrants miss their communal labor duties and on donations received for fiestas and religious events (2005, 97).

returning and are settling in the United States as unathorized immigrants, forming small communities in such places as Bakersfield, California, and Sun Valley, Idaho. Once established in the United States, they either bring their families there or obtain legal residence by marrying American citizens of Chicana or Mexican origin.

The aim of the fees on US labor migration was to generate revenue to improve community services and encourage return migrants to invest their savings in agriculture and stockbreeding. Nonetheless, the fees have turned out to be a double-edged sword. In recent years, the rate of return migration in Usibamba and Chaquicocha has been falling, an indication that many migrants have cut their ties with their villages and have either taken up residence in the United States or settled in Peru's cities. Instead of stimulating return migration, the fees and restrictions imposed on villagers' absences have led them to give up village life. Consequently, their communities back home are experiencing a drop in revenues and the loss of potential investments of migrants who, deprived of their status as *comuneros*, prefer to place their savings elsewhere.[17] Migrants who return and invest their savings in Usibamba and Chaquicocha also express discontent with the fees and time restrictions the communities have imposed on villagers' absences. They complain that the obstacles to migration cripple their opportunities to make money and say that the contributions they make to their communities should be voluntary instead of mandatory.

In recent years, a growing number of return migrants have even suggested that Usibamba and Chaquicocha should revoke private property in land. They argue that although a few return migrants invest their money in tractors and agricultural machinery that they rent to other villagers, the majority use their US earnings to construct new houses or buy vans, which they use to transport people in the area. Some even make a living as migration brokers, using their friendship with American sheep ranchers to obtain work contracts for young recruits in return for large amounts of money. Arguably, removing not only the fees and time restrictions on migration but also the *reestructuración de tierras* would channel more migrant investment into agriculture and stockbreeding and thus contribute to the development of Usibamba and Chaquicocha.

---

[17] For a comparison of rural and urban remittances in the Huancayo area, where Usibamba is located, see Alvarado, Gonzales, and Galarza (2005).

Fees on migration are a useful way to mitigate the effects of migration on inequality in Usibamba and Chaquicocha, but by imposing time restrictions on villagers' absences, these communities are discouraging migrant investments in their villages. The communal land system, which guarantees villagers equal access to land, also hampers the attempt to leverage migrant savings for development. Moreover, the communities' measures for controlling migration have created a divide within villages between those who are members of the migration networks and therefore can go on work contracts to the United States and those who cannot. Similarly, they have prompted a growing number of villagers either to leave their villages and move to the cities or settle in the United States or to spend their money on house construction, setting up a small business, transport, or other activities not related to agriculture or stockbreeding. In other words, instead of encouraging migrants to share their *voluntad* with the other villagers, migration regulations have created new divisions within communities in Peru.

The villagers of Usibamba and Chaquicocha have migrated to find work outside the villages for many decades. Up through the twentieth century, the mines and Peru's cities offered them the opportunity to make money, and in the past five decades US labor migration has been the most important source of cash income in the two villages. Whether migration is international or internal, it creates divides and accelerates existing relations of inequality within the village population. Both Usibamba and Chaquicocha have been able to contain these tensions and inequalities through strict regulations for community membership. These regulations limit the villagers' mobility and opportunities for making money, but until recently few objected to those restrictions. A strong territorial identity based on the districts' long history of struggles against encroaching haciendas and mining companies has generated a general consensus that membership regulations are the best means for fighting land usurpation and defending the community. Many migrants continue to feel attached to Usibamba and Chaquicocha even after many years of working in the United States, but as migration opens up new economic opportunities, a growing number of migrants settle outside the communities when they have completed their work contracts. As these former migrants lose or give up their right to land, their loyalty to Usibamba and Chaquicocha changes, and over the years that loyalty becomes less about a physical place of life experience than about imagined places of emotional attachment. However, as the price of land and the demand for meat and agricultural products rise in the wake of Peru's economic boom, many former migrants are now showing renewed interest in returning to Usibamba and Chaquicocha, at least temporarily, to invest their savings in the communities.

The Sponsorship

The migration history of Cabanaconde goes back to the colonial period, when the village was an immigration center for Spaniards and mestizos. Today, the district of Cabanaconde, which is located at 3,200 meters above sea level at the lower end of the Colca Valley in Peru's southern highlands, has 2,842 Quechua- and Spanish-speaking inhabitants, making it the second-largest population center in the region (Gelles 2000, 26–32; Paerregaard 1997, 39). Much like Usibamba, the occupational specialization of Cabanaconde is only rudimentarily developed, and the vast majority of the population makes a living from agricultural and pastoral activities, but in contrast to the former, which is integrated into the national market, the latter serves primarily for consumption in the district and barter in the neighboring districts (Gelles 2000, 36–37). The villagers of Cabanaconde have also formed a peasant community that is officially recognized by the Peruvian state.

In the twentieth century, Cabanaconde's population more than doubled, exerting growing pressure on the land, and after a road linking the village to the city of Arequipa was built in 1965 transportation and communication with the surrounding society improved dramatically (Gelles 2000, 36–37). In the years that followed, a canal was constructed from the Colca Valley to Majes on the nearby coast, and while this area was consequently irrigated and transformed into fertile land, the project's planners refused the population of Cabanaconde and neighboring villages access to the water of the canal. The Majes project caused much anger in Cabanaconde, for whom it recalled the policy that the Peruvian state had pursued since colonial times, which had ignored the vital needs of Andean peasants, such as water for irrigating their fields. In 1983, a year when water was particularly scarce, the villagers opened up the canal in what Gelles calls "a classic show of peasant resistance" (2000, 64). A police regiment was sent to Cabanaconde, and when they arrived the entire community confronted them and claimed the right to the water in the channel. The village's move was effective: it won increased access to irrigation water, and since 1988 the canal has brought more than 1,000 hectares of abandoned terraced fields back into production, doubling the land base. These changes have generated new incomes and more prosperity for the villagers, as well as a growing interest within the village's migrant population in defending their rights to land and other resources (2000, 66–74).

Unlike many rural communities in Peru's central highlands, Cabanaconde was not seriously affected by the political violence that plagued the country in the late 1980s and early 1990s. When social order returned in Peru in the mid-1990s, the community began to attract a growing number of tourists, who use it as a stopover when visiting the scenic canyon located just outside Cabanaconde (Feminias 2005, 71). In recent years, the villagers have seen the emergence of a tourist industry, including such services as hotels, restaurants, and tourist agencies, which has bolstered local economic development. Simultaneously, the introduction of parabolic antennas, video recorders, and other modern media and communication technologies, combined with electricity service around the clock, has allowed villagers to watch not merely national television channels but also American movies. Another important change was the installation of a permanent telephone service, and more recently Internet service became available in the village as well (Gelles 2000, 162–64). The new urban-inspired consumption practices spurred by the growing tourist industry and the introduction of new technologies are rapidly transforming Cabanaconde's traditional rural lifestyle and speeding up an already existing process of out-migration that began more than 70 years ago. Initially, this migration was directed toward Arequipa and Lima, Peru's two major urban centers, where people from Cabanaconde established migrant communities and formed migrant associations in the 1940s. Cabaneño migration grew steadily during the second half of the 20th century, and in 1987 the migrant populations of Arequipa and Lima numbered approximately 1,000 and 3,000, respectively (2000, 33).

In the 1970s, Cabaneños engaged in migration outside Peru as well (Paerregaard 2010b). The first Cabaneño to emigrate was a man who has spent most of his life outside Cabanaconde. At the age of eight, he went to live with a distant relative in a neighboring village, and a few years later he migrated to Arequipa to study and work. In 1969, he left for the United States with a friend and settled in New Jersey, where he found a job in a factory. After obtaining US citizenship and living more than 30 years in the United States, he retired and returned to Peru with his wife. Although their children were all born in New Jersey, where they currently live, this pioneering Cabaneño never invited any relatives or helped other villagers come to the United States. However, he was soon followed by a handful of young Cabaneño females. The first to leave Peru was a woman then living in Lima, who in 1970 traveled to Washington, D.C., with a neighbor. The same year another woman, who had migrated from Cabanaconde to Lima at the age of 14, immigrated first to Brazil and then to Washington, with the Peruvian diplomatic family she was working for as a domestic. A third woman, who had also left Cabanaconde and migrated to Lima in the mid-1960s, traveled first to Canada and then to Mexico to work as a domestic, and in 1974 she immigrated to Washington, when she learned that several of her fellow migrants were living there. In the following years, the women invited three more Cabañeño women to come, forming the roots of what became an organized migrant network over the next decade (Paerregaard 2012b). In the late 1970s and early 1980s, Cabanaconde's migration chain gained momentum, and throughout the 1990s women as well as men continued to arrive in Washington, D.C. By 2005, the Cabañeño community had approximately 500 members, and in 2010 more than 800 Cabañeños were living in Washington.[18]

In 1983, Cabañeños in Washington, D.C., formed the Cabanaconde City Association (CCA), which was recognized by the city's local authorities in 1997. The main purpose of this association is to organize social and cultural activities for the Cabañeño community, the annual soccer league being one of the most important. Other activities include social events during which the CCA gathers together Cabañeños in Washington and collects funds to finance the administration of the institution, help fellow migrants in need, and support village projects in Cabanaconde. At these events, the participants make individual contributions by paying an entrance fee and buying food prepared and cooked without charge by migrants. In 2005, the president of the CCA told me that the institution collects $5,000–$8,000 during such events. He also declared, "We only organize such events a couple of times a year, but we could easily do it every month and collect, say, $50,000–$80,000 a year." Compared with other Peruvian organizations in Washington, D.C., the CCA is a powerful association that musters considerable economic and social support from its members.

In the past decade, the institution has strengthened its role in two ways. First, until 2002 Cabañeño migrants participated in the soccer league organized by Peruvian and other Hispanic immigrant organizations in

---

[18] Another important group of Andean migrants in Washington, D.C., comes from Llamapsillón, an annex of Chongos Altos located several hours' drive west of the city of Huancayo. Like Cabañeños, they started to emigrate in the 1970s, and although their community in Washington is much smaller than the Cabeneño community, they have collected large amounts of money to finance projects in Llamapsillón, the most prominent being to construct a new church in the village.

Washington, and even though all the players on the team were Cabaneños, it was registered as a Peruvian team. In 2003, the CCA organized a separate soccer league exclusively for Cabaneños. Migrants told me that this decision was made in response to several incidents in which players from other Peruvian teams had injured Cabaneños while playing. They also claimed that soccer playing had become much more enjoyable since this separation. As one Cabaneño migrant said to me in 2005, "Before, we were only a few here in Washington. Now we're many, and we've been able to form a league only for Cabaneños. Every day we are more and more. We don't depend on other Peruvians anymore." During my stay in Washington in 2009–10, the Cabaneño soccer league could no longer accommodate the many newly arrived migrants, who therefore formed a second league that also included migrants from other Colca villages, such as Chivay, Coporaque, and Huambo.

A similar development occurred in the relationship between Cabaneños and other Peruvian organizations in Washington, D.C. Several migrants whom I interviewed in 2005 claimed that they used to take part in the religious processions of the Peruvian Hermandad del Señor de los Milagros [Brotherhood of the Lord of Miracles] (Paerregaard 2008b; 2011b) but now preferred to attend the celebration of the Virgin of Carmen that the CCA has organized for a number of years. The event—which takes place in a cave called the Gruta de Lourdes (Grotto of Lourdes) outside Washington on one of the Sundays around July 15 (the date of the fiesta in honor of the virgin in Cabanaconde)—includes food, music, and dancing and is the most important gathering of Cabaneños in Washington. A Cabaneño woman who arrived in Washington in 1996 said that she used to attend the procession of the Lord of the Miracles every year but that "as we don't live in downtown now, I don't go anymore. Now I go to the Virgin of Carmen. I think it is a very nice event. So why go to the Lord of the Miracles?" Many migrants felt the formation of their own league and the celebration of the Virgin of Carmen in Washington were milestones in an ongoing endeavor to strengthen the Cabaneño community and distance it from the Peruvian and Hispanic communities in Washington. Indeed, during my stay in Washington in 2005, I found that one of the topics most often discussed by Cabaneños was the continuous arrival of new migrants and the growth of the community that this migration flow was causing. When I returned in 2009, migrants told me that the number of Cabaneños was now so large that the CCA could no longer serve the entire community.

Second, although the CCA's leadership underscores the migrants' sense of belonging to Cabanaconde by creating a separate Cabaneño space within the Peruvian community in Washington, it also wants to reduce its economic support of Cabanaconde. According to the leaders I interviewed in 2005, the organization receives numerous requests every year from village authorities, schoolteachers, parents' organizations, and religious and civil associations for equipment (instruments, computers, and uniforms), furniture (chairs, benches, and tables), repairs to public buildings, and improvements to irrigation canals. They also reported that many individual villagers ask the CCA for help to pay hospital and medical bills when family members fall ill or suffer accidents. The CCA president felt that, rather than meet the many needs of the villagers in Cabanaconde, the main aim of the CCA should be to support fellow migrants in the United States. "For many years we've been supporting Cabanaconde and helped the authorities with money," he said. "But we don't want to continue doing that anymore because it hasn't helped at all. The money often disappears, and people in Cabanaconde believe that they can keep asking for more. For instance, one year we bought new instruments for the school band, but they have all disappeared. Another year we bought new benches for the church. But why give money to the church and not other things? So we have decided to use the money we collect to help Cabaneños who are in need here and perhaps buy a building lot for the organization." He also reported that the organization is considering offering loans to migrants who are planning to bring family members to Washington. Because most migrants travel overland from Panama to the United States without the required documentation, such a trip may cost up to $10,000.

The CCA's leadership, then, is currently strengthening the Cabaneño community in two ways. While carving out a separate Cabaneño space within the Peruvian community in Washington, D.C., it is redirecting the funds that were previously donated to Cabanaconde to support its own members in the United States. Although some, mostly elderly migrants who still hope to go back to Cabanaconde, disagree with this reorientation of the CCA's activities, many support it. Arguably, the shift in activities is a response to a more general change in the migration process. Since 2001, the US government has increased border controls and tightened its immigration policy, making it more difficult for Peruvians and other Latin Americans to enter the United States and regularize their status as immigrants. Whereas Cabaneños who were living in the United States as undocumented immigrants prior to 9/11 often obtained temporary or permanent work and residence permits within a number of years after their arrival, those who have arrived since that date have had fewer such opportunities. Many spend years living in the shadows, without a driver's license or a Social Security card and at risk of being detained and deported at any time (Paerregaard 2008a, 201–28). And, even worse, migrants who lack proper documentation or are in the process of regularizing their status jeopardize their chances of being granted residence or citizenship in the United States if they travel to Peru to visit relatives and participate in the fiestas.

A young Cabaneño man who had arrived in Washington, D.C., in 2004 told me that he had spent three months crossing all the borders between Central American countries, Mexico, and the United States as an undocumented immigrant, often at risk of being robbed and killed. The trip, which had cost him $8,000, had left him indebted to an uncle in Peru and several relatives in Washington for more than a year. When I interviewed the man in 2005, he claimed that he was finally free of his debts but could not leave the country because he was undocumented. He said, "I have no driver's license, but I need to drive to work. If I get caught I may be deported. Nor do I have a Social Security card, and if I get sick or have an accident I have to ask for help from other Cabaneños. But worst of all, I cannot travel to Peru to visit my family there." Similarly, one woman reported that she had not been back to Cabanaconde since she came to the United States in 1998. The Venezuelan family for which she was working as a domestic had brought her to Washington, but after some time she had quit her job. "They didn't treat me well," she said, "so I left and became illegal. Now I've hired a lawyer to get my residence, but I've been waiting for several years and don't know if I'll ever get the papers. My husband and daughter are going to Cabanaconde for the fiesta this year, but I have to stay here."

Even though the lack of proper documentation limits the mobility of immigrants in many ways, it does not prevent them from looking for work, finding a place to live, or sending their children to school. In fact, many undocumented Cabaneños live seemingly normal lives and engage in transnational activities such as sending remittances to their relatives in Peru just as other immigrants do. Yet, as the testimonies above clearly indicate, they are disturbed by the fact that they cannot travel to Cabanaconde to participate in the fiesta and visit family and friends. The testimonies also indicate that today the Cabaneño community in Washington is divided into two groups: those who have citizenship or a work and residence permit and therefore are free to travel and those who are undocumented and are not free to travel even though they engage in transnational activities such as remitting.

Although migrants in Washington, D.C., frequently donate substantial amounts of money to support projects in Cabanaconde, they make their presence felt in the village mostly during the annual fiestas. In particular, the celebration of the village's patron saint, the Virgin of Carmen, and lately also the Virgin of Candeleria have become a way for migrants to express and validate their identity and community membership. In recent years both fiestas have become important attractions, not only in Cabanaconde but also Arequipa, Lima, and Washington, D.C. As the migrant community in Washington becomes more established and migrants feel more distant from Cabanaconde and the transformation it is experiencing, they affirm their loyalty to the community by investing their prestige in celebrating its patron saint rather than trying to keep track of and engaging in the intricacies of its daily life.

Traditionally, the celebration of the Virgin of Carmen in Cabanaconde, which starts on July 15 and lasts four days, was a rural ritual that coincided with the sowing of the crops. By honoring the Virgin, the villagers hoped that the saint would guarantee them a good harvest in the coming year. This socioreligious reading of the fiesta is reflected in its dual structure, which delegates the responsibility for organizing the music, preparing the food, and financing these activities to the two sponsors, or *devotos*, those responsible for financing and organizing the fiesta. In the past 15 years, the economic and symbolic meaning of the fiesta has changed; whereas the competition between the two *devotos* previously took its meaning from the villagers' agro-religious calendar and was an occasion for ensuring the goodwill of the local religious forces, it is now a showcase for migrants' loyalty to their native village. They demonstrate their success in the metropolis by sponsoring the fiesta, which takes place in the village square and surrounding areas and involves eating, drinking, dancing, and bullfighting. Paul Gelles reports that "the two *devotos* compete throughout the fiesta: which has the best and largest group of musicians, which can recruit more dancers in the main plaza, whose bulls are the most valiant in the bullring, who has the best firework displays" (2005, 80).

For several years, villagers residing outside Cabanaconde have occupied the *devoto* posts. As Gelles puts it, "For the past several years at least one of the two sponsors has been a relatively affluent transmigrant. For example, in 2000 another family with members in Washington greatly outspent previous sponsors; they hired over 80 musicians and had the most extravagant display of fireworks ever seen in the region. More than 125 transmigrants attended. So, too, in 2001, another US-based transmigrant family sponsored the fiesta. Here the number of transmigrants attending exceeded 150, and the celebrations were more costly and extravagant than ever before" (2005, 79). In 2005, both *devotos* were migrants living in Washington, and with the support of their networks they spent almost $100,000 each on the fiesta. When I was interviewing migrants in Washington in 2005, one member of the network assisting in organizing the fiesta told me that the main task of the *devoto*'s core network is to cover the enormous cost of some of the activities and items required for the fiesta and that the *devoto* seldom makes the largest financial contribution. "Look at who sponsored the bulls and the bullfighters," he said. "The person responsible for this must have a lot of money, but he can also ask others for help. And look at who pays for the musicians. Of course, everybody knows it is the *devoto*, but often others help pay for them." When mobilizing the support network, then, the *devoto* creates a flow of exchange relations that crosses regional as well as national boundaries and reaches almost every corner of the Cabaneño migrant community, including Cabaneños living in Arequipa, Lima, and other places.

Although tensions have existed between rural and urban Cabaneños since villagers began to migrate on a large scale a half century ago, the emergence of transnational migrant communities in the United States and Spain has deepened this rift. Gelles describes this transformation as follows: "A combustible mix of envy and admiration that meets many of the return migrants is evident during the fiesta; the transmigrant sponsors are watched especially closely, and locals often prefer to honor the local sponsor, even though his sponsorship is not as grandiose as that of the transmigrant" (2005, 81–82). He reports that during one fiesta a conflict broke out between visiting migrants and local residents in the central plaza, where the latter burned an effigy of the former wearing a jacket with "U.S.A." written on it (Gelles 2000, 193). Other public events in Cabanaconde, such as the fiesta of the Virgin of Candlemas (La Virgen de Candelaria), celebrated in February, have undergone a similar change from a ritual anchored in rural religious life to an event supported by an urban consumption lifestyle.

The transformation of the village's Catholic institutions from a religious ritual into a secular fiesta that migrants use to gain prestige and confirm their ties to their home villages has not only created tensions and mistrust between rural and urban Cabaneños but also caused a new rift within the migrant population.[19] First, villagers in Cabanaconde are increasingly divided into

---

[19] Anthropologists report similar fiesta systems in other Catholic countries. George Foster describes how the responsibility for organizing the fiesta to celebrate Guadalupe has become an

those who belong to the networks that help villagers go to Spain or the United States and those who are excluded from these networks. This division becomes visible during the fiesta when migrants act as agents of change and role models for young villagers who yearn to emigrate and benefit from the opportunities migration entails but must also rely on the support network to arrange and finance their travel. Well-off and established migrant families that have obtained permanent residency or citizenship in Spain and the United States stand out particularly in the fiesta, which they use as a stage for expressing loyalty to their native village and for demonstrating their success as immigrants in their new countries of residence. In so doing, they reinforce the exclusiveness of the migrant networks they draw on to achieve physical and social mobility and to remind their fellow villagers and migrants of their new social status as both transnational villagers and global cosmopolitans.

Second, as a result of migration, more and more outsiders are taking up residence in the village and renting houses and fields from villagers who have migrated to Arequipa, Lima, Washington, D.C., and Spain. This influx has given rise to a new stratum of villagers in Cabanaconde that over the years has made claims to membership and rights in the community (Gelles 2000, 42–44). Since colonial times, Cabanaconde has experienced a constant flow of people, among them not only rural dwellers from other parts of the Andes but also mestizos and Spaniards from Peru's urban centers (Gelles 2000, 32). But unlike the previous influx of people in Cabanaconde, many of the migrants settling there today are former farm workers from the neighboring villages and other Andean regions who are benefiting from the community's recent land recovery project and growing tourist industry (Gelles 2000, 163). Newcomers must live five years in Cabanaconde to obtain rights to community land, and currently there are almost 30 people on the waiting list to become community members. In the meantime, many of them either rent or buy land in the village.

Not all newcomers settle in Cabanaconde to farm the land. In the past 10 years, trade and particularly tourism have become a very lucrative but also competitive business in the village, attracting many outsiders. These newcomers put up hotels and offer guided tours for the many international tourists who visit Cabanaconde, causing many locals to feel that the newcomers are seizing opportunities to make money at their expense. However,

---

opportunity for prosperous villagers to gain prestige in Tzintzuntzan, a village in Mexico (Foster 1979, 316–20), while Caroline Brettell writes that in the 1960s and 1970s, return migrants from France spent large amounts of money on the fiestas of their home villages in northern Portugal (Brettell 2003, 83–91).

the distinction between insiders and outsiders is increasingly blurred by the current out-migration, which includes former farm laborers who had recently settled in Cabanaconde but are now immigrating to the United States. A few have become members of the migrant community in Washington, D.C., and travel to Cabanaconde to participate in the fiesta.

Migrants play an ambiguous role in the ongoing processes of change and differentiation in Cabanaconde. On the one hand, they make important economic contributions to Cabanaconde in the form of their individual remittances and collective support. On the other hand, many of them come back to participate in the village's annual fiesta and invest thousands of their hard-earned dollars in the event, not only reaffirming their membership in Cabanaconde but also positioning themselves as guardians of the village's cultural heritage and promoters of its development. In particular, although tourism and new technologies and means of communication are rapidly changing the lives of Peru's Andean population, the transformation of the village's fiesta demonstrates that migrants and other outsiders who take up residence in the country's rural communities are altering the meaning of local traditions but at the same time are helping maintain a distinct Andean form of life. Moreover, the new role of the fiesta suggests that, apart from reaffirming migrants' loyalty to their home communities, it allows them to strengthen their ties to the networks they draw on to migrate and adapt to the receiving society and demonstrate their positions within these networks. Paradoxically, then, their participation in the fiesta simultaneously contributes to Cabaneños' sense of community and feeling of unity and to an emerging division of the villagers into those who have access to migrant networks and those who do not.

The Donation

Bolognesi is a rural district with 1,461 inhabitants located at 2,912 meters above sea level in the province of Pallasca and the region of Ancash in Peru's northern highlands. It is also the name of the capital of the district, a small town inhabited by approximately 800 individuals, the majority of whom are cattle breeders, agriculturalists, or traders. Before the Spanish conquest, the area formed part of the Inca Empire, but the colonial and republican past has significantly shaped the social and cultural life of the villagers. Although Bolognesi shares many cultural traits with communities in other parts of the Andean highlands, Bolognesinos are monolingual Spanish-speakers and are more influenced by Peru's coastal *criollo* culture than the villagers of Cabanaconde. Moreover, unlike Usibamba, which has abolished private property in land and formed a peasant community to defend the village's territory against the encroachment of neighboring mestizo towns and haciendas, Bolognesinos have not engaged in communal struggles over the village's land, which is owned by private individuals. Notwithstanding these differences, a strong sense of loyalty to the community is prevalent among the villagers, and even though the district can be accessed by two different dirt roads from Chimbote, the closest large coastal city, the trip takes almost a day, which gives the villagers a feeling of physical isolation and underscores their regional sense of belonging.

Out-migration from Bolognesi goes back to the beginning of the twentieth century, when young villagers started to migrate to Lima to study and work. In 1922, they created a migrant organization called Sociedad Representativa del Pueblo de Bolognesi, its aim being to provide economic and logistical support for their home village and promote its elevation to district in Peru's administrative hierarchy (*Wanda* 1960, 2). During the 1920s and 1930s, the organization helped Bolognesi obtain several government subsidies to buy materials to construct irrigation canals in the village and improve the infrastructure of the water system. In 1936, the government finally granted the village the status of district, which gave the inhabitants the right to appoint their own mayor and administrative representatives and to manage some of the communal land. To prepare Bolognesi to become a district, the Sociedad Representativa del Pueblo de Bolognesi equipped the village with office equipment. Migrants also proposed one of their number as the district's first mayor, but to their disappointment the suggestion was turned down. Even worse, during the festivities to celebrate Bolognesi's new status, the migrant organization was accused of being Apristas (that is, belonging to APRA, one of Peru's dominant political parties) (*Wanda* 1960, 3), and after the event it cut ties with the village.

A decade later, however, the migrant organization in Lima reestablished contact with the district authorities, and during the 1940s and 1950s it helped Bolognesi open a local post office, form an administrative unit to manage the district's water service, organize the privatization and division of the district's communal land, establish elementary schools, and improve the roads connecting the district capital with its outlying areas. In the 1960s and 1970s, migrants continued their support for Bolognesi, now concentrating their help on obtaining government money to construct a road from the nearby coast to the district and collecting funds to build a new church in the district capital. In 1958, migrants from Bolognesi and other districts of the province of Pallasca residing in Lima formed a new provincial organization to support these efforts, and in the following years this institution assisted the province in obtaining funds for numerous other projects (*Wanda* 1960, 14).

During the 1980s and 1990s, the migrant community continued to grow, which prompted Bolognesi migrants to seek help in buying a plot of land and constructing a building in the district where the organization could hold its meetings and keep its records. The plot also serves as the premises for the annual fiestas that the institution organizes to celebrate Bolognesi's patron saint, San Antonio de Padua. A century after Bolognesinos began migrating, they now make up an established community of many hundreds in Lima. A somewhat smaller group of Bolognesinos have taken up residence in the city of Chimbote, but their community is more recent. They are therefore not as well organized as migrants in Lima and do not have the means to engage in voluntary work in Bolognesi. The two migrant communities include not just second-generation migrants but also third- and fourth-generation migrants, some of whom have completed higher education and are well established. Although Bolognesi's first migrant institution in Lima was formed almost a century ago, it still regards support for the district's struggle to progress as its main aim, and in the 1990s a group of younger migrants in Lima formed a second district-based organization called Club Cultural de Bolognesi that seeks to strengthen migrants' support for Bolognesi. The election of Alejandro Toledo, a native of Cabana in the district of Bolognesi, as Peru's president in 2001 energized migrants' commitment and encouraged them to ask the government to construct a paved road from the coast to the provincial capital of Pallasca. The project has improved communication between Bolognesi and the outside world, and today a bus company owned by a Bolognesino offers daily services from the district to Chimbote and Lima.

Records kept by the Sociedad Representativa del Pueblo de Bolognesi reveal that a male villager was living in the United States as early as the 1930s (*Wanda* 1960, 2). Yet it was not until the 1960s that international migration from the district gained momentum. Among the first villagers to emigrate were a handful of young women who had left for Lima and found work as domestic servants for upper- and middle-class Peruvian and North American families in the city's uptown neighborhoods. When the employers returned to the United States in the 1950s and 1960s, they asked the women to come with them, and several took up the offer. One villager I interviewed in Bolognesi in 2005 told me that in 1950 his sister had migrated from Bolognesi to Lima, where she worked as a domestic for a North American family for two years. According to the man, in 1952 at age 20 his sister traveled with her employers to the United States and continued working for them in Miami. After a couple of years, she married a Cuban man with whom she had several children who are now living in Miami. She also invited her two sisters in Peru to come to the United States. In Miami, the women first found jobs as domestics, and later they invited their fiancés to come to the United States. The two men came to Miami in the early 1960s, but as they had difficulties finding work, they moved to Hartford, Connecticut, where it was easier for men to get factory jobs and where the salaries were higher. In 1965, the two sisters moved to Hartford, too, and over the following four decades the Bolognesino community in this city grew steadily.

When I visited Hartford in 2005, Bolognesi's migrant community included numerous second-generation immigrants of Bolognesino descent born in the United States and constituted one of the most prominent migrant groups within the Peruvian community in Connecticut and surrounding areas in Rhode Island, New York, and New Jersey.[20] Apart from Hartford, where Peruvians and Puerto Ricans make up the two largest immigrant populations, the Peruvian community in this part of the United States comprises scattered but numerous migrant groups in Bridgeport, Stamford, New Haven, Providence, and Norwich. According to the Peruvian consul in Hartford, more than 70 percent of these migrants come from the shantytowns of Lima and Chimbote and have arrived more recently as undocumented immigrants. By contrast, the vast majority of Bolognesinos in Hartford have traveled by legal means to the United States. Coming from a small group of families in Bolognesi, they use the family reunification program to invite close relatives to the United States, and even though they have to wait many years before they can travel to the United States, they obtain green cards and US citizenship much more quickly than other migrants. Family reunification serves as a safe strategy for migrants to bring close relatives to the United States, but it excludes a large number of Bolognesinos from their networks and from the opportunity to migrate. Migrants in Hartford are therefore viewed with envy in Bolognesi, and in recent years a growing number of villagers have started to migrate to new destinations, including Miami and Madrid.

In fact, many US migrants belonged to Bolognesi's better-off families before emigrating. Among these are Modesta and Mario, a couple who

---

[20] Hartford has a population of approximately 8,000 Peruvians. In 2002, former president Toledo opened a Peruvian consulate in Hartford. Other prominent Peruvian communities in Hartford are migrants from the province of Ocro located in the region of Ancash.

both have status as pioneers in Bolognesi's migrant community in Hartford, where they have lived for more than 20 years. The first in their families to emigrate was Luzvila, Modesta's older sister, who left for Miami in 1964 at the invitation of another young female villager living in this city. Upon her arrival, Luzvila found work as a domestic, but after a couple of years she moved to Hartford, where a group of Bolognesinos had formed a small migrant community. In the 1970s, she invited her five brothers to come to Hartford and in 1988 extended an invitation to Modesta too. All six siblings were granted residence visas in the United States through the family reunification program. During the 1990s, Modesta's mother and yet another brother also made it to Hartford, and today the only members of the family remaining in Peru are two brothers who have both formed families and established prosperous businesses in Lima. Two of Mario's sisters, who left for the United States when they were young in the early 1980s, are considered pioneers in Bolognesi's migrant community as well, and in 1988 they helped Mario migrate by applying for family reunification with their brother. Although Modesta and Mario lived in Lima before migrating and have spent most of their lives outside their village of origin, they still own 13 hectares of land and more than 15 cows in Bolognesi. According to Modesta, the couple did not migrate out of economic necessity but because they wanted their children to have better educational opportunities than they would have had in Peru. Today, they both have unskilled jobs that are well paid, which allow them to lead comfortable lives in the United States and travel frequently to Peru. However, they have no plans to stay in the United States for good. Mario says, "Our children both have academic degrees from prestigious universities in the United States and make good money. We don't want to stay here much longer but plan to return to stay in Bolognesi." Even though these two pioneering migrants have spent many years in the United States, they still dream of a future return to their native village. Although many share Modesta and Mario's dream, only a few have ever made it come true. Moreover, because those who actually do return often do so after they have reached retirement age, they use their savings to construct a new house rather than buy land, start a business, or otherwise contribute to Bolognesi's economic development. Thus, so far only one return migrant has invested his savings in agriculture. Migrants' dream of return is therefore closely associated with a wish to use their retirement savings from the United States to spend their last days in safety among relatives and fellow villagers.

In 1984, migrants in Hartford established an association called the Club Social Bolognesi (CSB). CSB's board of directors is elected from among Bolognesino migrants and holds meetings in a rented clubhouse in Hartford, where the organization also organizes family reunions and celebrates social events. One of CSB's main functions is to support Bolognesi's soccer team in Hartford, which for a number of years has played in a league consisting of Peruvian and Hispanic teams. Yet when I interviewed CSB's president in 2005, he told me that in the past 10 years the team has had difficulties recruiting new players, partly because the interest of young Bolognesinos in participating in migrant events has diminished and partly because the insurance that the players are required to buy has become too expensive. He also complained that migrant participation in the social activities they organize had dropped in the past decade and that they had been forced to sublease the clubhouse to pay the rent. Finally, the president pointed out that the majority of CSB's board members belonged to the older generation of Bolognesi migrants and that the younger generation had turned their backs on the institution. One member of the board said to me, "The younger generation is not concerned with Bolognesi anymore. We want them to step in and replace us as leaders of the institution, but they don't respond to our call."

Migrants' first organized attempt to support their home town occurred in response to the huge earthquake that hit the department (region) of Ancash in 1970, prompting Bolognesinos in the United States to form a committee to collect money to help the victims of the disaster. Migrants continued to show concern for their home region in the years after the earthquake, and when they established CSB in 1984 the organization became an important instrument for organizing aid for Bolognesi. Migrant donations are used mostly to organize *chocolatadas* (a social event that includes a snack of hot chocolate and cake) and buy toys for the schoolchildren in Bolognesi on Mother's Day and Christmas or to help individual villagers who have fallen ill or been injured. However, during my visit in Hartford several migrants complained that CSB lacks guidelines for the use of the money it raises and that many of the donations they make to Bolognesi through the organization are therefore mismanaged. They also pointed out to me that this lack of clarity in CSB's work generates frustration not only within the migrant community but also among the villagers in Bolognesi, who do not know what kinds of projects the organization is supporting. Not surprisingly, tension frequently breaks out between CSB and the municipal authorities in Bolognesi, whose misuse of migrant donations adds fuel to the troubled relationship.

In 2005, a CSB board member told me that the organization had donated toys to Bolognesi's schoolchildren for Christmas for several years but that the authorities of Bolognesi had led the villagers to believe the donation came from them and not the migrants of Hartford. During my visit, another senior migrant explained that the mayor of the district once took credit for a *chocolatada* that CSB had donated to Bolognesi, claiming that he personally had sponsored the event. The migrant, who had come to the United States in 1964 and is one of the pioneers of the Bolognesi migrant community in Hartford, angrily exclaimed, "Imagine, the mayor was even my own cousin!"

More recently, CSB's board decided to concentrate its donations on fewer but bigger projects. During the past decade, the organization has given money to improve the road connecting Bolognesi with the provincial capital of Pallasca and to repair the district school. Both projects received donations of several thousand dollars from CSB to buy tools, equipment, and materials. In return, the villagers provided manual work. Other, larger-scale projects include renovating the church of Bolognesi, which in 2005 had so far cost $120,000 and was still incomplete, and setting up a computer center, which was completed in 2003 and cost about $45,000. Several migrants in Hartford told me that the idea of renovating the church came from a female migrant who had resettled in Bolognesi upon her return from the United States. Once reintegrated into the village, the woman argued that it was migrants' moral responsibility to pay for the project, as the church serves as the main location for the annual fiestas that celebrate Bolognesi's patron saint. The money to carry out the project has mainly been collected mainly during the social events that CSB organizes in Hartford, but migrants have also made significant individual donations, one as much as $20,000.

Unlike the renovation of the church, which was suggested by the villagers of Bolognesi, the computer center is a project conceived and promoted entirely by migrants in Hartford. The center, which is located in a newly constructed two-story building, has seven computers and a separate space for cultural events; it is the result of an initiative of a group of young migrants who wanted to give schoolchildren in Bolognesi the opportunity to use modern information technology. After the center was completed, the Peruvian Ministry of Education supported the project by providing instruction to Bolognesi's schoolteachers on the use of the computers. Today, the center stands as a symbolic monument not only of migrants' support for Bolognesi but also of the district's connection to the globalized world and its quest for modernity. However, when I visited Bolognesi in 2005, the computers had not yet been connected to the Internet, and several teachers were still waiting to receive instruction on how to teach the schoolchildren to use them.

The renovation of the church and the construction of the computer center have required not only substantial financial contributions from migrants in Hartford but also much organizational work. For more than a decade, migrants have traveled constantly between the United States and Peru to pay the bills and monitor the projects and have also formed committees in Hartford, Lima, and Bolognesi to coordinate the execution. Yet migrants in Hartford assert that cooperation between these committees has often been difficult and that Bolognesino migrants in Lima have offered little assistance. According to one migrant leader in Hartford, "The migrant institutions in Lima are incapable of carrying out projects and we have not been able to work with them. That's why we have to do everything on our own." A young migrant who has returned from Hartford to live in Lima and who shows great interest in Bolognesi's future expressed a similar mistrust of the village's migrant organizations in Lima, pointing out that the group is inefficient and needs to rethink its role as a voluntary association. Migrants also claimed that the local authorities in Bolognesi have been reluctant to support the two projects. One migrant in Hartford who had traveled to Peru to assist in setting up the center recalled that on the day of its inauguration the mayor of Bolognesi paid the center only a short visit and then disappeared. According to this migrant, the mayor considered the center a potential threat to his authority in Bolognesi and therefore did all he could to distance himself from it and the migrants who had supported it. The migrant explained that "that's how the authorities in Bolognesi react when we try to help. They get jealous." Although the majority of Bolognesi's migrant community in Hartford has been committed wholeheartedly to the two projects, some members are concerned that they have drained CSB of its financial resources and worn out its members. A former CSB leader told me that the church project in particular had exhausted the migrant community in Hartford and that in its future work the institution needs to define lower-profile and shorter-term projects. He also suggested that CSB should use the money it collects to buy its own clubhouse in Hartford and support its own migrant community instead of giving donations to Bolognesi.

The church renovation and the computer center are examples of how migrants in Hartford show support, individually as well as collectively, to the progress and modernization of Bolognesi. But migrants also engage in other projects in their hometown and spend large amounts of money on social events and ritual activities in Bolognesi. Indeed, many migrants regard sponsoring the annual celebration of Bolognesi's patron saint as the most tangible way of paying respect to the village. In contrast to the money migrants give to CSB—and which the leaders of the organization then remit to the authorities in Bolognesi—their patronage of the fiesta in honor of San Antonio de Padua, June 9 through 15, is conceived as an individual contribution and is visible to everyone. During the five days of the fiesta, the migrant who has volunteered as *prioste*—the person in charge of sponsoring and arranging the event—is the center of attention of hundreds of townsmen and visiting migrants from Chimbote, Lima, and Hartford (and recently also Spain), for whom the fiesta is an opportunity to drink, dance, reconnect with distant relatives and old classmates, and thus reaffirm ties to Bolognesi. Therefore, while the projects financed by CSB do not allow migrants to display their individual *voluntad*, sponsoring the fiesta is an important way of gaining personal prestige and building up social capital among both villagers and migrants.

Both the celebration of San Antonio de Padua in Bolognesi and the fiesta of La Virgen del Carmen in Cabanaconde offer migrants a way to showcase and affirm their ties to their villages of origin. Yet at a closer glance, the social meaning of the two events varies. Unlike the extravagant amounts of money that migrants from Cabanaconde spend on their fiestas, the cost of assuming the duties of *prioste* rarely exceeds $20,000. Moreover, whereas entering *devotos* in Cabanaconde announce their candidature on the last day of the fiesta (often competing with other candidates) without further notice, in Bolognesi potential sponsors of the fiesta must first be approved by the *mayordomo*: the person appointed to keep a record of the *priostes* of previous years. The office of *mayordomo* and the institutionalization of the appointment of new *priostes* (and allowing only one per year) reduce the competition inherent in the fiesta system that drives up the cost of celebrating these religious events. Nevertheless, to most Bolognesinos, assuming the responsibility for celebrating their patron saint implies a big personal sacrifice and, just as the *devotos* in Cabanaconde mobilize their networks to help finance the fiesta, the *prioste* asks kin and friends for support. To do this, the incoming *prioste* hosts the *huillana*, a social gathering where the participants are offered plenty of food and drink in return for making contributions to the fiesta and assuming the many duties it entails. The *huillana* is critical to the *priostes* not only because it shows them the support they can expect to receive but also because it allows them to draw up a budget for their own expenditure. As in Cabanaconde, it is the sponsor's job to pay for the music, whereas their support network usually covers most of the remaining costs. Once *priostes* receive the commitment of their network, they can focus on other tasks, which mainly involve traveling to Peru to make preparations in Bolognesi, such as hiring cooks, musicians, and assistants.

Although the main event in the celebration of San Antonio de Padua takes place in Bolognesi, migrants in Lima and Hartford also honor the village's patron saint. The costs of organizing the fiesta, as well as the prestige that migrants win by volunteering as *prioste* in these cities, are less than what they would be for the same event in Bolognesi. Yet whether Bolognesinos volunteer to arrange the fiesta in Bolognesi, Lima, or Hartford, the *prioste* spends far less money than the *devoto* in Cabanaconde. Indeed, the lower cost of celebrating San Antonio de Padua allows Bolognesinos living in Lima to volunteer as *prioste* in Bolognesi as often as migrants from Hartford and makes the post affordable not only for the established and well-off but also for newly arrived migrants in the city. Thus, in 2005 the *prioste* in Bolognesi was a young female migrant who had lived in the United States for only one year and therefore had had little time to save money or mobilize a support network. Nevertheless, according to migrants, the fiesta she put on was up to the standards of previous years. Even though celebrating San Antonio de Padua is less costly than celebrating La Virgen de Carmen, honoring the patron saint of Bolognesi has become more expensive in recent years. Once the renovation of Bolognesi's church is completed, it is likely that migrants will capitalize on this project and use the fiesta as an opportunity for demonstrating their loyalty to their home village in the same way as migrants from Cabanaconde do.

Saving the Andean World

Throughout the twentieth century, Andean people have struggled to defend their territories against encroaching haciendas and to win their rights as citizens of Peru and other countries. The three case studies in this subsection give evidence of these struggles. In particular, the villagers of Usibamba, Chaquicocha, and Cabanaconde have long histories of conflict with neighboring landholders and law enforcement institutions. In the 1970s and 1980s, the Peruvian state interfered in village affairs in the three communities in very dramatic ways. The land reform introduced by the Peruvian government in the 1970s encouraged Usibambinos and Chaquicochanos not merely to restructure the community organization and abolish private ownership of land but also to engage in new struggles for power in the area, which had important implications for their response to the entry of Shining Path into the communities in the 1980s. By the same token, the Majes project described earlier, which the Peruvian government implemented in the Colca Valley in the 1970s and 1980s and which was constructed within the communal territory of the Cabaneños, inspired the villagers to claim their rights to the water in the canal. Eventually, they had to take things into their own hands and confront the police to achieve their goal. Even though the villagers in Usibamba, Chaquicocha, and Cabanaconde experienced these encounters with the Peruvian state very differently, the outcome of their struggle was the same: a large group of villagers gained access to more irrigated land, and the political organization of the communities was strengthened.

Bolognesinos do not base their community identity on land conflicts, but they nevertheless have had the same experience of rural-urban migration and social exclusion as the villagers of Usibamba, Chaquicocha, and Cabanaconde. For several generations, they have migrated internally in Peru to make themselves visible in the urban landscape, redefine their inferior status as indigenous peasants, and thus claim recognition as Peruvian citizens. Indeed, it is the struggle not only for land and territory against neighboring haciendas and the Peruvian state but also for social and legal rights in Peruvian society that has spurred Usibambinos, Chaquicochanos, Cabaneños, and Bolognesinos first to settle in the cities of Arequipa, Huancayo, Chimbote, and Lima and later to immigrate to such places as Spain and the United States.

More recently, globalization in the form of development agencies, new technologies, external market forces, and international tourism has encouraged villagers to adopt a modern lifestyle and to create new links to the national and global worlds (Paerregaard 2010a). Unlike the changes that occurred in Usibamba, Chaquicocha, Cabanaconde, and Bolognesi in the twentieth century, which strengthened the economy of many rural districts and reinforced the communities' political authority, the growing modernization and globalization of Andean society in the past 20 years have prompted the younger generation to look beyond their native communities in search of new livelihoods and economic opportunities and to view its institutions and leadership as obstacles to improved living conditions. This opening toward the national and global worlds has pushed out-migration to destinations inside and outside Peru to new heights and cast migrants as important agents of change. In contrast to rural-urban migrants who lack the financial capacity to finance large-scale projects, migrants based in the United States and other countries in the developed world are able to provide substantial economic support to their places of origin. In Usibamba, Chaquicocha, Cabanaconde, and Bolognesi, this engagement is manifested in migrants' contributions to communal activities and projects and participation in religious fiestas; it has also paved the way for new divisions between villagers with access to the networks that migrants control (and the flows of resources and information these generate) and those without such access.

The three case studies reveal that in their endeavor to donate money and organize activities in Peru migrants face a difficult predicament between, on the one hand, sponsoring development projects and helping those in their native rural districts and, on the other hand, providing support for their fellow migrants in the new settings. They also show that migrants' engagement in rural development is shaped not only by their sense of belonging to their places of origin but also by their migration histories and the networks they create and draw on to "pull" in newcomers. For migrants who travel by illegal means, as in the case of Cabanaconde, migration is more costly and risky than for other migrants. The lack of legal status also prevents them from traveling to Peru and cripples their ability to communicate with community leaders and fellow villagers in their native districts and to channel support and organize and manage development projects in Peru. Yet even though undocumented immigration curbs the mobility of Cabaneño migrants in the United States, their community in Washington, D.C., is growing much faster than the Bolognesi community in Hartford, which almost exclusively brings in newcomers through family reunification.

Cabañeños' migration experiences also differ from those of Usibambinos, who travel by legal means like the Bolognesinos but live scattered and isolated in rural areas and therefore rarely gather together. Moreover, unlike both Cabañenos and Bolognesinos, Usibambinos engage in circular migration, traveling back and forth between Peru and the United States, which prevents them from forming stable immigrant communities. This difference in migration practices and settlement patterns is reflected in the migrant networks of the four districts and their contribution to the development of their communities. The CCA leaders, for example, have demonstrated on several occasions that they are capable of collecting large amounts of money; but because of their troubled relationship with the authorities in Cabanaconde and their fragile links to the district's migrant organizations in Arequipa and Lima, they prefer to use their funds to help the many newly arrived undocumented immigrants in Washington, D.C., rather than contribute to development projects in Peru. Moreover, many migrants in Washington spend huge amounts of money on their district's annual fiestas, this being viewed as proof of their individual loyalty to Cabanaconde. As legal immigrants, however, migrants in Hartford encounter few obstacles in traveling between the United States and Peru, and although Bolognesinos also use their savings for fiestas in their home district, they feel more committed than Cabaneños to supporting the development projects in their home community.

My data illustrate that migrants who are undocumented face many obstacles in organizing development projects in their country of origin. But the case studies also show that even when migrants obtain legal status and become citizens in the receiving country, they encounter serious difficulties in coordinating their support with their fellow migrants and villagers back home. Thus, the leaders of both CCA and CSB complain that their efforts to promote development are hampered by the lack of support and cooperation of other migrant institutions in Peru and, more important, the local authorities in Cabanaconde and Bolognesi. By the same token, the local populations of the two districts feel that migrants tend to ignore their needs and mainly seek influence in village affairs to promote their own interests and gain prestige at the annual fiestas. These different perspectives suggest that an organizational framework to facilitate transnational migrants' engagement in their native villages and ease their communications with the local authorities is warranted; such a framework could be provided by the regional governments of Peru or external actors such as NGOs. Finally, the case studies indicate that the Peruvian government could play a beneficial role by engaging in a dialogue with migrant groups in the United States and other parts of the world to make them more sensitive to the needs and wishes of their fellow villagers.

Although migrants' engagement is leading to increasing economic and social inequality in all four communities, the strategies they use to contribute to development and to gain influence in Usibamba, Chaquicocha, Cabanaconde, and Bolognesi differ in significant ways. In Usibamba and Chaquicocha, where migration is legal, temporary, and entirely a male activity, most migrants either remit their earnings to their families in Peru or save them to construct new houses in the district upon their return. In recent years, a growing number of return migrants have also used their savings to set up a business in the nearby city of Huancayo or in Lima, where they settle with their families. Some do not even return to Peru but stay in the United States, where they form small communities and marry local women. In other words, international migration in Usibamba and Chaquicocha has not only speeded up an ongoing process of rural-urban migration that started more than 40 years ago but has also contributed to the division of the district population into those who are part of the networks that recommend new villagers to sheep ranchers in the United States and those who have no access to them and therefore cannot migrate.

By contrast, in Cabanaconde, where migration was initiated by women and is permanent, migrants prefer to use their earnings to bring their relatives to the United States to offer them a new and more prosperous life instead of saving those earnings to construct a new house or set up a business upon their return to Peru. Moreover, migrants in the United States who no longer have relatives in Cabanaconde and have obtained legal residence or citizenship in the United States are therefore free to travel to Peru and spend their money on the fiesta system to affirm their loyalty to the village. The presence of these migrants during the fiesta and the influx of information and resources they create have deepened the rift in the village population between those connected to migrant networks and those not connected. In Bolognesi, migrants also sponsor the village's fiestas, but unlike in Cabanaconde, where the costs of assuming the post of *devoto* have skyrocketed in the past decade, rural-urban migrants and other villagers too can afford to be *prioste*. Arguably, Bolognesinos in Hartford, who have traveled mainly by legal means and therefore constitute a more homogeneous community than the Cabaneños in Washington, D.C., feel less need to demonstrate their success as immigrants in the United States by spending money on symbolic events such as the village's patron saint. The mere fact that relatives in Hartford have invited them to the United States through family reunification is proof of their privileged status as members of the district's migrant networks.

The community leaders of Usibamba, Chaquicocha, Cabanaconde, and Bolognesi have responded to migrants' engagement very differently. To discourage migration and thus reduce the growing socioeconomic inequalities in the districts, the leaders of Usibamba and Chaquicocha charge migrants annual fees to maintain their membership in the village and their rights to communal land. Yet, rather than encouraging young villagers to stay in Usibamba and Chaquicocha as intended, this policy has prompted a growing number of return migrants to invest their savings in businesses outside the districts. This pattern of return migration has not only widened the gap between those who are linked to migrant networks and those who are not, but also created a division among return migrants themselves between those who enter into rural life in Usibamba or Chaquicocha upon their return and become reincorporated into the communities and those who invest their savings outside Usibamba and Chaquicocha and pursue new urban lives outside the districts. Cabanaconde, however, has not adopted any measures to discourage transnational migration or reduce its impact on social differentiation in the district. Instead, the general expectation among community leaders as well as villagers is that everybody in Cabanaconde profits from the current migration stream to Washington. The activities organized by CCA have to some extent fulfilled these expectations, but in the past decade disagreements within the migrant community over how to use the funds that the organization raises has weakened them. This division becomes starkly clear during the fiesta in Cabanaconde, which highlights the boundary between two groups of migrants: those who have prospered and achieved status as legal immigrants in the United States, and those who are either too poor to sponsor the fiesta or who are prevented from visiting Cabanaconde because they lack the proper documents to travel. Community leaders in Usibamba, Chaquicocha and Cabanaconde, then, have used different means to reduce the impact of migrants' engagement, but the outcome is the same in the three districts: the distance between villagers and migrants has widened. Even though Bolognesinos' expectations of their migrant institutions often exceed its donations, CSB has mustered much more support for Bolognesi than CCA for Cabanaconde. Yet, just as rural-urban migrants from Bolognesi complained that the district authorities excluded them from participating in the celebration of the village's elevation to district in 1936, Bolognesinos in Hartford report that they find it difficult to involve the mayor of Bolognesi in their projects. Migrants have therefore planned and implemented most of their projects for Bolognesi without the support of the district authorities or of Bolognesi's migrant community in Lima.

In contrast to the changes introduced by such external agents as the Peruvian state and international NGOs, migrants' engagement is undirected and covers a broad variety of activities, including the celebration of the village saint and the creation of new economic livelihoods outside the community. Whereas in Cabanaconde migrants devote most of their savings to the village's fiesta, in Usibamba and Chaquicocha they place them in transport and businesses outside the districts in nearby cities. Even though these kinds of involvement differ from more conventional forms of intervention in the Peruvian highlands, the impacts of migrants and external agents of change on social stratification and differentiation in the local population are very similar. In fact, in the past 30 years migration and the many engagements it has generated have left Usibambinos, Chaquicochanos, Cabaneños, and

Bolognesinos more unequal economically and more divided socially than other forms of intervention by external agents of change in the three villages. This suggests that Peru's peasant communities and district leaders lack the necessary authority and capacity to channel the resources and information that transnational migrants provide into activities and projects that will benefit migrants as well as villagers. In addition, it suggests that the Peruvian state and international development organizations could play a more active role by establishing an institutional framework that brings migrants and community leaders together to discuss and negotiate exactly how their involvement can contribute to the development of these communities.

The Ambivalence of Volition

Unlike *compromiso*, which to most migrants is an obligation that they cannot fail to keep, *voluntad* is a commitment that migrants regard as optional. The contributions provided by migrants from rural districts constitute the most significant share of these commitments. Not only do they make up the bulk of all the money that migrant organizations send home, but they also have a more important bearing on Peru's socioeconomic development than the contributions or donations of other migrants. Nevertheless, as demonstrated in this chapter, migrants often experience difficulties in cooperating with the local authorities in their home districts, who may take credit for the activities financed by migrant organizations. In fact, such tensions are rooted in the relations of power and dominance that migration causes, and in some regions they tap into conflicts between village and town authorities and rural-urban migrants that are centuries old. In some places, the local authorities try to control the impact that migration is having on rural development in the district by charging fees to villagers who are absent. In most districts, though, migrants are allowed to spend and invest their savings as they want. In US cities with large Peruvian communities, migrant organizations regularly collect considerable amounts of money that they either donate to the children in their home districts for Christmas or other important holidays or use to boost development. But even though many of the projects that migrants undertake in their home villages meet the needs of the local population, the latter seldom feel that their voices are being heard, and they therefore often regard the donations as symbolic gestures of the sponsors. Paradoxically, the most generous contributions are made by migrants who volunteer as organizers of the fiestas: rather than contributing to the progress of their fellow villagers and townsmen, the money spent on these events serves as a means to display the donors' wealth and power. Migrants' commitment to help their home villages and towns is therefore a Janus-faced engagement generated by a wish both to share their savings and to ensure their continuous personal influence.

Chapter 5

Superación:
The Personal Commitment

As demonstrated in the two previous chapters, many migrants send large amounts of money to their relatives during their first years abroad, and some continue to donate and sponsor activities in their home regions for the rest of their lives. However, migrants also spend their earnings in other ways, such as constructing new houses, investing in various economic activities, starting businesses, or saving for retirement. Moreover, to many Peruvians the purpose of migration is to satisfy personal aims rather than to support their close relatives or show their dedication to the communities they came from in Peru. In this chapter, I explore how migrants invest their savings in activities that serve their own rather than others' interests and thus use their migration experience to make their own dreams of a better life come true. For some, this means changing their social status; for others, it means changing the world, fighting for justice, or simply preparing for their retirement. A common thread in these endeavors is the struggle to *superarse*, literally, "to overcome oneself," or, in the vernacular, to overcome the obstacles that prevent individuals from achieving social mobility and obtaining the goals they have set for their lives. Related terms are *progresar* (to progress) and *sacarse adelante* (to take oneself forward), which both connote the individual's efforts to improve himself or herself, overcome hardships, and achieve progress.

Superación is part of most Peruvians' daily vocabulary, but people used it mainly to describe their efforts to obtain an education, find work, and improve their economic status. In the migration context, *superación* and its emphasis on pursuing personal dreams have taken on special meaning, as migrants are viewed as individuals equipped not only with the personal courage to travel to foreign places but also with the special skills needed to profit from that undertaking. Migration, in other words, epitomizes the idea of *superación*. Hence, whereas in the previous two chapters I drew on the term *compromiso* to analyze the commitment migrants make to their families and *voluntad* to examine the commitment they make to their communities, in this chapter I explore the commitment they make to themselves through the lens of *superación*. I do this by asking several questions. Once migrants have fulfilled the promises they have made to their families and once they have demonstrated their readiness to support their communities in Peru, how do they spend their savings on themselves and make plans for the future? Moreover, how does migration lead to economic and social mobility, and how do migrants contribute to the prosperity and welfare of the sending and the receiving societies? In short, the chapter explores how migrants mobilize their talents and skills, how they use them to pursue individual goals, and how their newly acquired agency affects the sending and receiving societies.

Obviously, the dreams that drive Peruvians to emigrate and forge new lives are multiple, and some migrants fare better and are more successful than others in making progress in their new environment. The analytical scope of this chapter is therefore broad, and I am claiming to have captured only a few of the many personal goals Peruvian migrants pursue and the many ways in which they contribute to the surrounding society. However, I have selected 18 case studies in this chapter that illustrate some of the most important dreams that fuel Peruvian migration. It is organized into five sections describing how migrants achieve *superación*: (1) by saving for their retirement, (2) by investing in economic activities, (3) by starting new businesses, (4) by making career shifts, and (5) by engaging in politics. Although the five sections represent distinct forms of *superación*, some of them overlap; for example, the second and third both deal with migrants who use their savings to invest—the former investing in existing businesses and the latter establishing new businesses but also investing in their home countries. I call the migrants who try to attain these five goals migrant savers, migrant investors, migrant entrepreneurs, migrant innovators, and migrant transformers.

The first section offers case studies of three migrants (two females and one male) in Argentina, Chile, and the United States who are using their savings to construct houses for their retirement. In the second section, I show how three male labor migrants from rural areas and three male migrants from urban areas spend their earnings on farming, commerce, transport, and services in Peru. The third section explores how three male migrants with very different social and cultural backgrounds in Peru are creating new livelihoods as businessmen in Chile, Japan, Spain, and the United States. The fourth section examines how three migrants (two males and one female) in Spain and the United States are reinventing their professional identities and challenging conventional ideas of how to make a living and practice their professions. Finally, in the fifth section, I describe how three male migrants have assumed the role of political and organizational leaders to change the world for the better.

To assess the contribution that migration makes to the development of both the migrants' home regions and the receiving societies, this chapter argues, we need to examine the resources, skills, and talents they draw on to become savers, investors, entrepreneurs, innovators, and transformers. To show exactly how migrants mobilize their abilities and use them to overcome the obstacles they encounter in their struggle to achieve *superación*, I employ the concepts of economic, social, cultural, and human capital. Starting with economic capital, money is the reason why most Peruvians emigrate; and as most of them become indebted to pay their travel costs, they spent the first years in their new countries of settlement in almost chronic need of cash. Thrift is therefore an important virtue for many migrants, especially migrant savers, migrant investors, and migrant entrepreneurs, although they save money for different purposes. For migrant savers, thrift is almost a goal in itself to ensure their retirement; by contrast, for migrant investors and entrepreneurs, saving is merely a means to accumulate capital and invest it. Migrant investors and migrant entrepreneurs must also possess other talents such as endurance and decisiveness, just as they must be adept at commanding and managing financial capital, although they use this skill for different purposes. While migrant investors often invest their capital back home in the same types of business that they specialized in before emigrating, migrant entrepreneurs use their capital to open a new business (restaurants, shops, agencies, or clinics, for example) in the receiving countries.

Migration scholars often point to migrants' networks of trust and support as the most effective and sometimes the only resource available for accumulating the financial capital needed to start such a business.[1] Peruvian entrepreneurs are no exception to this practice. An even more important talent of this group of migrants, however, is the willingness to take risk, both economic and social, which often implies jeopardizing not only their own savings but also their families' household economy. To become self-employed, an entrepreneur also needs cultural capital, including knowledge of the laws and customs of the receiving country, language proficiency, and a good feeling for the cultural values and traditions of the migrant's own ethnic group (Adler 2002, 145; Zhou 2004), which together with other Latin Americans makes up the core clientele of most Peruvian entrepreneurs. Human capital constitutes another critical resource in achieving *superación*, especially for migrant entrepreneurs and migrant innovators, who can draw on their previous experiences as cooks, managers, salesmen, businessmen, brokers, and so on to estimate economic risks, organize business activities, manage employees, and raise financing in their new country of settlement. In a similar vein, imagination, creativity, and communication skills are the resources required to conceive and introduce new ideas and are essential for migrant innovators. Finally, migrant transformers must possess not only the courage to stand up against exploitation and injustice but also the personal charisma to mobilize and lead others.

Migrants as Savers

In the literature on remittances, it is often assumed that migrants direct their savings into business. Although this is true in many cases, migrant savers also have other goals in mind, such as sponsoring the migration of a

---

[1] The concept of social capital was introduced in the social sciences by scholars such as Pierre Bourdieu and James Coleman to explain how individual actors draw on the bounded solidarity and enforceable trust invested in social relations to mobilize material as well as human resources and reach personal or collective ends (Portes 1998). Bourdieu's idea of different forms of capital and how these can be converted from one to another is of particular interest to migration scholars because it allows them to describe how newly arrived migrants as well as already established entrepreneurs use the ties of reciprocity that forge migrant networks to access economic and cultural capital (Bourdieu 1986).

close relative, helping family members who have fallen ill, paying for their children's education, or renovating their houses. As migrants grow older, however, other concerns take over: What will happen when I can no longer work? Who will take care of me when I grow old? Where will I spend my last days? These questions, of course, are critical to anyone who is reaching the age of retirement, but for migrants they force them to face concerns of even greater importance: Where do I belong? Should I stay or return? Where will I be buried? The following three case studies, which shed light on what happens when migrants grow old, show how one male and two females are preparing for their retirement. Although the first is living in the United States, the second in Argentina, and the third in Chile, they all plan to spend their last days in Peru.

Enjoying Seniority

Livio, age 64, was born in Chacapalca, a little town in Peru's central highlands. In 1951, after finishing school, he moved to Oroya, where he got a job selling tickets on the city's urban buses. At age 18, he was granted a driver's license, allowing him to assist his father, who made a living as a driver offering a service known as *colectivo* (transport in privately owned cars). A few years later, he married a woman from Pichos, a village not far from Chacapalca that has large migrant communities in both Lima and Miami. In the 1960s, Livio, his wife, and their three children moved to Moquegua in southern Peru, where he opened a small shop selling groceries to the workers in Southern, an American-owned copper mine. When the company laid off a large number of workers in the early 1980s, Livio and his wife decided to close the shop and move to Lima, where they bought a house and made a living buying and selling merchandise. However, the business did not prosper, and they then decided to go to Florida, where one of their daughters and her husband had been living for several years. They had both entered the United States illegally but later obtained stay and work permits with the help of a lawyer. Thus, in 1985 Livio and his wife entered the United States on a tourist visa, which they later overstayed, becoming unauthorized immigrants. During my interview with Livio, he explained, "I was lucky to get a tourist visa. I got it because of my wife's business. They [US officials] thought I entered the country not because I needed work but because I was a tourist." In Miami, their daughter and her husband helped them find a place to live. A couple of years later, Livio's two other daughters followed them and also settled in Miami.

His wife immediately found a job as a domestic servant with an American family in Miami, but Livio spent several months unemployed. Being an unauthorized immigrant who spoke only Spanish, he did not know where or how to look for work. He recalled, "I just walked around asking anyone who looked like they spoke Spanish where to find work. I felt ashamed that my wife and daughters were making money but I wasn't." Eventually, he got a job as an unskilled construction worker. He said, "One day, someone told me where they were looking for construction workers, and when I got there they asked me whether I could start working the following day. I said yes, and the next day I worked for 10 hours. I didn't even ask what the salary was." Later, he got a job in a 7-Eleven but had to quit because there were too many violent attacks. Four years ago, he found a job as a table cleaner in a fast-food restaurant in Ventura Mall in northeast Miami.

Although Livio and his family were all American citizens and all his children were living in the United States at the time I interviewed him in 1998, he felt ambivalent about returning to Peru and had not made up his mind where to spend his retirement. His wife was living in Lima, where she supported herself by renting out rooms in the house and the flat they own. Livio and his three children, meanwhile, were living in Miami. At the time of the interview, two of their daughters were studying at college, while the third was working. Livio pointed out that he was content with his life in the United States and grateful to the country. He added, "Look, you don't have to work as hard as me because you're a professional. If not, you would have to work like me." He continued, "I like living here. But my wife is in Lima, and I may go back to live there too when I retire." He said that he had been saving for retirement for several years and that he owned some real estate: "I have three houses, one in Miami, one in Lima, and one in Chacapalca. As an American citizen, I can go anywhere I want once I retire." Indeed, Livio's network is far-reaching: his daughters all live in Florida, his wife is in Lima, and he still has close relatives in Chacapalca. For him, retirement means the freedom to live in any of the three places.

Dreaming of Retirement

Maritza, who was 42 when I interviewed her in Buenos Aires in 2000, has lived most of her life in Lima. She was born in Canto Grande, a shantytown on Lima's eastern outskirts, in a family of eight children, whose parents came from Arequipa and Ayacucho. Once Maritza finished school, she got a job in the nearby prison of Castro Castro, where she met her future husband, a policeman also working in the prison. Although their salaries were low, the newly wedded couple managed to make ends meet throughout the 1980s, but as Peru's economic situation went from bad to worse at the end of president Alan García's first administration (1985–90), Maritza decided to go to Argentina, where one of her sisters and one of her cousins were working. Before emigrating in 1993, she and her husband agreed that he should follow her once she had settled and found work in Buenos Aires. Soon after her arrival in Argentina, however, Maritza was told that her husband had found a new woman in Peru. In 2000, she said to me, "I left for Argentina because I thought my husband would come after me. But now I don't care. I'm doing fine without him." She later met an Argentinian man, but he also left her for another Peruvian woman. As Maritza ironically pointed out, "The woman was illegal, and she only married him because she needed the papers. As soon as she got her stay permit, she left him." When I interviewed Maritza, she was still single and living by herself. Moreover, as Maritza's parents were both dead and she has no children, the only close relatives she has are her siblings, three of whom were working in Buenos Aires at the time of the interview.

When Maritza came to Argentina, her sister and cousin helped her find work as a domestic and nanny for a prosperous Bolivian family that not only paid her well ($700 a month) but also helped her legalize her stay and obtain a work permit in Argentina. As a live-in domestic, Maritza had few daily needs and saved most of her earnings except for the money she spent on weekends when she stayed in the flat she shared with her sisters and cousins in Buenos Aires. Even though Maritza made more money than most other domestic workers and her employer treated her well, she did not plan to stay forever in Argentina. "I don't like Argentina," she said. "People are very cold here. I miss Peru, but I don't want to go home now because my work here is good and well paid." In fact, a few years before I met Maritza, she had considered going to Europe. On a trip back to Peru, a remote relative had tried to coax Maritza into going to Italy, where the relative was working. However, rather than spending the savings she had brought home with her from Argentina on a ticket to Europe, Maritza decided to spend her money in Peru. As she explained, "I had saved $1,700, which was enough to arrange the trip and buy the ticket to Milan, but instead of going to Italy I decided to spend it on presents and living a good life in Peru." Maritza told me that she does not regret forgoing the opportunity to go to Italy. Rather than planning a future life somewhere else, she prefers to use her savings to visit Peru and reconstruct the house she owns in Lima. "When I go to Peru, I spend my savings on the house, and when I'm in Argentina I send home money to pay for the bills," she said. "That's how I use my savings—to make sure I have a place to return to when I retire."

Ensuring the Future

Julia was 61 when I interviewed her in Chile in 2005. She was born in Chimbote, where she spent her childhood and also most of her adulthood. Like most people living in Chimbote, Julia started working in the fishing industry after she finished school in the late 1950s at a time when Peru was one of the world's leading fishing nations. At age 21, she married a man who was working in the same factory. When Chimbote's fishing industry went into decline in the 1970s, they both lost their jobs. While Julia soon found work in a local hospital as an unskilled health assistant, her husband made a living doing different part-time jobs. Meanwhile, the couple had four children who all grew up in Chimbote. Three of them got married in the late 1990s, and at the time of the interview Julia and her husband had numerous grandchildren. Although they managed to provide for their children with their meager incomes in the early 1980s, the economic crisis that hit Peru in the last decade of the twentieth century had left them both without work. Like thousands of Peruvians in search of a better life in other parts of the world, Julia and her children explored the possibility of emigrating, but with very few resources for travel and with no relatives or friends to help them in such places as Italy or Spain, their only option was to go to Chile. The first to leave was Julia's unmarried daughter, who traveled to Santiago in 1997. Shortly upon her arrival, she found work as a domestic, and after two years she married a Peruvian man who was also working in Santiago. The couple has two children, both born in Chile. During my interview with Julia in Santiago in 2007, she told me, "My grandchildren were born in Chile. They go to school in Chile and they're Chileans. They only know Peru because they have visited Chimbote a few times."

In 1999, Julia, who had divorced her husband, also left for Santiago, where she found work as a live-in domestic in the home of a Chilean family. In 2007, Julia told me that she was content with the salary but not with her employer. According to Julia, the woman not only insisted that she cook Chilean food for the family she worked for but also for herself. Julia said, "I have to cook Chilean-style every day. She doesn't even allow me to cook Peruvian food for myself." She added, "When I started to work the woman taught me how to cook Chilean food. But I know how to cook and I'm a better cook than she is. Chileans don't know how to cook. The only thing they add is salt and occasionally garlic." Although Julia was not content with the treatment and the food, she had stayed with the same employer since she came to Chile. With a salary of $300 a month and almost no expenses except what she spent on her days off, Julia had been able to save a considerable amount of money during her years in Chile. Moreover, because Julia had no stay or work permit, the possibility of finding another job was low. When I asked her how she intends to spend her savings, she replied, "I don't have to support my children anymore. They are married and can take care of themselves. I only give them money when they ask for it. The rest I put into the Seguro Social. That's the retirement money I've saved since I started to work in the hospital in Chimbote." Indeed, during my interview Julia revealed that she plans to return to Peru in the close future and never go back to Chile again. She said, "It's time for me to retire."

The Thrifty Migrant

Most migrants spend their first years outside Peru struggling to find work and a place to live, to acquire new identity papers, and so forth. Once migrants are established, they begin to make plans for the future and, as they grow older, their retirement. This concern has prompted the three migrants discussed above to save and spend their earnings on land or homes in their place of origin, which shows that the question of return is pivotal to migrants when they consider their retirement. However, the three migrants imagine their lives in retirement very differently. Livio, who has lived in the United States since 1985 and is a US citizen, keeps several options open, including living in Miami when he retires. He has houses and family in both the United States and Peru and can travel between the two countries without legal restrictions. Moreover, over the years he has lived in several places where he has created attachments: Chacapalca, his home town in the Peruvian Andes; Lima, where he lived before emigrating and where his wife currently works; and Miami, where he has spent most of his migrant life and where his daughters live.

Maritza and Julia have spent less time outside Peru than Livio and are therefore less prepared for their retirement. Moreover, unlike Livio, who has obtained US citizenship and says that he feels grateful to the United States for offering him the opportunity to work and create a new life, both women say they dislike Argentina and Chile and wish to return to Peru when they stop working. In fact, for Julia, who is undocumented, staying in Chile is not even an option. However, both women have fared well economically and have been able to save for their retirement. Julia started putting money in a pension fund in Peru before emigrating, and as she has continued to save most of her income in Chile, she plans to go back to Chimbote and retire next year. Maritza, however, is single and well paid in Argentina and can even afford to spend some of her income on her yearly visits to Peru to inspect the construction work on the house that will be her home when she retires.

The three migrants discussed in this section are remarkable because all three have saved for their retirement; one even has a new house to live in when she returns to Peru.[2] Most migrants, however, cannot afford to save for their retirement and construct a house in Peru. Their modest earnings are used to pay back loans, remit money to their families in Peru, sponsor the migration of relatives, or finance fiestas and other events in their home region. Livio, Maritza, and Julia are not troubled by such burdens and can therefore spend the money they make on themselves. To save for retirement requires hard work, vision and, it should not be forgotten, thrift, but even so only migrants who have fulfilled their family and community commitments are able to achieve such a *superación*. Livio, Maritza, and Julia, then, stand out because of their ability to save. Yet, thrift is a virtue of other migrants too, as the following section demonstrates.

Migrants as Investors

In the world of policymakers and development planners, migration is regarded as a way for rural poor in the global south to save money and invest in economic activities such as agriculture when they return and thus not only improve the living standards of their families but also contribute to the development of their home country. The following six case studies examine migrants' potential for saving and investing their earnings in economic activities in Peru. I have chosen to present six and not three case studies (as elsewhere) because the migration and development literature often places such great importance on investments in migrants' home countries. The first part, "Rural Investors," describes how labor migration to the United States

---

[2] Equally important, but not discussed in detail here, are the national migration and labor market policies that have an enormous impact on where migrants decide to invest and retire as a demonstration of their commitment to the country where they reside (Paerregaard 2008a).

has provided three male villagers from Peru's central highlands with an opportunity to invest in agriculture, cattle ranching, and land. In the second part, "Urban Investors," I explore how three other male migrants are investing their money in transport, commerce, and service for their return to Peru. The case studies demonstrate that, while migration offers many rural poor an opportunity to invest, the price of their endeavors is sometimes much higher and the outcome much lower than expected. However, the cases also show that, even though investing savings in an urban business is risky, such a strategy may be more profitable than investing in agriculture.

Rural Investors

Many labor migrants come from remote rural areas in the global south that suffer from poorly developed public services and infrastructure. The lack of modernization and absence of state institutions, combined with widespread poverty, prompt them to seek regions and countries where salaries are higher and where they can save money to invest in agriculture, cattle ranching, and land when they return. The three cases that follow illustrate both the costs and the gains of rural labor migration.

ONCE MORE

Remigio, age 31, was born and raised in the village of Usibamba in Peru's central highlands. After he graduated from *secundaria*, his father taught him agriculture and cattle herding, and when he turned 18 he became a *comunero* (that is, member) of Usibamba's peasant community (see chapter 4). Remigio spent the next three years in the nearby city of Huancayo, where he worked in transport, and at age 24 he married a local woman and moved back to his home village, where he and his wife had three children. As a *comunero* who had formed his own household, he obtained the right of use of 2.5 hectares of irrigated land in the community with the possibility that this would allocate him another 2.5 hectares when more land became available. The family lived off the land for several years, but as their needs grew, Remigio began to search for new ways of earning an income. With no start-up capital to buy land or cattle, his prospects for improving the household economy looked very bleak. Although the Peruvian economy was recovering, jobs were still few and badly paid, which made Remigio think of going abroad to work.

Since 2000, two of Remigio's brothers had been working in the United States as shepherds, and in 2006 one of them coaxed his employer to hire Remigio. At age 26, he left on his first contract to work for three years as a shepherd in Colorado. Although Remigio spent most of his time alone in the mountains, the solitude and the cold did not bother him. In my 2011 interview with him in Usibamba, he said, "I only thought of one thing: to save money. I thought this is my opportunity to buy land and cattle in Peru." He also told me that his employer treated him well and that the isolation allowed him to remit $300 to his wife monthly and to save most of the remaining part of his salary of $800. During his absence, Remigio also paid the mandatory annual fee of $200 that the community charges its members who work on contracts in the United States. Once the contract expired, Remigio returned to Peru with $15,000, which he used to buy cattle and reconstruct the family's house in Usibamba. "I bought 12 milk cows that cost 3,000 soles a head and spent the rest of my savings on the house and my family," he said. In 2009, Remigio returned to the United States, this time to work in agriculture on a short-term contract arranged by a lawyer in the United States. Remigio also pointed out that although the contract lasted only three months, it offered him much better working conditions than his first contract for three years. He also said he made better money. The next year Remigio went back to work on two more short-term contracts that allowed him to save another $5,000. Upon his return, Remigio used the money to buy eight more milk cows. He also bought a building lot in Huancayo, where he plans to construct a house for his family when the children come of age. Meanwhile, Remigio rents out the land, providing him with a small extra income.

In 2011, Remigio was elected president of the community, the most important political office in Usibamba and one that commands great respect from the villagers. Clearly, his years in the United States and investments in his home village have given him a reputation as a successful migrant worker. One of Remigio's priorities as village president is to privatize the community's irrigated land. Such an initiative will allow him and other return migrants to use their savings to buy land from other *comuneros* and acquire more cattle. Indeed, Remigio is already planning to go for another contract in the United States to make more money. He told me, "When I step down as president, I'll go back. But only on short-term contracts to buy five or ten more cows." Like many of Usibamba's returning *comuneros*, Remigio uses the dollars he has earned in the United States to move from agriculture into cattle herding, which has improved his and his family's economic status.

That's It

Eugenio, age 42, comes from Chala Nueva, a community close to Chaquicocha in the Alto Cunas area. He has four brothers, all of whom have worked or currently work in the United States. The first to leave was the oldest brother. Recommended by a brother-in-law, he left on his first contract in 1981 and continued to travel another three times in the 1980s and early 1990s. After a total of 12 years in the United States, the brother eventually bought a piece of land, constructed a house, and set up a business in Huancayo, where he now lives with his family. Another brother spent nine years in the United States on three different contracts before eventually settling in Chala with his family. He managed to save $17,000, which he used to buy a tractor and some plots of land in the village. The brother now makes a living by renting the tractor and part of the land to other villagers. To supplement this income, he tills the rest of the land by contracting local labor to plant carrots, garlic, or other cash crops, which he sells in the regional markets. Two more brothers are currently working in the United States on their second contracts. Even though the brothers send home remittances every month to support their families, they also save some of their income with the aim of buying a piece of land, constructing a house, and starting a business in Huancayo when they return.

Eugenio left on his first contract in 1981 at age 21, having been recommended by his oldest brother. He spent three years working for a Mormon rancher in Utah, who treated him well. In 1984, he returned to Peru, where he stayed for seven months until he left on another contract in the United States. This time Eugenio worked for a Basque rancher in California who exploited and mistreated his workers, an experience that prompted Eugenio to return to Peru and settle in his native community when the contract expired in 1988. During his six years in the United States, Eugenio saved enough capital to buy several hectares of land in Chala, and in 1989 he married a local woman with whom he had several children. Unfortunately, the political violence that troubled Peru after 1980 reached the Alto Cunas area in the late 1980s, spreading fear and terror among the local population and constraining their economic activities. By 1993, Eugenio had spent his savings and decided to go to the United States for a third time. Three years later, in 1996, he returned and stayed in Peru for four months until he left on his fourth contract. When I first met Eugenio, he was grazing sheep in the cold Californian desert in April 1998. Speaking about his plans for the future, he explained that it was time to settle down for good in Peru when his fourth contract expired the following year. He also said that his wife had a little shop in Chala and that he wanted to follow his brother's example by spending his savings on a tractor, which he would rent to other villagers.[3] In January 2000, we met again, this time in Chala. During our conversation, Eugenio told me that he had just bought a used tractor for $18,000 from another return migrant in neighboring Usibamba. Now that he had achieved the dream of his life and the fruit of many years' hard work, Eugenio said he would never return to the United States again.

NEVER AGAIN

Juan Pablo, age 30, is a Cabaneño who has spent most of his life in his native village (see chapter 4). After graduating from *secundaria* at age 16, he went to Arequipa and Lima to work for several years, but in 2000 he returned to Cabanaconde, where he married a local woman. In the following years, the couple had four children, and as the family's needs grew, Juan Pablo started to contemplate other ways to make money. Although he inherited several small pieces of irrigated land in Cabanaconde, the crops they produce were barely enough to support his children. Hence, when rumors started circulating that a Spanish company was recruiting agricultural workers in one of the neighboring villages, Juan Pablo signed up for an interview. Within a few months, he had obtained not only a work contract but also a temporary visa to enter Spain, and in 2008 he boarded a flight to Madrid together with a hundred other agricultural workers from his home region.[4] In 2010, he told me, "I passed the exam without problems and the Spanish embassy in Lima issued the visa in a few weeks. In less than three months I was on my way to Spain. I was the only worker from Cabanaconde, but I knew most of the others as they came from the neighboring villages." In Madrid, two buses took the workers to Almería, where they were accommodated in lodgings that hosted workers from other Latin American and several African countries as well. The following day they started to work in the fields planting lettuce eight hours a day, five days a week. Even though Juan Pablo was

---

[3] While shepherding in the United States is an entirely male migration practice, for a number of years Peruvian women have been migrating to Argentina, Chile, Italy, and Spain. Thus, one of Eugenio's sisters left for Buenos Aires in 1996, where she makes a living as a street seller.

[4] The workers were all males, expect for two women who both escaped from the farm after a couple of days. Using a temporary work permit issued by the Spanish embassy in Lima to enter Spain legally, they both traveled to Barcelona, where they were reunited with Peruvian relatives living in the city.

used to hard work in the fields of Cabanaconde, planting lettuce in Spain required him to pass most of the day bending, causing a constant backache. As Juan Pablo explained, "We were supposed to plant 30,000 plants a day and we were not allowed to work for more than eight hours. The only way to do this is to work like crazy from morning to afternoon." The pay was €850 a month, but as the company deducted €310 to cover the costs of his travel and lodging during his stay in Spain, he received only €440. In addition, he had to buy his own food, and since the contract offered him work for only nine months in the year, he bought an airline ticket to Peru to spend the remaining three months with his family in Cabanaconde. As a result, Juan Pablo's savings were much less than expected.

Although Juan Pablo's contract lasted for five years, he stayed in Spain for only two. In 2010, he returned to Cabanaconde for good with the $8,000 he had managed to save. When I interviewed him in Cabanaconde, he said, "It wasn't worth the effort. The work was too hard for my health and I saved less money that I had been told. See, when we arrived in Almería, we were told to sign a new contract, and when we said that we had already signed one in Peru, the employer replied that it wasn't valid because we're going to work for another company." However, the working conditions and the employer's invalidation of the contract signed in Peru were not the worst part of his migration experience. It was his homesickness for his children that eventually prompted him to return before the contract expired. "I thought of them all the time," Juan Pablo said, "and when I visited Cabanaconde after the first nine months I was really shocked when the smallest called me uncle instead of father." In Cabanaconde, Juan Pablo spent his savings on a used tractor, which he rents out during the planting season from June to October. Charging 50 soles ($22) an hour, this business provides him with an average income of 200 soles a day.

Urban Investors

In the literature, labor migration is generally portrayed as the temporary movement of people from poor rural areas to more developed regions or countries to save capital. However, many labor migrants have come from urban areas, and in my study some have even belonged to Peru's middle classes before migrating. Their decision to migrate was often triggered by the economic difficulties they faced when they lost their jobs or when their business failed, as the three examples below show. These case studies describe three men from urban areas in Peru, two from the country's central highlands and one from the northern coast, who emigrated at different times and to different places, but all three have invested their savings in their hometowns, with the aim of returning and living off their investments.

AT ALL COSTS

Teógenes, age 44, was born in a small village outside Huancayo. He moved to the city with his parents at the age of four to attend school. At age 17, he entered the University of Huancayo, but because the family lacked the means to support him, he had to interrupt his studies and become a schoolteacher. In my first interview with Teógenes in 1998, he said, "My parents couldn't afford to pay for my studies, so I had to find work and make my own money." To supplement his salary, Teógenes took out a loan to set up a small printing workshop. Within a short time, he started delivering printing materials to the municipality of Huancayo, and the following year he got married and later had two children. In the late 1980s, he got into debt because the municipality delayed his payments, and as a result of Peru's economic crisis, he lost his clientele. Teógenes told me, "I always wanted to set up my own business and become independent and the print shop was doing fine. But then the crisis deteriorated and I had to find a new way to support my family." He then asked his brother-in-law, who had just returned from the United States, to help him obtain a work contract as a shepherd. In 1989, he was contacted by the brother-in-law's former employer, who offered Teógenes work on his sheep ranch in California. The same year he traveled to Los Angeles and began working on the employer's ranch. As Teógenes got along well with his employer, the latter agreed to renew his contract. Teógenes accepted the offer and stayed in California for another three years.

In 1995, after six years in the United States, Teógenes returned to Peru. Although he had saved most of his income, Teógenes found the situation in Peru too unstable for him to invest his money in starting up a business as he had planned and so decided to leave on a third contract. Tragically, Teógenes never completed it. Shortly after he started work again, he had an accident. While putting up fences around the pastures where the sheep he was looking after were grazing, Teógenes fell and slipped a disc. In Los Angeles, he received surgery and was hospitalized for three months. In the hospital, Teógenes also had an eye operation due to an infection he had contracted on the ranch. Even though the insurance company covered the costs of both operations, he never received financial compensation for the injuries he had suffered.

When I met Teógenes in California in 1998, he said that he hoped to return to Huancayo the same year and invest his savings in a hardware business. However, he also told me that he was deeply concerned about his family in Peru, who not had received any remittances since the operation. He said, "When I was in hospital, I thought of my family all the time. I also made plans for the future and decided never to go abroad to work again. The worst part of it was that I knew my wife and children depended on the money I was sending home, but I couldn't do anything. The insurance only paid for my surgery, and as I didn't make any money my wife had to make ends meet on her own." In January 2000, I met Teógenes again in Huancayo. He had returned as planned the year before and invested his savings in a printing workshop that provides himself and his wife with a small but regular income.

WALKING ON TWO FEET

Melvin, age 51, was born and raised in a well-off middle-class family in Huancayo, where he and his siblings studied in a private school. After school, he found work in a bank in Huancayo and invested his savings in a shop. At age 25, he married a woman also from Huancayo. Peru's economic crisis and the growing political violence in Huancayo in the 1980s prompted Melvin to sell his shop and use the money to travel to Spain together with his wife. After entering the country on tourist visas in 1987, they settled in Barcelona, where a number of his wife's former classmates were living.

Melvin's first job in Spain was as a vegetable and fruit picker for a farmer in Reus south of Barcelona, making $4 an hour. When I met him in 1997, he recounted, "It was really tough. I had never worked with my hands before, and in the summer it was so hot. But I had to do it to make money. Peruvians no longer do that kind of work. Today only Moroccans work in the fields." Later he worked as a waiter in a bar owned by a Spaniard, and shortly afterward he was offered a job running a restaurant in downtown Barcelona. The job taught Melvin how to manage restaurants in Spain, and in 1993 he used his savings to buy his own business in the Olympic Port, a modern district with many offices frequented mostly by Catalan businessmen.

When I first visited Melvin and his wife in their restaurant, they told me that during the week the customers are mainly Catalans. On Sundays, however, when business in the Olympic Port is at a standstill and the usual customers stay away, Melvin's wife and the Peruvian cook she has hired to assist her serve typical Peruvian dishes. This attracts many Peruvians, who use their days off to enjoy a moment in the company of their fellow countrymen. As Melvin's wife explained, "I always cook Peruvian food on Sundays. Mostly dishes like *seco de carnero* [lamb stew] or *escaveche* [marinated fish or chicken in a sauce of onion and other ingredients]. Sometimes Peruvians ask me to prepare food on Saturdays, too." Although Melvin's wife cooks Peruvian style, she acquires all the ingredients locally. She said, "You don't need to go to Peru to cook Peruvian style. I buy everything here. Even *culandro* [coriander]."

In 2002, I returned to Barcelona and learned that Melvin and his wife had separated. Melvin complained that since they had opened the restaurant in the Olympic Port, he and his wife had been working seven days a week and never took a day off to rest. He explained that they paid too much in taxes and were reluctant to hire local people to help them because the unions are too powerful in Spain. Their only employee was an undocumented Peruvian immigrant. Melvin said that he had invested his savings in a small shopping mall in his hometown of Huancayo, hoping that it would provide him with an income when he returns to Peru. "I'm looking for a better place to invest my money," Melvin said. "The restaurant in Barcelona requires too much work, and now I've divorced my wife." However, the shopping mall turned out to be a bad investment. "The man I left in charge of the mall has not done anything, and now I can't even sell it," Melvin explained. "There are no buyers." In 2004, I visited Barcelona again and found that Melvin had just opened a new restaurant downtown selling *pollo a la braza* (fried chicken, a Peruvian specialty), and when I came back again in 2006 he had bought a bar in Hospitalet on the outskirts of the city. Melvin invited me for a drink and updated me on his plans: "It's not time to go back to Peru yet but I still have the shopping mall in Huancayo. If Peru makes more progress, I may go back."

Don't Count on Me

Ever, age 34, was born in Trujillo into a middle-class family. His father owned a factory in Trujillo until he retired a few years ago, while his mother takes care of the house. Ever and his two brothers all went to a private school in Trujillo, and after graduating they went to Lima to continue their studies. In Lima, Ever and his brothers took English classes in a private language school for several years while exploring the possibility of emigrating. In 2006, Ever told me, "I always wanted to go to the United States, and when

I came to Lima in 1993, everybody was trying to find ways to get out of the country. My brothers also wanted to leave the country." As Ever and his brothers did not have any relatives abroad to help them emigrate, they tried to get to the United States by other means. Ever recalled, "Someone had told me that it was easy to get a job in the tourist industry in the United States, so I started to look for job advertisements in English." In 1996, Ever was hired as a waiter on a cruiser owned by an American company, which also helped him obtain a work and temporary residence permit in the United States. Instead of returning to Peru when his contract expired, Ever stayed in Miami, where the company was based, and when the visa expired, he crossed the US-Mexican border and asked to have it extended. In this way, Ever remained a legal immigrant in the United States for more than a year, making a living as a waiter in a Miami restaurant. He also helped his brothers obtain work contracts with the American company that had brought him to the United States.

The immigration reform that the Clinton administration introduced in 1996 speeded up the legalization process for immigrants with temporary stay permits and opened a new door in Ever's life. In 1998, he was granted a green card, which not only allowed him to take any work he wanted but also permitted him to travel back and forth between the United States and Peru. In the following years, Ever worked as a salesman in different companies in Miami and traveled to Trujillo to visit his parents. On one of his visits to Peru, he married a woman from Huanchaco, a small town close to Trujillo, with whom he had a child. Ever recalled how his life changed after he obtained the green card: "I used to worry whether they would extend my visa or whether I would become illegal. My life changed when they gave me the green card. Now I can go home when I want and make better money. My plan is to bring my wife and child to the United States." When I interviewed Ever in Huanchaco in 2004, he told me that he was applying for family reunification with his wife and child in the United States and that he had returned to live in Peru while waiting for the reply, which he said may take several years.

During his stay in Peru, Ever invested his savings in two businesses in Huanchaco. The first is an Internet cafe equipped with 15 computers and five videogames, which he bought in Miami and brought to Peru. Although there were already several competing Internet cafes in Huanchaco in 2004, Ever felt confident that the business would pay off. "I charge one sol an hour for the computers and a little more for the videogames," he said. "I'm surprised how the kids and young people spend their money here." Ever has also bought two used vans (*combis*), which he uses as buses to transport passengers from Huanchaco to Trujillo. Although he paid the drivers 30 soles a day, he told me that the two vans generated an average daily profit of 40 soles. "I've invested $20,000 in the Internet cafe and the vans, and that provides me with enough money to support my family while we're in Peru," he said, adding, "but I really don't want to stay. I'll go to the United States as soon as the papers for my wife and child are ready."

The Enduring Migrant

The subjects of these six case studies come from different socioeconomic and cultural environments in Peru, four from poor rural families and two from urban middle-class families. Although the different backgrounds have clearly shaped their migration experiences, the six migrants were driven by the same goal: to save money and invest it upon their return to Peru. In fact, when asked what initially impelled them to leave Peru, most migrants usually say it was the dream of saving capital to set up a business in their hometown or region, and some continue to cling to it after they have settled and formed families outside Peru. Nevertheless, few ever carry out the dream of returning, and even if they do their investments rarely pay off, whether because they lack the necessary expertise to run a business, they have been robbed or cheated, or they neglect to reinvest their earnings. Successful investments therefore represent the exception rather than the rule in Peruvian migration. But even though these six case studies provide proof that some migrants actually manage to save enough money to make a significant investment in agriculture (Eugenio), cattle ranching (Remigio), or a business in the city (Teógenes and Ever), they also indicate that the physical and psychological costs of achieving this dream are often far higher than expected. Indeed, when I interviewed Juan Pablo and Teógenes in Peru they both said they regretted having migrated.

The case studies also show that the investments migrants make upon their return are influenced by how they migrate. Thus, Remigio, Eugenio, Juan Pablo, and Teógenes traveled on visas that allowed them to work only in agriculture or cattle herding for a limited period of time. In chapter 3, I discussed how Bernardo became an unauthorized immigrant after he ran away from the ranch he was working on. Many shepherds leave repeatedly on new contracts, and a growing number follow Bernardo and others to settle in the United States; but even so, most return to Peru, where they invest their savings in either a tractor, a new house, a vehicle, or a small business in a nearby city. Conversely, Melvin and Ever have not decided where to live yet, and although they have both made investments in Peru, they also have other plans. Melvin, who is older and has lived outside Peru for much longer than Ever, still hopes that the shopping mall will one day yield an income so that he can return to Huancayo. Meanwhile, he owns a restaurant and a bar in Barcelona. Ever, in contrast, wants to go back to the United States in the near future, and although he has invested his savings in an Internet cafe and two vans in Peru, this investment merely serves to support his family until they can all go to the United States.

In the remittance and migration literature, migrants such as Remigio, Eugenio, Juan Pablo, and Teógenes are often pictured as examples of labor migrants from poor rural families who invest their savings in agriculture and cattle herding upon their return and whose earnings leverage development in their home regions. At first glance, they all fit this image, but a closer look at the migration experiences of these four men also reveals that, even though labor migrants spend long periods away from their families and toil hard to save capital, their plans seldom materialize. As low-paid labor migrants, their savings are small, and even though the investments they make on their return allow them to establish new businesses, their success relies entirely on their capacity to continuously save, reinvest, and survive competition from fellow former migrants. Thus both Eugenio and Juan Pablo have bought used tractors that provide them with a steady income but also require maintenance; also, within the next five to seven years both will need more capital to renew their tractors and, even more important, other villagers are likely to follow their example, making their business ever more competitive. Moreover, as Teógenes's case shows, even though many migrants come from remote Andean villages, they have spent some of their lives in the city and are therefore more likely to invest in urban rather than in rural activities when they return to Peru. Remigio stands out as the single case of labor migration that has paid off and led to a profitable rural investment. However, his plan to go back on yet another contract reveals that even successful labor migrants become dependent on their earnings in dollars. Indeed, as discussed in chapter 4, a growing community of former labor migrants from Usibamba has emerged in several places in the United States.

In contrast, migrants such as Melvin and Ever who lived an urban middle-class lifestyle before emigrating and who found work outside their previous professions in Spain and the United States have fared much better economically. Ironically, their opportunities to make money are much better than those of Remigio, Eugenio, Juan Pablo, and Teógenes, but the likelihood that they will ever end up as businessmen in Peru is much smaller. The six case studies therefore point to the need to rethink conventional ideas about labor migration as a means to leverage rural development.

Migrants as Entrepreneurs

As demonstrated above, exploitation, solitude, and unhealthy living conditions are some of the many hardships that labor migrants must endure, even as they have to work hard and save almost every penny of their earnings. Endurance and thrift are virtues among migrant entrepreneurs as well, but as self-employed immigrants making a living as businessmen, their main concern is not to endure in order to save but to access capital and create a network of business contacts and customers in the receiving society. How do they raise capital? How do they create a business network? And, most important, what do they sell, and how they attract a clientele?

The Taste of Peru

Segundo, age 40, was born in Cajamarca, a northern Andean region of Peru where he grew up in a family with seven brothers and one sister. From the time the boys were young children, his mother trained her sons in domestic work, which, according to Segundo, stimulated his interest in cooking. At the age of seven, he migrated to Lima with his family. After finishing school, he attended a course in gastronomy that taught him not only how to cook but also how to run a restaurant. For a number of years, he and one of his brothers worked for a businessman who had several restaurants in Lima. In 1993, the man sent Segundo's brother to Chile to work in a restaurant he owned in Santiago, and in 1994 Segundo followed him. After a couple of years working as a cook for the Peruvian employer in Santiago, Segundo was hired in a Chilean restaurant. Four years later, he decided to quit the job and use his savings to open up his own restaurant, following the example of his brother, who had opened a restaurant in an upper-class neighborhood of Santiago not long before. Segundo took out a loan with a Chilean bank, and with economic support from his siblings he rented and restored a restaurant located in downtown Santiago. The businesses of both brothers turned out to be profitable, and in the late 1990s two more brothers came to Santiago to help them.

Today, the brothers own a total of four restaurants in the city. Two are located in downtown Santiago and specialize in *pollo broaster* (barbecued chickens), a Peruvian dish appreciated by migrants in Chile, and other so-called *platos típicos* (typical dishes). Most of the clients are Peruvians who either eat their lunch during the week at the restaurants or spend Sundays or other days off in the company of other Peruvians enjoying the taste of Peruvian food and beverages. The two other restaurants are located in Seminario, an uptown neighborhood of Santiago. One specializes in Peruvian seafood, while the other primarily serves barbecued meat. Unlike the two restaurants in downtown Santiago, which attract mainly Peruvian customers, most of the clients of these two restaurants are better-off Chileans, who are showing increasing interest in ethnic cuisine.

Initially, Segundo and his brothers brought the beverages (soft drinks and beer) and the ingredients (herbs, spices, and the like) that they use to prepare their food directly from Peru. However, in the past five years several wholesale dealers have emerged that specialize in the import and sale of these items in Chile. The dramatic increase in the number of Peruvian restaurants in Santiago is clearly indicative of this development. Yet, Segundo insists that, in order to guarantee the authentic taste of Peruvian food in the restaurants, he and his brothers continue to bring their cooks from Peru. He says, "The cooks always end up finding work somewhere else, but then we go looking for a new cook in Peru. It's not difficult to find someone who wants to leave the country to work." Segundo also says that all their employees are Peruvians.

According to Segundo, the four brothers are *socios* (partners), which means that they all own a share in the restaurants and divide the profits. He also told me that they were the first in the family to start an independent business. "We knew how to cook, but we didn't know how to run a business," Segundo said, adding, "it's only a question of believing in what you're doing. I have even been thinking of setting up a business in another country—maybe in Spain, where one of my cousins has a restaurant, or in the United States."

Soap Operas + Inca Kola = Business

In Japan, migrants face many difficulties in trying to start up their own businesses. One of the requirements is proficiency in Japanese so that the owner can communicate with the local authorities, financial agencies, customers, and the like. Another challenge is acquiring a stay and work permit, which is needed for renting or buying a property and for gaining permission to open a shop or engage in other forms of commerce. Familiarity with Japanese codes of conduct and business management is, of course, also an advantage.

Marco, age 35, is clear evidence of these difficulties. He originates from the city of Huacho north of Lima. Both he and his wife are *sansei*, that is, third-generation Japanese. In 1989, they migrated to Japan with the first wave of Japanese Peruvians who went to the land of their parents or grandparents in search of a better future in the wake of a Japanese immigration law aimed at attracting foreign workers. After several jobs as a factory worker, Marco decided to try his luck as an independent businessman and opened a shop in Isesaki, northwest of Tokyo. Trained as a butcher by his father, Marco started selling meat to Peruvians in the neighborhood where he lives. He also sells imported Peruvian products such as Inca Kola, Cuzqueña beer, and canned spices, herbs, and beans that are not available in ordinary shops in Japan. Later, he began to rent videotapes of Peruvian television programs.

The videotapes are the product of a transnational business network organized by Marco and his two brothers. One lives in Lima, where he records more than 50 percent of all programs broadcast by television channels available in Peru. Three times a week, a messenger travels from Lima to Tokyo, where Marco's second brother receives the master tapes. He rents a small workshop 15 minutes from Narita Airport, where he copies the videos. As the transpacific flights usually arrive in the afternoons, the brother in Narita has approximately 15 hours to copy the master tapes brought in from Lima. In the morning of the following day, Marco drives from Isesaki to Narita—a trip that takes him three hours—and collects the 500 tapes that his brother has made from the masters. Around midday, he returns to Isesaki, where he offers the tapes for rent in his shop. The charge is 1,000 yen for eight tapes to be returned after a couple of days. In the late afternoon, he fills up a van with Peruvian products and, of course, the videotapes and drives around Isesaki, Takasaki (the closest large city), and sometimes Nagano, which is several hours away, to offer his products to the local Peruvian migrant community.

Marco's business is based on the mutual trust and ethnic solidarity that he creates when touring the Gunma and Nagano prefectures in his mobile shop delivering Peruvian products.[5] Over the years, he has assembled a list

---

[5] According to Marco, at least four other Peruvians are reported to have created similar transnational business networks.

of phone numbers and addresses of hundreds of migrant families, allowing him to tell his clients where and when to wait for him during these trips. Although Inca Kola, *salsa de culandro* or *huacatay* (sauce of coriander or of an Andean herb), *ajínomoto* (Chinese salt), *salchicha tipo Huacho* (sausage from Huacho), and a personal service in Spanish provide Marco with a regular income, the most profitable part of his business is the videos of the most recent television programs in Lima, including the news (*Noticiaras*), sports events (*Goles en acción*), Latin American soap operas (*Los ricos también lloran*), Peruvian talk shows (*Laura en América*), and movies and cartoons in Spanish translation that lend Peruvians in Japan a sense of proximity to Peru, despite the differences in the time zones and miles.

Recently, however, the videotape business has become more competitive. Introduced by innovative Japanese Brazilian businessmen in the early 1990s, renting videotapes was initially targeted at the Portuguese-speaking immigrant community in Japan. In the late 1990s, Japanese Peruvian businessmen also started renting videotapes in Spanish, a market that in the beginning was controlled by five Peruvian shop owners, one of them being Marco. But later the business became much more competitive. On my last trip to Japan in 2004, Marco told me that the price of renting videos had fallen in half and that the introduction of new technologies such as cable television was making it a dying business. He said that there were now more than a hundred Peruvians renting out videos in Japan and that instead of importing master tapes from Peru, he had started to download some of them. Moreover, Marco had recently tried to reach a deal with several Peruvian television channels giving him and a couple of other Peruvian businessmen in Japan the right to download their programs. However, the attempt had failed, and he was therefore considering new ways of doing business in either Japan or the United States.

Richer Than the President

Oscar, age 61, was born and raised in the region of Amazonas in northern Peru but left for Lima before coming of age. In Lima, he studied dentistry at Peru's San Marcos University. After graduating, he married a woman who also came from Amazonas and began working in a public hospital. Once he had saved enough money, he opened a private clinic in Lima. The economic and political crisis during the first García government (1985–90) had a disastrous effect on his business, however, and in 1989 he and his wife decided to emigrate. The same year Oscar applied for and was granted a tourist visa at the American embassy in Lima, and soon afterward he left for Miami, where several remote relatives of his were living. One month later, his wife followed with their two children. When their tourist visas expired, all four became unauthorized immigrants.

Unlike most other migrants, Oscar brought his own savings from Peru, which he used to pay for the courses he needed for revalidation of his professional credentials and thus for obtaining a license to practice dentistry in the United States. In Miami, a friend helped Oscar get a job at the airport in a catering company delivering food. He worked from 2 p.m. to 11 p.m., allowing him to study English in the morning, the first step in his plan to regain his professional standing. "The job was really tiring," he explained. "I wasn't used to manual work. I worked together with a Salvadoran, who said it was real easy. You see, he used to work in agriculture, so to him it was easy." Oscar's wife, Silvia, however, found work as a domestic while taking care of the children. "Our first years in the United States were extremely tough," she recalled. "I will never forget it. We only had one car, which Oscar needed because he worked late at night. So I had to take the bus to go to work with the kids. Can you imagine standing there waiting for the bus for one hour with two small children in the heat in Miami? Fortunately, the children behaved really well and never made trouble while I was working."

After a year and a half, the family moved to Los Angeles, where a brother of Silvia's was living. In Los Angeles, Oscar got a job assisting an American dentist in her clinic. Meanwhile, he enrolled in a study program to update his professional skills and to prepare for the exams that the health authorities offer immigrants who have received a degree in dentistry outside the United States. "All those years I had to hush the children every evening so they didn't disturb Oscar while he studied after coming home from work," Silvia remembered. Three years later, Oscar felt he was ready to take the exams, which were held in San Francisco, lasted three days, and required Oscar to bring two people to act as his patients. "I spent my last savings to cover the expenses for the exams," he said. "Not only did I have to pay the two patients to go with me, but I also had to spend money on transport, hotels and food for all three of us. Apart from that I lost three days' salary." He continued, "The exam started at seven in the morning, so I got up really early to have breakfast. But one morning, the waiter was too slow bringing me the food I had ordered, so I had to go to the exam on an empty stomach. I don't how I did it. But I held out for the rest of the day."

Eventually, Oscar passed the exams and was granted a license to practice dentistry in California. He told me that when he came back from San

Francisco, the dentist he was working for congratulated him and offered him a salary increase. But he declined her offer and took out a loan to open his own clinic. Today, Oscar has two clinics in Huntington Park, Los Angeles, with a handful of dentists working for him. The majority of his patients are Hispanics, who prefer to be treated by a Spanish-speaking rather than an English-speaking dentist. When I visited the family in Long Beach in 1998, he said, "I make more money than President Clinton. When I turn 50, I plan to retire. I hope my oldest daughter will study dentistry here in the United States so she can take over my clinics. Then my wife and I can enjoy our retirement in Peru."

The Audacious Migrant

Marco, Segundo, and Oscar started their new lives as immigrants in Japan, Chile, and the United States, taking low-paid jobs as unskilled, blue-collar workers, as immigrants in these countries often do. After a few years, they started their own businesses as restaurant, shop, and clinic owners, drawing on their previous experiences as a cook, butcher, and dentist in Peru. While Oscar used his savings from Peru to pay for the exam that gave him a license to practice his profession in the United States and to establish his own clinic, Segundo took out a bank loan and borrowed money from his relatives to start his restaurant in Chile. Marco, however, spent the money he had made as a factory worker in Japan to buy the shop and the van he uses to market his merchandise and rent out videotapes.

Starting a business, however, requires not only economic capital but also customers. By using Spanish as their working language and their knowledge of Latin and Peruvian culture and taste, Segundo, Marco, and Oscar created networks of business contacts and a clientele mostly but not only of co-ethnics. The clientele of the three businessmen is important for their economic success. The customers in Segundo's restaurants include Peruvian migrants as well as middle-class Chileans, while Oscar's clinics treat both Peruvians and other Hispanics, of whom there is a large population in Los Angeles. Marco, however, only serves Peruvians, which restricts his opportunities for opening new markets and reaching a wider clientele. In Mark Granovetter's terms, only Melvin and Segundo have profited from the strength of the weak ties (that is, ties reaching beyond the close family relations) and succeeded in creating bridging as well as bonding capital (that is, social capital based on weak as well as strong ties). Marco, conversely, mainly draws on his strong ties, which generate only bonding capital (that is, social capital based on strong ties) (Granovetter 1973).

Migrants as Innovators

Networking, a good sense of the needs and demands of other migrants, and, most of all, daring are important qualities for the success of migrant entrepreneurs, as shown above. Even though the three migrants discussed in this section also possess some of these qualities, their principal virtue is the capacity to generate and carry out new ideas. As the following case studies illustrate, the professional experience that migrant innovators bring with them from Peru or acquire outside the country is a critically important resource for their endeavors, as are their creativity and their ability to use their potential in a new context. The next three migrants come from very different locations in Peru: the first, a man from the northern highlands; the second, a woman from the northeastern lowlands; and the third, a man from the southern highlands.

Imagining the Future

Hilmer was only 14 years old when he traveled with his parents and younger sister to the United States in 1988. Born and raised in Bolognesi (see chapter 4), he had just finished *primaria* (elementary school) when his parents decided to emigrate. For his parents, the decision was far from easy, as they had 13 hectares of agricultural land and more than 15 cows in Bolognesi, which they left in the charge of relatives. However, like many other Bolognesinos, Hilmer's parents thought that ensuring their children's future by emigrating was more important than taking care of their properties in their native village.

One of the pioneers in the Bolognesino community in Hartford is the older sister of Modesta, Hilmer's mother, who came to the United States in 1964 and in the 1970s and 1980s brought five of her seven brothers to Hartford. Hence, when Modesta's sister invited her to come to Hartford, she immediately accepted the invitation, using this as an opportunity to bring Mario, Hilmer's father, and their two children to the United States. During my stay in Hartford in 2006, I interviewed Modesta. "We were living a good life in Bolognesi before we left for Hartford and we didn't leave Peru because of economic need," she told me. "Mario raised cattle in Bolognesi and sold them to the butchers in Lima at a very good price. We thought of our children and the possibilities we could offer them in the United States." Modesta also told me that she and Mario had both worked hard to support their family in Hartford and that both she and her husband plan to return to Peru when they retire.

Modesta and Mario's struggle to offer their children a better future has indeed paid off. Hilmer and his sister both went to high school in Hartford, and after graduating his sister studied to become a medical doctor, while he went to Cornell University, where he received a degree in engineering. Once out of school, Hilmer worked for a company in Canada for several years, enjoying a trouble-free and well-paid bachelor life. However, Hilmer did not feel content with his career and lifestyle, and in 2002 he enrolled in a master's program at Harvard Business School to study management, using his savings to finance his degree. In 2006, he explained to me, "I didn't find my work in Canada very interesting. At Harvard I learned how to start up and manage a business, and my plan is to use this knowledge in Peru. I'm currently trying to form a local branch of a worldwide organization called GEN [Global Entrepreneurship Network, an organization that supports entrepreneurs around the world] in Peru." In fact, when I interviewed Hilmer in Hartford he had already moved to Peru and was just paying his parents a visit. "Before going back to Peru, I bought the house in Hartford where my parents live," he said. "I didn't know how my return to Peru would turn out, whether I could use my management knowledge or not." Apart from introducing GEN in Peru, Hilmer also had other ideas. One was to extend the loan service that Peruvian banks offer their customers to remote rural areas by using modern credit card technologies and other ways to supervise and support the projects that migrants in Hartford employ in the home village of Bolognesi.

In 2007, I visited Hilmer again, this time in Lima, where he had bought a flat and opened an office to promote the message and activities of GEN in Peru. My latest encounter with Hilmer was in 2011, when he told me his involvement in Peru had changed and that he was now concentrating his efforts on supporting a congressional candidate from his home province who was running in the 2011 elections. "Her campaign is focused on such questions as education and health, which are very important," he said. "But my own interest to push for water is the principal issue to be addressed. Peru's main problem is water." When I asked him whether he ever thought of going back to the United States, he replied, "I still have many ideas of how to introduce changes in Peru and I have no plans to go back in the near future."

Making a Better World

Chavica, age 63, was born in Mendoza, a provincial town in Peru's northeastern highlands. She and her eight siblings all went to school in Mendoza and moved to Lima when they came of age. Several of her siblings worked as schoolteachers in Mendoza, a profession they continued practicing after migrating, while the rest took up studies at different universities in Lima. Chavica, however, never finished her studies in educational psychology. In 1969, she traveled to Europe, where she first spent several years in England making a living as a waitress while continuing to study psychology. Later she moved to Barcelona, where she completed her studies and started working as a children's speech therapist. In the mid-1970s, she married a Catalan man but was widowed 10 years later when her husband died of cancer.

In the late 1990s, the Spanish government implemented a policy called codevelopment, requiring the country's municipalities to dedicate 0.7 percent of their budgets to development projects in the home countries of their immigrant populations. It also encouraged these migrants to apply for money to finance such projects. Peruvians in Barcelona and other cities in Spain responded by forming migrant organizations and suggesting projects that could be cofinanced by the municipalities and private funders. In 2001, Chavica and a group of migrants from Mendoza managed to obtain funding from public and private funds in Barcelona to support an agricultural project in their home community to improve the environment.[6] Although the project encountered difficulties because of a lack of support from the local leaders in Peru, Chavica and a group of fellow migrants decided to continue their efforts to implement change in their native province. The same year they formed an organization called Solidaridad con la Amazonía, which seeks to strengthen sustainable development in the Peruvian jungle, and in 2002 they received €30,000 from the municipality of Tarragona to finance several small projects in Mendoza. Among these projects were the production of conserved fruit such as *guayawa*, one of the main products of the area; the formation of a cooperative owning sewing machines that local women could use to generate an income of their own; and efforts to clean the town's drinking water and protect the area's trees. In the following years, Chavica received more public as well as private funds to train the schoolteachers of

---

[6] The same year Peruvians from the community of Sarhua in Ayacucho also formed an nongovernmental organization (NGO) and used money from the municipality of Hospitalet to invite a group of schoolchildren from their home village to visit Barcelona. However, the NGO never received money for the project.

Mendoza in how to work with children with physical and mental disabilities. She also obtained funding to build a resort of bungalows made of sustainable construction materials to house tourists and visiting migrants and teach the local population how to take care of the environment. To disseminate the ideas and objectives of Solidaridad con la Amazonía, Chavica has repeatedly participated in regional television programs in Catalonia that introduce their viewers to remote places such as Mendoza and the activities of the organization. In these programs, Chavica encourages Catalans to *apadrinar* children ("adopt" them as godchildren) in Mendoza, committing to sending them €15 in return for a letter of gratitude. During her many visits to Mendoza, Chavica has acted as a guide for such "godparents" who travel to Peru to visit their "godchildren."

In the past 10 years, Chavica has dedicated most of her free time to raising funds and managing the many activities of the nongovernmental organization (NGO) she is in charge of. Although she continues to feel committed to the goals of the organization, Chavica also recognizes that the changes she is trying to introduce in Mendoza will not come easily. In my interview with her in 2006, she said, "The difficult part is to change the attitude of people in Mendoza. They still live with the old ideas and don't listen when we offer them new ways of solving their problems." Chavica also complains that the local authorities, including the mayor, are corrupt and involved in drug smuggling. "Once the mayor visited Barcelona to promote the development of Mendoza," she told me. "He caused a scandal when he attended a meeting with the Peruvian consul and the authorities here in Barcelona." Indeed, raising money in Spain is the easiest part of Chavica's struggle to modernize life in Mendoza; the struggle to alter the lifestyles of her fellow townsmen is much harder.

I Did It My Way

Nicario Jiménez was born in Alqaminka, a Quechua-speaking peasant community in the Ayacucho region, in 1957. He was raised in a group of seven siblings. In 1968, he moved to Huamanga, the capital of the Ayacucho region, together with his family, the first move in a long chain of migration that eventually brought him to Lima and finally to the United States. In Huamanga, he finished elementary school and began receiving training as a folk artisan in accordance with the family's tradition. As both his father and grandfather were *retablistas*, Nicario learned to make *retablos*—rectangular wooden boxes with two painted doors, which contain small figures representing people and animals engaged in social and ritual activities, such as agricultural work, cattle herding, trade and exchange, and religious celebrations of mostly Christian events.[7]

In 1986, Nicario was invited by a North American historian to lecture about his work as a folk artisan at one of Miami's universities. In the years that followed, he continued traveling to the United States to participate in academic events. However, he also started showing his works, which he produced at his workshop in Barranco, at local art exhibitions in Florida. When he was granted a temporary residence visa in 1997, he decided to move permanently to Miami together with one of his daughters. While lecturing in Miami, Nicario changed his notion of what it means to be a *retablista*. He learned that the distinction between folk art and fine art is very fuzzy and that his *retablos* are valued not only because he manufactures them according to an Andean folk art tradition but also because of his own individual ingenuity and creativity. In other words, he discovered that the *retablos* he makes are not just a reproduction of a native tradition (folk art), but a unique creation, the value of which can only be determined by its inherent, artistic quality. This reconceptualization of his own identity as an artisan encouraged Nicario to engage in what he considers a personal struggle to win recognition as an artist, not only within the Peruvian community in Miami but also in the broader art world

In 1997, he established a workshop in a rented flat in Miami, which served as his main base for producing *retablos*. He later moved the workshop to Naples in western Florida, where he currently lives with his daughter. Periodically, he travels all over the United States to display his works at art festivals, which over the years have won him numerous prizes and opened doors to the North American market. However, Nicario does not feel that his works have won the recognition they deserve. When I interviewed him in Miami in 1998, he said, "They always try to place me in a special section of folk art and they gave me all those prizes. But I wanted them to recognize my work as real art. So I ask them to place it in the section for art. Sometimes they let me do it. See, they think I'm a folk artisan because I'm Peruvian and make *retablos*. But I want them to understand that I'm an artist."

To Nicario, however, the artistic value of his *retablos* consists in their quality and originality rather than in their motifs and symbolic meanings. A good *retablo* can depict North America's modern urban world and Peru's

---

[7] *Retablos* began as portable altars used to proselytize and then became a folk art.

political history as well as the rural life of the Andes. He conceives of the *retablo* as a genre of art that is constantly changing and that can be adapted to new environments. He also believes that its transformation from a sacred object used for ritual purposes first into a commercial folk product symbolizing Andean culture and then into an individual artistic expression revives rather than jeopardizes the folk art history of Ayacucho. He also thinks that the folklore tradition of his family validates his attempts to win recognition as an artist. Whereas his grandfather was a local producer of the Cajón de San Marcos (boxes of St. Mark), his father manufactured mainly modern *retablos*. And just as his father trained him as a *retablista*, so Nicario has instructed his son and daughter in the production of *retablos* as a folk art. To Nicario, then, the struggle to be acknowledged as an artist embodies the artistic spirit of his father and grandfather, a vision to which he gave testimony in an exhibition he arranged displaying the works of his family's four generations of *retablistas*.

The Creative Migrant

Thrift, endurance, and assertiveness are resources that not only savers, investors, and entrepreneurs need to acquire, but also other migrants too. As shown in this section, Hilmer spent several years working to save for his studies at Harvard, just as Chavica's experience as a fund-raiser and an accountant was critical to her work in her NGO. Like them, Nicario has invested both time and money in his effort to enter the mainstream American art market. They have also encountered many challenges in convincing others of the importance of their ideas and the value of their work. Finally, the three case studies show daring to be a driving force in the work of all three. Nonetheless, it is their receptivity to new ideas and their ability to incorporate those ideas into specific projects or art forms that are the true virtues of the three innovators.

Hilmer is Peruvian but spent most of his childhood and youth in the United States, where he studied and received a business degree from one of the country's most prestigious universities. Rather than pursue a conventional and promising career in North America, he decided to return to Peru after graduating to help develop the country's fast-growing economy. His professional potential is great, and apart from supporting several development projects in his home community of Bolognesi, Hilmer has created a local branch of a global network of business entrepreneurs and is currently advising the congressional candidate from his home region of Ancash. Chavica has also studied abroad, and, like Hilmer, she has decided to use her professional skills to promote the development of her home community in Peru. In Spain, Chavica has raised money from the city where she lives to carry out projects that aim to improve the living conditions in Mendoza and introduce a modern lifestyle. She has also created projects that make it possible for Spaniards to sponsor the education of children in Mendoza and organized tours that bring Spaniards to Peru. Finally, Nicario, who was trained as a folk artist in Peru, is part of a transnational network that allows him to renegotiate his role as a *retablista* in Peru and redefine the meaning of folklore and art. Although he invests most of his time in exhibiting *retablos* at art festivals in North America, where he has gained recognition as an artist, he also acknowledges the cultural roots of his *retablos*. These fluid and apparently contradictory identities as traditionalist, rural folklore artisan, and modern artist emerge from a migratory process that links Nicario to his home community of Alqaminka, as well as to Lima and Miami.

Even though the professional and migratory trajectories of Hilmer, Chavica, and Nicario vary and they engage in very different projects and endeavors, their contributions to the larger society are all driven by their imaginations, creative talents, and ability to challenge conventional ways of thinking and foster new ideas. Hilmer and Chavica acquired these skills after they emigrated, while Nicario had already been trained as an artisan before leaving Peru. However, their migration experiences have been critical in inspiring them to rethink their professional skills and use them in new and innovative ways. Their case studies suggest that migration allows people not only to develop their personal talents but also to bring them to bear in ways that contribute to both the sending and the receiving societies.

Migrants as Transformers

Peruvians seek *superación* in a variety of ways. Some spend many years abroad saving for a better life for when they retire or return. Others try to realize their migration dreams by opening a business or recasting their professional talents in the receiving society. In this section, I present three case studies of Peruvians, all males, who have dedicated their lives as migrants to the struggle for social justice and to bettering the working and living conditions of other migrants. The first comes from Peru's second-largest city of Arequipa, the second from the tropical lowlands, and the third from the country's central highlands. The three migrants have engaged in politics at different levels of society and in different kinds of social struggles in the receiving countries, but they all share an ability to lead and mobilize their fellow migrants.

Legislating Dreams

Felipe, age 61, was born in Arequipa and lived in Peru until he was 20 years old. In 1969, he migrated to the United States, where he first studied English. Later he enrolled in Sacred Heart University in Connecticut, where he studied to be a professional educator. Meanwhile, he worked to pay his school fees. After graduating from college, he worked in business for a while until he took up his studies again, now at Fairfield University, where he completed graduate studies. He also obtained American citizenship after marrying a Puerto Rican woman with whom he had several children who were born in the United States and are American citizens. The experience of pursuing his own goals while supporting himself at an early age shaped Felipe's personality and taught him how to achieve mobility in the United States. It also showed him the barriers immigrants and minorities encounter when they pursue the American dream and try to change their social status in North America. In particular, he became aware of the importance of obtaining an education, which prompted him to dedicate his professional career to supporting and mentoring young Hispanics in Connecticut in their struggle to realize the American dream for themselves.

For many years, the focus of Felipe's work was Bridgeport, Connecticut, where he has spent most of his years in the United States. In 1989, Felipe started a project in the city to help high school students and reduce the dropout rate of the children of Hispanic immigrants. The following year, he initiated a program called "See the Government in Action," which prepares students for a week-long leadership training program in Washington, D.C. In 1997, he also cofounded a charter school, the Bridge Academy, which is managed by a nonprofit organization and receives funding from the state. In the following years, Felipe was director of the school, which serves mainly children from low-income families in Bridgeport and mostly those from a Hispanic background. Felipe's social commitment also extended beyond Bridgeport, and he has served as a board member for such organizations as the American Red Cross and Community Responding to Others in Poverty, which earned him the President's Service Award (the highest award for volunteerism), presented to Felipe by President Bill Clinton in 1998. He has also been appointed to the board of directors of the National Council of La Raza, a Mexican and Hispanic advocacy organization.

Because of Felipe's dedication to volunteerism and community work, he is a well-known and respected person among the Hispanic community in Bridgeport. Moreover, in his role as principal of Bridge Academy and board member of numerous organizations, Felipe has created an extensive network of contacts within the Democratic Party, not only in Connecticut but also in the rest of the United States. In 2001, he used this political experience to run for and win a seat in Connecticut's General Assembly, and the same year he received an award for being the first Peruvian to be elected to a state legislature in the United States. In the following decade, he was reelected three times, supported primarily by Hispanics in his home district of Bridgeport. During his years as a legislator, Felipe became particularly well known for introducing bills such as the Dream Act and the Student Adjustment Act, which aimed to make it possible for students living in the United States illegally to pay in-state tuition rates at all public colleges and universities in Connecticut, rather than the pricier out-of-state rates they would otherwise pay.

When I interviewed Felipe at Connecticut's capitol building in Hartford in 2006, he was halfway through his fourth term as a legislator. Felipe told me that although he is Peruvian, his constituency is mainly Puerto Rican and other Hispanics of various nationalities and that his main commitment was to fight for the rights of minorities and immigrants, regardless of their ethnic or national backgrounds.[8] "I know how it is to start from the bottom and work your way up in the United States," he said. "That's why I've dedicated my work to helping young people get an education, even if they are undocumented." On my visit to Peru in 2011, I was told that Felipe had ceased working as a legislator in Connecticut after completing his fourth term and that he had returned to Peru to use his political contacts and act as a link between the United States and Peru to promote the free trade agreement and other issues. I was also told that Felipe had expressed an interest in Peru's presidential politics, with the idea of finding a candidate he could support. Whatever he decides, his experience represents a huge potential for the development of Peru's relations with the United States.

---

[8] Felipe, whose family name is Reinoso, also served as president of the Association of Peruvian Organizations in the United States and Canada from 2001 to 2002.

Breaking the Wave

Alfonso was born in San Martin, a region in Peru's tropical lowlands. In 1980, at age 22, he moved to Lima, where he studied psychology for several years, and in 1987 he and his wife traveled to Spain. The couple entered the country on tourist visas that they later overstayed. After a couple of years, he obtained permanent residence and a work permit in Spain, and in 1997 Alfonso, his wife, and their Spanish-born daughter all had dual citizenship as Peruvians and Spaniards. In the early 1990s, Alfonso's two brothers also came to Spain, where they too formed families. As political refugees, they were granted Spanish citizenship, and like Alfonso they live in Cornellá, a working-class municipality on the southern outskirts of Barcelona that for many years has been a PSOE (Spanish Socialist Workers' Party) stronghold. Until the early 1990s, Cornellá was inhabited almost exclusively by Spaniards (although ethnically mixed, including Catalans, Andalucians, and other Iberian minorities), but due to its liberal public housing policies the municipality received large numbers of immigrants throughout the 1990s. As a result, it is one of the Barcelona municipalities with a high percentage of foreign-born residents, among whom the Peruvian community is one of the most notorious.[9]

From a young age, Alfonso has been a member of APRA (American Popular Revolutionary Alliance, the center-left party that ruled Peru from 1985 to 1990 and from 2006 to 2011), and before migrating, he engaged in local politics in San Martín and Lima. In Spain, he has continued this engagement in his local PSOE branch, and in 1993 he formed a migrant association called Asociación Cultural Deportiva de Peruanos, which aims to promote Peruvians' integration into the municipality of Cornellá and their contact with the Catalan and Spanish population. Alfonso, who is also president of the APRA section in Barcelona, explained, "This is a working-class neighborhood, so this is where immigrants like us belong. As an Aprista [APRA party member], I have a lot in common with PSOE. We are fighting for the same ideas." In the mid-1990s, the association began arranging weekly soccer matches between different immigrant groups and organizing parties with Latin music at one of the municipality's public facilities. At the same time, Alfonso opened a bar in the neighborhood, which within a few months became an important rendezvous for Peruvians in Cornellá. During

---

[9] The Peruvian community in Cornellá became particularly notorious in the late 1990s because a group of migrants known as the Peruvian Band (*la banda peruana*) that lived in the municipality used it as a base for assaulting and robbing tourists in the Barcelona area.

my first interview with Alfonso in 1997, he told me, "I don't drink much myself, and I know we have to be careful that our compatriots don't make too much trouble. But I know people in the municipality, and they support us. I even know the mayor." However, in the late 1990s, the municipality suspended permission for the association to use municipal facilities for soccer games and parties because of complaints from the neighbors over the trouble that these activities had caused.

The Asociación Cultural Deportiva de Peruano is emblematic of the challenges that the Peruvian community faced in Catalonia in the late 1990s and early 2000s. For several years, a small group of migrants were involved in organized crime and had given Peruvians a reputation as thieves and troublemakers. Initially, Alfonso and the association he had formed tried to mediate and downplay the growing tensions between the Peruvian community on the one hand and the municipality and local population on the other. However, when the conflict increased rather than decreased, the association became identified with the very problem it had aimed to solve: the stigmatized image of Peruvians. Alfonso therefore encouraged association members to be more cautious in their public behavior, and he withdrew as leader.

In 2004, I interviewed Alfonso again. He told me he wanted to return to Peru and run for mayor in his native district in San Martin, where he has invested his savings in a chicken farm and an orange orchard. "I don't believe in all those organizations for migrants from the same country or region anymore," he said. "That only leads to regionalism. I believe in organizing politically." Alfonso added that when Cornellá experienced extensive immigration of Ecuadorians and Colombians after 2000, things got out of hand, and the relationship between the immigrants and the municipality had deteriorated. He concluded, "I'd rather do something for my people back home than try to help solve the problems in Cornellá."

Fighting the System

Victor, age 45, was born in a village close to Junín in the central highlands of Peru. As a young man, he moved to Lima, where he made a living as a tailor, got married, and had several children. The economic crisis in the late 1980s had a disastrous effect on Victor's business and induced him to change livelihoods. In 1991, one of his brothers, who was working as a shepherd in the United States, helped him enter into a contract with a rancher of Basque origin, and in 1991 he traveled to California, where he spent the next three years herding sheep. Although Victor usually stayed on the ranch and was able to avoid the hard life in the desert and mountains, this work experience changed his view of labor migration and sheep ranching. In my interview with him in 1998, he stressed how the employers exploited the herders and from time to time committed physical abuse against them. Victor's contract expired in 1994, but instead of returning to Peru, he overstayed his H-2A visa and became an unauthorized immigrant. He settled in Bakersfield, California, where a community of more than a hundred Peruvians lived. Some were shepherds who had completed their work contracts, while others were newcomers who had only recently arrived from Peru. Yet others were herders who had been hospitalized because of accidents at work or diseases caught on the ranches. Victor also met a group of shepherds who, like himself, had overstayed their H-2A visas and become unauthorized immigrants. The following year, he obtained a stay and work permit by marrying a Chicano women.

To fight for the shepherds' rights, Victor formed an organization called Unión de Pastores Ovejeros in 1995, which a few years later was recognized by the United Farm Workers AFL-CIO. In the late 1990s, the organization helped several herders file suits against the ranchers' insurance company for payment for medical treatment they had received after they had fallen ill or been victims of accidents on the ranches. The union also received public attention when a Peruvian newspaper in Los Angeles, *Perú de los 90*, started to document the herders' critical situation. The news caused a heated debate over the moral and legal rights of immigrants within the Peruvian community in California and the dismissal of the Peruvian consul in Los Angeles because of his neglect of the herders' complaints. The news also reached Peru, where the media reported on missing and ill-treated Peruvian herders in the United States and where the government blamed the US administration for ignoring immigrants' human rights. Similar reports on Spanish-language television channels in the United States caused moral indignation among Peruvians and other Hispanics, prompting the Peruvian ambassador, together with officials from the US Department of Labor, to visit sheep ranches that used Peruvian labor.

Victor's efforts to improve the herders' working conditions in the United States have been unique. A small group of fellow migrants joined the struggle, but the vast majority (including Victor's own brothers) has either ignored his appeals to join the organization or even taken the side of the ranchers. Moreover, Victor told me that he had received death threats from several ranchers and that he had been disappointed by the response of some of the herders that his organization had helped by suing the ranchers' insurance company. He also said that he was concerned about his family in Peru, who no longer received remittances. When I visited Peru in 2004, I was told that Victor had returned there and been reunited with his family. The fighter had laid down his arms and gone home.

The Charismatic Migrant

For the bulk of Peruvians, migration is a means for improving their living conditions and for achieving social mobility and economic progress. As demonstrated above, migrants pursue this aim in different ways: some invest their earnings in a house for their retirement years, while others save their capital for investing when they return, for starting a business in their new place of settlement, or for inventing new ways of making use of their talents. However, a small group of migrants seek *superación* by bettering not only their own lives but also the lives of others. Their engagement evolves both inside and outside the political system, and their struggle is dedicated to righting the social injustices that Peruvians suffer in the receiving societies and to encouraging other migrants to organize, fight for their rights, and seek integration into their new country of settlement.

The desire to change society and make it more tolerant and open to immigrants is the impetus behind the struggles of Felipe, Alfonso, and Victor, but the means they used and the avenues they have taken to attain this goal are very different. Felipe is the first Peruvian ever to have been elected a congressman in the United States, and even though he is known primarily among the Peruvians and other Hispanics who voted for him in Connecticut, he is a role model for migrants throughout the United States. Indeed, his own migration trajectory makes him the incarnation of the American dream, and interestingly, as a congressman, he gained recognition in the Hispanic community (but also was the target of the condemnation by political voices outside that community) when he proposed the Dream Act, legislation intended to give undocumented and unauthorized immigrants the right to attend state colleges and universities for the same tuition as other in-state students. Alfonso, by contrast, was not an elected leader but a local bar owner who attained his political position by articulating the needs of the Peruvian community in public and, at the same time, creating a personal network within the municipality of Cornellá that he used to mediate conflicts between migrants and the wider society. Finally, whereas Felipe worked within the political system and Alfonso served as broker between the system and the migrant community, Victor went his own way. A migrant laborer himself, he decided to take up the fight against the sheep ranchers' exploitation and abuse of migrants. A true grassroots fighter, Victor challenged not only the sheep ranching industry in the United States but also the political system that legitimizes its use of cheap, unskilled, migrant labor. Although his struggle briefly drew the attention of the wider society, the labor migration he tried to change continues as before.

Migrant transformers engage in politics at different levels in the receiving society and employ different means to challenge the system. Nevertheless, whether their battleground is Connecticut's General Assembly, Cornellá's working-class bars, or California's desolate deserts, the transformers can achieve their goals only by mobilizing their followers and gaining their support. As this discussion illustrates, charisma is essential to creating such leadership.

The Added Value of Migration

In the contemporary world, migrants are often portrayed in two opposing images. In many developed countries, they are viewed as uninvited troublemakers who disturb the public order and represent an economic burden on the host society. Conversely, in the policy world of international organizations and in many sending countries, they are regarded as the answer to the development problems of their home regions. This chapter offers a different picture of migration. Analytically, I have examined migrants' savings, investments, and accumulation of social and symbolic capital as yet another way of living up to their commitments, in this case, the promise they made to themselves to *superarse*. However, in contrast to the previous chapters that focused on migrants' contribution to their home country, this chapter demonstrates a less recognized potential of contemporary migration. By focusing on how migrants use their resources and talents to achieve social mobility and change the surrounding world, rather than on how they spend their earnings on their families or communities back home, I have tried to shed light on the many ways in which migration enriches modern life. From this perspective, migrants are not easily assigned to categories such as intruder, victim, or savior, as the public debate and the media in both the sending and the receiving countries tend to do, but are seen as social agents driven by the same personal desire to progress and endowed with the same individual talents as the other members of the societies in which they reside. In other words, the chapter has explored how migration empowers individuals and how they use this empowerment not only to improve their own lives but also to contribute to society as a whole.

The 18 case studies presented here suggest that the talents migrants draw on to mobilize the economic, social, human, and cultural capital they need to *superarse* are multiple and include thrift, endurance, boldness, creativity, and charisma. The case studies also show that migrants use these qualities for very different purposes. Some migrants are particularly good at saving, which allows them to enjoy a well-deserved retirement. Others endure many years of hardship in foreign countries to save capital that they then use to invest in their home country or risk their economic security and that of their families to establish ethnic businesses in the receiving country. Yet others think of migration as an opportunity to make a career shift or improve their professional skills and in this way draw on unused creative talents or develop new ones. Finally, some find that migration opens up avenues for them to engage in politics and employ their organizational and leadership talents to make the world a better place for their fellow migrants. By highlighting migrants' various talents and human potential and illustrating the many ways in which they use them, both abroad and at home, these case studies provide an alternative image of migration and remind us that migrants are skillful and resourceful actors in the modern world who contribute to their own welfare and quality of life, as well as to the good of society in general.

The analysis in this chapter has focused on migrants' own empowering capacities while deemphasizing the structural constraints they are up against and the vulnerabilities these barriers cause. However, it is important to acknowledge the many obstacles that even the most gifted and talented migrants face in both the receiving and the sending countries, an aspect I have discussed in more detail in previous works (see, for example, Paerregaard 2008a); in particular, it is important to evaluate how migrants assess the risks they are taking when they embark on their new lives. In the next and concluding chapter, I take up that issue.

Chapter 6

After Remittances

For centuries, people have remitted money to relatives in other parts of the world. A century ago, the British aristocracy sent money to support their sons who were living in North America, Australia, and elsewhere. Today, millions of labor migrants remit their savings to families and communities in their home countries. To those unfamiliar with the concerns and exigencies of migrants, the meaning and implications of these money transfers have changed little. To some, remittances still carry an aura of mystery and desire (where did that money come from?), just as they provoke envy and disdain in others (what kind of people would live off others' money?). These images prompted Robert Service to write his poems about the "men who don't fit in," individuals whose *raison d'être* was called into question because they lived off the money of others.

Present-day migrants suffer from the prejudices of the surrounding world, too. Because labor migrants often work on temporary work contracts or without proper identity papers and remit most of their earnings home, the receiving society sometimes views them with distrust (why do they send all their money away?). Yet even though remittances continue to flow from the developed to the developing world, the roles of the senders and the recipients have been reversed. The subjects of Service's poems were remittance *receivers*, the unwanted sons of Britain's aristocracy who had been exiled to the country's former colonies. The people portrayed in this book are remittance *senders*, breadwinners of the developing countries who go abroad to work and send money home to their parents, spouses, and children.

Remittance Policy Prescriptions

For many years, migrants were also viewed with suspicion in their home countries, even though governments used migration as a safety valve for social and political unrest. Indeed, some regimes even portrayed them as "traitors"—and a few continue to do so. Migration, however, is increasingly seen as a source of wealth and prosperity by national governments, whose mistrust of migrants is therefore decreasing. Equally important, the category of migrant is acquiring new meaning. Many of today's "remittance men" are not men but women, and unlike their predecessors they do not live on others' money but are hardworking people struggling to make a living and maintain their families. In fact, they work so hard that the money they send home constitutes the second-largest capital flow in the contemporary world, surpassed only by private investment. Far from being the "men who don't fit in," migrants are in high demand in many countries that lack workers, caregivers, businessmen, doctors, and scientists. The new image of migrants as stakeholders and contributors rather than troublemakers and outsiders is emerging at a time when the world is experiencing the growing mobility of both people and capital and when international organizations and governments in the developing world are taking more and more interest in migrants' remittances.[1] Recast as development "saviors" and "heroes," today's migrants therefore occupy critical positions in the policy prescriptions of experts, planners, and politicians, who see migrants' earnings and talents as important resources for generating growth in their home countries.

---

[1] According to de Haas (2006, 18), the Multilateral Investment Fund of the Inter-American Development Bank was the first international organization to promote the idea of using migrant remittances to leverage development. De Haas also points out that World Bank researchers began to study and promote migrant remittances only in 2003; before then, the institution attributed little importance to the "migration and development" issue.

Common to all remittance policy prescriptions is the expectation that remittances are an endless flow of money that governments have the moral right to tap into to boost the development of migrants' home regions and thus shed some of their own responsibility. Some of the first attempts to reach out to migrants and capture their remittances were made in the 1970s and 1980s by North African countries in response to the growing emigration of their people to Europe and later to the Persian Gulf area. Recognizing that migrants returned a large part of their earnings to their families at home, the governments on this region tried to ease remittance flows and channel them into productive activities (de Haas 2006). In the 1980s and 1990s, several Asian countries also designed migration policies to stimulate economic growth through the remittances that migrants send home to their families. Among the most prominent cases is the Philippines, which for several decades has promoted temporary labor migration as a means to generate economic growth (O'Neil 2004; Le Espiritu 2005; Asis 2008). As a result, today the country's economy relies heavily on migrant remittances. To encourage its population to migrate and use their savings to support their families and invest them upon their return, the Philippine government has created an institutional framework that regulates labor migration, facilitates remittance activities, and encourages migrants to return once they have completed their contracts. The government has also created a program to protect its citizens during their stays overseas.

Similar attempts to capture migrant remittances and strengthen migrants' participation in the development of their countries of origin have been made in Latin America. Mexico, for example, has created a program that encourages the involvement of its US-based migrant population in their hometowns (Canales 2007; Garcia Zamorra 2005; Orozco 2002). In this program, the money that migrants collect through hometown associations (HTAs) for investment in infrastructure, schools, and the like in Mexico will be matched by the local authorities in their regions of origin. The program, which today receives support from migrants' local, regional, and national governments, has been coined "3x1" (Garcia Zamorra 2006). At the other end of the migration chain, some receiving countries have also started designing policies that encourage immigrants to invest their savings in development projects in their home regions. In Europe, several countries have created codevelopment programs that invite their immigrant populations to engage in the development of their countries of origin (de Haas 2007a). The first country to introduce a codevelopment program was France, which directs most of its development assistance to its former colonies in West Africa (de Haas 2006). Several years ago, Spain also adopted a codevelopment policy, and today Catalonia and several of the country's other regional governments offer financial support to immigrant groups that present plans for implementing development projects in their home regions (Béjar 2011; Østergaard-Nielsen 2011; Maisonave Cortés 2011). Local governments in other southern European countries, such as Italy, also encourage immigrants to participate.

Today, national governments in the developed and developing worlds are pursuing many migration and development policies, which often differ in means as well as in goals. Similarly, the policy recommendations made by international institutions such as the World Bank, the International Organization for Migration, the Organisation for Economic Co-operation and Development, and the regional offices of Inter-American Development Bank vary in scope and aims. However, remittance policy approaches all share the same illusion: that migrants' resources in the form of earnings, professional skills, and innovative talents can be converted into "development." So how does Peruvian migration fit into these prescriptions, and what can policymakers learn from this study?

Peru and Mexico Compared

Before answering these questions, let us sum up the main features of Peruvian migration and remittances. Geographically, Peruvian migrants are dispersed across several continents, although they tend to cluster in the major cities in the countries where they settle. The main destination is the United States, but Argentina, Chile, Italy, Japan, and Spain receive many migrants, too. Migration is also diverse; migrants come from all social strata of Peruvian society and have very different occupational backgrounds. Despite these variations, Peruvian migration is predominantly a female activity, and the vast majority of migrants come from urban areas, the country's capital being the main center of emigration. The educational level is also high, and many migrants are either single or live in informal partnerships. Even though such arrangements are common and are often preferred to formal marriages in Peru, they indicate that migrants enjoy a high degree of individual independence and agency.

While Peruvian migration is geographically dispersed and socially diverse, remittances are concentrated in a few locations in Peru and unequally distributed within the Peruvian population. The prevalence of Peru's urban middle and upper classes in Peruvian migration clearly shapes migrant remittances, which are captured mostly by households from the middle and higher income groups and rarely reach the country's rural and impoverished areas. Women are the main recipients of Peruvian remittances, which are spent primarily on conspicuous consumption and education. Moreover, my data demonstrate that the remittances flow predominantly into the developed part of Peru, to its urban areas, and, in particular, to Lima and its surroundings, thus deepening existing divisions and differences in Peruvian society. They also show that relatively few Peruvians benefit from remittances, which tend to favor the economically better-off households by expanding their capacity to spend on private consumption and education. Although the less privileged sectors of Peruvian society also receive remittances, their migration-remittance balance is "negative"; that is, migrants from Peru's poorest households remit less than migrants from the better-off households.

To highlight the development potential of Peruvian remittances, let us compare them with Mexican remittances. Mexico has the largest migrant population in Latin America and captures more migrant remittances than any other country in the region. Furthermore, remittance policymakers often refer to its remittance policies as a model for Latin America and the rest of the world to emulate. Finally, and perhaps most important, in spite of the disparate scale of migration and volume of remittances Mexico and Peru are comparable when their migrations are viewed as a percentage of their total populations and their remittance economies are viewed as a percentage of gross domestic product. A brief look at Mexican history gives us an idea of why the country often is associated with migration and remittances.

Mexican migration goes back to the first half of the nineteenth century, when the country lost almost half of its territory to the United States and many of its citizens suddenly became American (Rosenblum and Brick 2011, 3–5). In the twentieth century, Mexicans continued to migrate in response to the American economy's demand for unskilled and cheap labor, which is clearly reflected in US immigration policy. While the *bracero* program, which lasted from 1942 to 1964, encouraged Mexicans to work in the United States, later immigration acts have tried to control migration, and in the past four decades migration from Mexico has become increasingly illegal. Other Latin Americans have migrated to the United States, too, but Mexicans make up the largest immigrant group in the country by far. Today, "Hispanics" or "Latinos" account for 40.4 million (14 percent) of the American population. People of Mexican origin account for 66 percent of this group, and 40 percent of them were born in Mexico, the remainder being first- or second-generation immigrants or more distantly descended (Delgado Wise and Márquez Covarrubias 2008, 116–18). Mexican immigrants tend to be wage-earners occupying the lowest rung of the US income ladder, and because many are undocumented, poverty rates are high, just as their access to schooling, health care, and other public services is low. In response to poor social integration, many migrants are forced to rely on their social networks. More recently, they have established a number of organizations, ranging from HTAs and federations to trade unions and media outlets, that all strive to bring political, social, economic, and cultural influence to bear on the areas in which they work.

Peruvian and Mexican remittances differ in many respects although they also share some commonalities. The chief statistics on Mexican and Peruvian migration appear in table 6.1. Demographically, Mexico's population of 121 million is four times that of Peru, which is 30 million (World Bank 2013b). Mexico's migrant stock of 11.7 million is also much bigger than Peru's 2.6 million (MPI 2014; INEI, IOM and MIGRACIONES 2013, 15). Nevertheless, as a percentage of the total population the migrant stocks of the two countries' are comparable, in Mexico 9.6 percent and in Peru 8.5 percent. Similarly, the two migration populations have almost the same age-spread: in Mexico, 89 percent are between ages 15 and 64, while in Peru 86 percent belong to that age group. However, a closer glance at the gender pattern reveals an important difference. Migration in Mexico is predominantly a male activity, with men making up 55 percent of the migrant population. In Peru, the gender bias is reversed: 52 percent of its migrants are female.

In table 6.2, we observe the key numbers for Mexico's and Peru's remittance economies. Obviously, the countries capture very different volumes

Table 6.1. Selected Demographic Data on Mexico and Peru, 2010–2012

Demographic Data	Mexico	Peru
Total population (millions)	121*	30*
Migrant population (millions)	11.7*	2.6*
Migrants (%)	9.6	8.5
Migrants ages 15–64 (%)	89**	86**
Male migrants (%)	55**	48**
Female migrants (%)	45**	52**

Sources: CONAPO 2010; INEI, IOM, and DIGEMIN 2010, 20–21; INEI, MIGRACIONES, and IOM 2013; World Bank 2013b; MPI 2014.
Notes: *2012, **2010

Table 6.2. Data on the Remittance Economies in Mexico and Peru, 2008–2012

Remittances Captured	Mexico	Peru
US dollars (billions)	23.4*	2.8*
Remittances as % of GDP	2.0*	1.4*
% of population receiving remittances	4.7**	3.8***

Source: CONAPO 2010; INEI and IOM 2008, 50; World Bank 2013b.
Notes: *2012; **2010, ***2008

of remittances: for Mexico, $23.4 billion and for Peru $2.8 billion. Despite the huge difference in volume, the number is not so different as a percentage of gross domestic product: in Mexico it is 2.0 percent and in Peru it is 1.4 percent. This difference is reflected in the distribution of remittances: in Mexico, 4.7 percent of the population receives remittances; in Peru, only 3.8 percent receive remittances.

Table 6.3 shows how remittances are distributed geographically in Mexico and Peru. The differences are huge. Mexico City captures only 4.6 percent of its remittances, while Lima receives 57.2 percent. Moreover, 44 percent of Mexico's remittances flow into urban areas, while the country's rural areas capture 56 percent. By contrast, in Peru 95 percent of the country's remittances ends up in urban areas and only 5 percent in rural areas.

In both Mexico and Peru, migrants constitute less than 10 percent of the total population (9.6 percent in Mexico and 8.5 percent in Peru), and the ages of these populations differ little: 89 percent of Mexican migrants and 86 percent of Peruvian migrants are between ages 15 and 64. Similarly, Mexico's and Peru's remittances make up a similar contribution to the countries' gross domestic product (2.0 percent in Mexico and 1.4 percent in Peru). Comparing the two countries, therefore, allows us to identify the

Table 6.3. Remittance Distribution by Region in Mexico and Peru, 2009 (percent)

Remittance Distribution	Mexico	Peru
National capital	4.6	57.2
Urban areas	44	95
Rural areas	56	5

Sources: CONAPO 2009a, 2009b; INEI and IOM 2010, 92.
Note: "National capital" refers to the Federal District in Mexico and to Lima and Callao in Peru.

particularities of the Peruvian case, one of which is the strong presence of women (in contrast to the male-dominated Mexican migration), a dominance that is especially apparent in the country's remittance economy. As shown in chapter 2, 68 percent of Peru's remittance recipients are women. Another salient feature of Peruvian migration is that migrants overwhelmingly (92 percent) come from urban areas in Peru. In Mexico, the proportion of migrants from rural and urban areas is much more even (51 percent rural and 49 percent urban). The urban bias of Peruvian migration is particularly evident in the concentration of Peru's remittances, which reach only 3.8 percent of the country's households. By contrast, in Mexico 4.7 percent of the households receive remittances. The geographical bias of Peruvian remittances is even more obvious when one looks at the volume of remittances captured by Peru's capital, which Lima captures 57.2 percent of the country's remittances, while Mexico's capital captures only 4.6 percent of Mexico's remittances. Unfortunately, comparable data on the distribution of Mexican and Peruvian migration with respect to profession, occupation, and income groups are not available.

Unlike Mexican remittances, then, Peruvian remittances are an urban middle-class phenomenon that contributes little to the development of country's impoverished rural areas. Nevertheless, policymakers would be wise to take lessons from Peruvian migration. As this study has shown, the size and scope of Peruvian migration (2.6 million migrants spread around the world representing 8.5 percent of the country's total population) and the social composition (different age groups, women as well as men, variety of ethnic backgrounds, rural and urban unskilled workers, as well as semiprofessionals and professionals) allow us to revise the assumptions about remittances that policy planners make when analyzing the data. The data here are particularly relevant because they shed light on the many motives that drive people to migrate and remit and bring to the fore the circumstances and concerns in migrants' lives that induce them to remit (or not remit) and, in a broader perspective, contribute to a better world. To learn from Peruvian migration, policymakers must start by asking several questions: (1) what risk and cost assessments do people make before emigrating, and what are migrants' primary concerns when remitting? (2) how do remittances affect the relations between migrants and their relatives and communities? (3) when in migrants' lives do remittances commence, peak, and dry up? (4) what are migrants' personal aspirations? and (5) how do migrants contribute to the sending and receiving countries apart from remitting?

The Vapor of Remittances

Peruvians migrate to improve the conditions of their lives, and many pursue this goal by remitting money home. But their migratory endeavors often change direction and aims over time, and quite a few migrants bring their relatives to their receiving countries, making it difficult to predict Peruvian remittance flows. As demonstrated in chapter 3, many remit considerable amounts of money home in response to family needs but reduce and stop their remittances once those necessities are taken care of. While some continue to remit on a weekly or monthly basis for decades, others do so only once or twice in their lives. Remittances can therefore be a routine in migrants' daily activities or a simple money transfer along with other expenditures, just as they can be the result of savings of many years finally remitted for a specific purpose. Moreover, remittances often flow in several directions, and sometimes migrants even find themselves in the role of remittance-receivers. And although most remittances are earmarked, the receivers sometimes use them for other aims or re-remit them to other family members, which makes it difficult to track the flow of a given remittance and account for its path.

To create a relationship of trust between remittance-senders and -receivers, communication is of crucial importance, and over the years remittances can become the very issue that brings migrants and their families together, a critical sign that the relationship is still valid (Pribilsky 2004, 2007). However, disagreements over the amount of money sent and the way it is spent are inevitable, particularly when migrants and their spouses are divorced or feel committed to supporting members of different families. Strife can also arise between migrants and their relatives and home communities because they have different ideas on how remittances should be used. These tensions reveal that remittances are always "special" money (Vogel and Korinek 2012) that migrants take out of their earnings or savings and send home with an invisible tag indicating how they expect the receiver to spend it. Even though money has no smell, as Paul Stoller writes in his study of African traders in New York (Stoller 2002), figuratively speaking, the vapor of migrants' sweat and the echo of their last phone call home linger in the minds of the senders and recipients long after the money is remitted, donated, saved, invested, or otherwise spent. In this study, I have tried to convey a sense of that vapor and echo by focusing my analysis on the commitments migrants make to their relatives, to their communities, and to themselves rather than on the money transfers those commitments entail. Gender and generational relations are particularly important for the way in which migrants' money is negotiated and distributed; to ensure that it is properly used, migrants often ask female relatives or family members of different generations to act as stewards of the money they send. These arrangements change the power structure of the household, and while some family members may gain voice, others lose agency as they see their roles changed in the wake of migrants' absence. In a wider context, remittances are viewed as a symbol of social status defined not only by the amount of money they receive but also by the places from which it is sent. Thus just as remittances are embedded in the personal history of the senders, they transmit the prestige the receivers associate with the countries where migrants live and work, the most prestigious remittances coming from countries with high salaries and the less prestigious from countries with low salaries.

Remittances sent by migrant organizations to their home communities can also be controversial. The lion's share of collective remittances is rarely invested in development (schools, roads, and the like) but in religious events and prestige projects such as fiestas and churches; and even though migrants put large amounts of money into these activities, their main concern is to affirm their continuous membership in their home communities and ensure their legacy rather than contributing to real change. Financing fiestas and building new churches are also important symbolic actions by which migrants demonstrate their newly gained success in the receiving society. Furthermore, many migrant organizations find themselves in a dilemma between supporting their home communities and helping newly arrived migrants who depend on the help of those who are more established. In fact, it can take many years until migrant organizations become capable of collecting money to support the development of their places of origin, and even when they succeed, that support is likely to dry up once out-migration has peaked and a new generation takes over.

The Volatility of Remittances

Migration scholars and international institutions often point out the resilience of remittances to economic changes, arguing that because remittances are family money, migrants continue to remit even when their wages are cut or they lose their jobs (Bagasao 2005, 134; Ratha 2005, 26). The field research for this book was conducted in a time of progress and prosperity in most of the receiving countries of Peruvian migration, and it is therefore difficult to use my data to validate this assertion. I did, however, observe a few cases of migrants remitting in moments of economic hardship. The crisis that hit Argentina in 2001 had a devastating impact on the country's unemployment rates and living standards, and, as often happens in times of depression, migrants were the ones to suffer most. Peruvians were particularly vulnerable, as they had generally found work as domestics and caregivers, jobs that are easily lost when money is short in the household economy. The majority, however, stayed in Argentina and continued sending money home simply because they had no alternative. In 2001, Peru was in a state of political and economic disarray, and a return home was therefore not a feasible option nor was remigration to Italy, Japan, Spain, or the United States because of the high cost of travel to those destinations. While collecting field data in Washington, D.C., in 2009–10, I also noted the impact the economic crisis was having on Peruvian migrants in the United States. Except for 2009, Peru's economy has boomed over the past 10 years and the prospects for returning migrants were therefore far more promising. Nevertheless, return rates were only just starting to gather speed and, apparently, Peruvians not only in the United States but also in Italy, Japan, and Spain were reluctant to give up on creating new lives as immigrants and supporting their relatives in Peru. Remittances are certainly less volatile than other money flows, but promoting development policies on the assumption that migrants can keep on remitting forever, notwithstanding economic and political changes in the world, can be a risky business, as the ethnographic insights in this book demonstrate.

These data reveal that the Peruvians most inclined to remit are those with children in Peru. Yet they also show great variation, including those who continue to remit for decades, despite no longer having contact with their children, as well as those who form new families in the receiving society and therefore cut their ties with their original families and stop remitting. Peruvians who have left their elderly parents back home are also frequent remitters, although some send money home only very irregularly. Others stop remitting upon obtaining family reunification. Remitting money to younger siblings or nephews or nieces is also common among Peruvian migrants. However, the aim of these remittances is mostly the education of their relatives, and they therefore stop after a couple of years when the young people have completed their training. Peruvians also remit to other family members but mostly on special occasions, when someone falls ill or they need to pay off loans. Another target of Peruvian remittances is the construction of family homes and the acquisition of electronic devices, vehicles, and other consumer goods. Often such money is saved over a longer period of time and either brought home by migrants personally or sent in smaller sums.

Whether remittances are used to buy food, finance education, acquire cars, or pay medical bills, they are migrants' individual earnings spent on family needs. In essence, they represent money exchanged between relatives who are bound up in a timeless web of exchange relations, economically as well as morally and emotionally. Indeed, as this study also demonstrates, instead of sending remittances, some migrants actually receive money from relatives in Peru (as did the "remittance men" Robert Service wrote about). Remittances therefore embody the spirit of the gift, and they last only as long as migrants and their families live apart or recognize their mutual dependence. The argument of this book is that it is only by studying remittance biographies (the migration histories of individual remittance-senders and -recipients), remittance flows (migrants' remittance practices in time and space), and remittance economies (the use and importance of remittances within migrant households) that can we understand the underlying reasons for the fluctuations in migrant remittances and grasp why migrants continue to remit in times of crisis and change those practices for reasons that have little to do with macroeconomic causes. More bluntly, my message to policymakers and development planners is not to view migrants' money as a cash cow ready to be milked but to focus on migrants' many commitments and then to design migration policies that support their efforts to meet those commitments, even when those flows fall short of yielding the short-term economic output expected by the sending or receiving governments.

Peruvian migrants send money not only to their families but also to their home communities. Compared to family remittances, however, collective remittances are rather insignificant. The figures presented in chapter 2 show that only 5 percent of Peru's remittances reach rural areas, the chief recipient of Peru's collective remittances. Moreover, as demonstrated by other studies, using collective remittances to generate sustainable development requires an institutional framework that can define projects that meet the needs of the local population and ensure accountability and transparency in the management of migrant donations. Such frameworks have not been established in Peru's rural areas, and while migrants complain that corruption is common among village authorities in their hometowns, the villagers deplore the fact that the migrants prefer to spend their money on fiestas and other nonproductive activities. Migrants' collective remittances therefore tend to deepen the distrust between migrants and villagers and enhance economic inequality between families with migrant members and families without migrant members. These findings also show that, even when the community authorities create a framework for channeling remittances into rural development by charging fees to migrants during their absence, those migrants prefer to invest their money elsewhere or settle in the receiving country instead of returning. As a result, only a few migrants return home and use their remittances to invest in agriculture or cattle herding. In other words, the country's poorest regions capture only a tiny fraction of Peruvian remittances, and the few remittances that actually reach rural areas are rarely invested in sustainable development.

Overall, this study suggests that in a country like Peru, which already suffers from a huge gap between rich and poor, remittances enhance existing inequalities, even in regions where they have a positive impact on migrant households. Hence, designing remittance-driven development policies in Peru makes sense only in times of crisis and falling incomes, as a way to cope with acute needs and compensate for lost opportunities. In the past decade, however, the country has experienced an economic bonanza, with growth rates of between 5 and 10 percent. For that reason, Peru is far better off pursuing development strategies other than encouraging its population to migrate and remit.

Global Heroes

How, then, does Peruvian migration contribute to Peru and the receiving countries? Remittances represent hard-earned money that belongs to migrants and their families, not to national governments and international organizations. The Philippine model therefore builds on a troubled relationship between migrants and their governments. The Mexican experience, in contrast, reveals that remittances can empower migrants and their hometowns in negotiating access to public resources and citizens' rights with the government authorities of the sending society. The European model also indicates that encouraging migrants to adopt the role of co-actors in development assistance can strengthen that empowerment. Rather than viewing migrants' capacity to earn a living and remit money home as their major achievement, scholars, planners, and politicians should acknowledge that migrants have at their command many other skills that help them acquire influence and pursue their goals. Chapter 5 showed how Peruvian migrants prepare for retirement, achieve social mobility, start a business, make career shifts, introduce change, and transform society. To achieve those goals, they mobilize a variety of talents: thrift, endurance, daring, creativity, and charisma. The Peruvian model illuminates these efforts and highlights the multiple resources that migrants use when settling in foreign countries. The remittance man of the twentieth century was despised and ostracized; the migrant of the twenty-first century is a hero heralded by the rest of the world.

References

Abdih, Yaser, Ralph Chami, Jihad Dagher, and Peter Montiel. 2011. "Remittances and Institutions: Are Remittances a Curse?" *World Development* 40 (4): 657–66.
Acosta, Pablo, Cesar Calderón, Pablo Fajnzylber, and Humberto López. 2006. "Remittances and Development in Latin America." *World Economy* 29 (6): 957–87.
Adams, Richard. 2006. "International Remittances and the Household: Analysis and Review of Global Evidence," supplement 2. *Journal of African Economies* 15: 396–425.
Adams, Richard, and John Page. 2005. "Do International Migration and Remittances Reduce Poverty in Developing Countries?" *World Development* 33 (10): 1645–69.
Adler, Rachel. 2002. "Patron-Client Ties, Ethnic Entrepreneurship and Transnational Migration: The Case of Yucatecans in Dallas, Texas." *Urban Anthropology and Studies of Cultural Systems and World Economic Development* 31 (2): 129–61.
Agarwal, Reena, and Andrew Horowitz. 2002. "Are International Remittances Altruism or Insurance? Evidence from Guyana Using Multiple-Migrant Households." *World Development* 30 (11): 2033–44.
Agunías, Dovelyn Rannveig. 2006. *From a Zero-Sum to a Win-Win Scenario: Literature Review on Circular Migration*. Washington, DC: Migration Policy Institute.
———, ed. 2009. *Closing the Distance: How Governments Strengthen Ties with Their Diasporas*. Washington, DC: Migration Policy Institute.

Airola, Jim. 2007. "The Use of Remittance Income in Mexico." *International Migration Review* 41 (4): 850–59.
Åkesson, Lisa. 2009. "Remittances and Inequality in Cape Verde: The Impact of Changing Family Organization." *Global Networks* 9 (3): 381–98.
Altamirano, Teófilo. 2006. *Remesas y nueva "fuga de cerebros": Impactos transnacionales.* Lima: PUCP.
———. 2010. *In Times of Crisis: Migration, Remittances and Development.* Lima: UNFPA/CISEPA/PUCP.
Alvarado, Javier, David Gonzales, and Francisco Galarza. 2005. "Ahorro y Remesas Familares: el caso de Huancayo." *Debate Agrario: Análisis y Alternativas* 38: 19–51.
Ansion, Juan, Luis Mujica, and Ana María Villacorta. 2008. *Los que se quedan. Familias de emigrados de un distrito de Lima.* Lima: FIUC/CISEPA.
———. 2009. "En el aeropuerto me dijo que cuidara a mi madre." In *Más allá de las remesas. Familias de migrantes en América Latina*, edited by J. Ansion, R. Aparicio, and P. N. Medina, 25–85. Lima: FIUC/CISEPA.
Aparicio, Rosa. 2007. "The Integration of the Second and 1.5 Generations of Moroccan, Dominican and Peruvian Origin in Madrid and Barcelona." *Journal of Ethnic and Migration Studies* 33 (7): 1169–93.
Arroyo Alejandre, Jesús, and Isabel Corvera Valenzuela. 2003. "Actividad económica, migración a Estados Unidos y remesas en el occidente de México." *Migraciones Internacionales* 2 (1): 36–58.
Asis, Maruja M. B. 2008. "How International Migration Can Support Development: A Challenge for the Philippines." In *Migration and Development: Perspectives from the South*, edited by S. Castles and R. Delgado Wise, 175–200. Geneva: IOM.
Bagasao, Ildefonso F. 2005. "Migration and Development: The Philippine Experience." In *Development Impact and Future Prospects*, edited by S. M. Maimbo and R. Dilip, 133–42. Washington, DC: World Bank.
Batniztsky, Adina, Linda McDowell, and Sarah Dyer. 2012. "Remittances and the Maintenance of Dual Social Worlds: The Transnational Working Lives of Migrants in Greater London." *International Migration* 50 (4): 141–56.
Béjar, Miryam Hazam. 2011. "Beyond 3x1: Linking Sending and Receiving Societies in the Development Process." Working Paper 2011/08, National Centre of Competence in Research Trade Regulation, Bern, Switzerland.
Bendixen, Segion, and Erin Onge. 2005. "Remittances from the United States and Japan to Latin America: An In-depth Look Using Public Opinion Research." In *Beyond Small Change: Making Migrant Remittances Count*, edited by D. Terry and S. R. Wilson, 41–70. Washington, DC: Inter-American Development Bank.
Berg, Ulla Dalum. 2008. "In the Defence of Community: Long Distance Localism and Transnational Political Engagement between the US and the Peruvian Andes." *Journal of Ethnic and Migration Studies* 34 (7): 1091–1108.
Binford, Leigh. 2003. "Migrant Remittances and (Under)Development in Mexico." *Critique of Anthropology* 23 (3): 305–36.
Boccagni, Paolo. 2010. "Whom Should We Help First? Transnational Helping Practices in Ecuadorian Migration." *International Migration* 51 (2): 192–208.
Bourdieu, Pierre. 1986. "The Forms of Capital." In *Handbook of Theory and Research in the Sociology of Education*, edited by J. G. Richardson, 241–58. New York and London: Greenwood Press.

Bracking, Sarah, and Lloyd Sachikonye. 2009. "Migrant Remittances and Household Wellbeing in Urban Zimbabwe." *International Migration* 48 (5): 204–27.

Brettell, Caroline. 2003. *Anthropology and Migration: Essays on Transnationalism, Ethnicity and Identity.* Walnut Creek, CA: Altamira Press.

Canales, Alejandro. 2007. "Remesas, desarrollo y pobreza. Una vision crítica desde América Latina." In *Nuevas migraciones latinamericanas a Europa. Balances y desafío*, edited by Isabel Y. del Castillo and Gioconda Herrera, 363–89. Quito: FLACSO/OBREAL/UCL/UB.

Carling, Jørgen. 2008. "Interrogating Remittances: Core Questions for Deeper Insight and Better Policies." In *Migration and Development: Perspectives from the South*, edited by S. Castles and R. Delgado Wise, 45–64. Geneva: IOM.

Carling, Jørgen, and Kristian Hoelscher. 2013. "The Capacity and Desire to Remit: Comparing Local and Transnational Influences." *Journal of Ethnic and Migration Studies* 39 (6): 939–58.

Castles, Stephen, and Raúl Delgado Wise, eds. 2008. *Migration and Development: Perspectives from the South.* Geneva: IOM.

Cavaco, Carminda. 1993. "A Place in the Sun: Return Migration and Rural Change in Portugal." In *Mass Migrations in Europe: The Legacy and the Future*, edited by R. King, 174–91. London: Belhaven Press.

Caycho, Hernán. 1977. *Las SAIS de la sierra central.* Lima: ESAN (Escuela de Administración de Negocios para Graduados).

Chami, Ralph, Adolfo Barajas, Thomas Cosimano, Connel Fullemkamp, Michael Gapen, and Peter Montiel. 2008. "Macroeconomic Consequences of Remittances." Occasional Paper 259, International Monetary Fund, Washington, DC.

Cohen, Jeffrey H. 2005. "Remittance Outcomes and Migration: Theoretical Contests, Real Opportunities." *Studies in Comparative International Development* 40 (1): 88–112.

———. 2010. "Oaxacan Migration and Remittances as They Relate to Mexican Migration Patterns." *Journal of Ethnic and Migration Studies* 36 (1): 149–61.

Colloredo-Mansfeld, Rudi. 1999. *The Native Leisure Class: Consumption and Cultural Creativity in the Andes.* Chicago: University of Chicago Press.

CONAPO (Consejo Nacional de Población). 2009a. *Remesas familiares y su distribución por entidad federativa 2009.* Mexico City: CONAPO and SEGOB (Secretaría de Gobernación), http://www.conapo.gob.mx.

———. 2009b. Gráfica VIII.2.1. *Porcentaje de hogares que reciben remesas, 1992–2008.* Mexico City: CONAPO and CONAPO and SEGOB, http://www.diputados.gob.mx/cedia/sia/se/SE-ISS-31-09.pdf.

———. 2010. *Remesas y Población residente en Estados Unidos.* Mexico City: CONAPO and SEGOB, http://www.conapo.gob.mx; http://www.conapo.gob.mx/es/CONAPO/Remesas; http://www.conapo.gob.mx/es/CONAPO/Poblacion_residente_en_Estados_Unidos.

Cox-Edwards, Alejandra, and Eduardo Rodríguez-Oreggia. 2008. "Remittances and Labor Force Participation in Mexico: An Analysis Using Propensity Score Matching." *World Development* 37 (5): 1004–14.

Datta, Kavita, Cathy McIlwaine, Jane Wills, Yara Evans, Joanna Herbert, and Jon May. 2007. "The New Development Finance or Exploiting Migrant Labour? Remittance Sending among Low-Paid Migrant Workers in London." *International Development Planning Review* 29 (1): 43–67.

de Haas, Hein. 2005. "International Migration, Remittances and Development: Myths and Facts." *Third World Quarterly* 26 (8): 1269–84.

———. 2006. *Engaging Diasporas: How Governments and Development Agencies Can Support Diaspora Involvement in the Development of Origin Countries*. Oxford: International Migration Institute.

———. 2007a. "Turning the Tide? Why Development Will Not Stop Migration." *Development and Change* 38 (5): 819–41.

———. 2007b. "Migration and Development: A Theoretical Perspective." *International Migration Review* 44 (1): 227–64.

———. 2012. "The Migration and Development Pendulum: A Critical View on Research and Policy." *International Migration* 50 (3): 9–25.

Delgado Wise, Raúl, and Humberto Márquez Covarrubias. 2008. "The Mexico-United States Migratory System: Dilemmas of Regional Integration, Development, and Emigration." In *Migration and Development: Perspectives from the South*, edited by S. Castles and R. Delgado Wise, 113–36. Geneva: IOM.

Departamento de Extranjería y Migración (Chile). 2010. *Informe Annual*. Santiago: Ministerio del Interior y Seguridad Publica.

Dias Garay, Alejandro, and María del Carmen Juárez Gutiérrez. 2008. "Migración internacional y remesas: impacto socioeconómico en Guerrero." *Papeles de Población*, 113–33. Mexico: Red de Revistas Científicas de Améria Latina y el Caribe, España y Portugal.

DNM (Dirección Nacional de Migración) (Argentina). 2010. *Periódico Migraciones* 3 (30): 1–8 December. Buenos Aires: Dirección Nacional de Migración/Ministerio del Interior.

Eckstein, Susan. 2010. "Immigration, Remittances, and Transnational Social Capital Formation: A Cuban Case Study." *Ethnic and Racial Studies* 39 (9): 1648–67.

Ellerman, David. 2005. "Labour Migration: A Development Path or a Low-level Trap?" *Development in Practice* 15 (5): 617–30.

ERCOF (Economic Resource Center for Overseas Filipinos). 2010. *Harnessing the Development Potential of Remittances: The Italy-Philippines Migration and Remittance Corridor*. Manila: IOM.

Escobar Latapí, Agustín. 2009. "Can Migration Foster Development in Mexico? The Case of Poverty and Inequality." *International Migration* 47 (5): 75–113.

Fajnzylber, Pablo, and Humberto López. 2007. *Close to Home: The Development Impact of Remittances in Latin America*. Washington, DC: World Bank.

Femenias, Blenda. 2005. *Gender and the Boundaries of Dress in Contemporary Peru*. Austin: University of Texas Press.

Ferrero-Turrión, Ruth, and Ana López Sala. 2010. "Spain." In *Migration and the Economic Crisis: Implications for Policy in the European Union*. Geneva: IOM.

Fokkema, Tineke, Eralba Cela, and Elena Ambrosetti. 2013. "Giving from the Heart or from the Ego? Motives behind Remittances of the Second Generation in Europe." *International Migration Review* 47 (1): 1–34.

Foster, George. 1979. *Tzintzuntzan: Mexican Peasants in a Changing World*. Prospect Heights: Waveland Press.

Fox, Jonathan, and Xochitl Bada. 2008. "Migrant Organization and Hometown Impacts in Rural Mexico." *Journal of Agrarian Change* 8 (2/3): 435–561.

García Zamora, Rodolfo. 2005. *Migración, remesas y desarrollo. Los retos de las organizaciones migrantes mexicanas en Estados Unidos*. México: UAZ.
———. 2006. "El Programa 3×1 y los retos de los proyectos productivos en Zacatecas." In *El programa 3x1 para migrantes: ¿primer política transnacional en México?*, coordinated by Rafael Fernández de Castro, Rodolfo García Zamora, and Ana Vila Freyer. México, ITAM, UAZ, Miguel Ángel Porrúa.
GDF (Global Development Finance) (database), World Bank, Washington, DC, http://data.worldbank.org/data-catalog/international-debt-statistics.
Gelles, Paul. 2000. *Water and Power in Highland Peru: The Cultural Politics of Irrigation and Development*. New Brunswick: Rutgers.
———. 2005. "Transformaciones en una comunidad andina transnacional." In *El Quinto Suyo. Transnacionalidad y formaciones diaspóricas en la migración peruana*, edited by U. Berg and K. Paerregaard, 69–96. Lima: Instituto de Estudios Peruanos.
Gmelch, George. 1980. "Return Migration." *Annual Review of Anthropology* 9: 135–59.
Goldring, Luin. 2004. "Family and Collective Remittances to Mexico: A Multidimensional Typology." *Development and Change* 35 (4): 799–840.
Goldstein, Daniel. 2004. *The Spectacular City: Violence and Performance in Urban Bolivia*. Durham: Duke University Press.
Goza, Franklin, and Igor Ryabov. 2010. "Remittance Activity among Brazilians in the US and Canada." *International Migration* 50 (4): 157–85.
Granovetter, Mark. 1973. "The Strength of Weak Ties." *American Journal of Sociology* 78 (6): 1360–80.
Guarnizo, Luis. 2003. "The Economics of Transnational Living." *International Migration Review* 37 (3): 666–99.
———. 2006. "El Estado y la migración global columbiana." *Migración y desarrollo* 6: 79–101.
Hansen, Peter. 2012. "Revisiting the Remittance Mantra: A Study of Migration-Development Policy Formation in Tanzania." *International Migration* 50 (3): 77–91.
INE (Instituto Nacional de Estadística, Spain). 2009. *Avance del Padrón a 1 de enero de 2009. Datos provisionales*. Madrid: Ministerio de Trabajo e Inmigración.
INEI (Instituto Nacional de Estadística e Información). 2007. *Censo Nacional 2007, XI de población y VI de vivienda*. Lima: INEI.
INEI and IOM (International Organization for Migration). 2008. *Perú. Remesas y desarollo*. Lima: INEI.
———. 2009. *Perú. Migración Internacional en las familias peruanas y perfil del peruano retornante*. Lima: INEI.
———. 2010. *Peru. Remesas y desarrollo*. Lima: INEI.
INEI, IOM, and DIGEMIN (Dirección General de Migraciones y Naturalización). 2010. *Perú. Estadísticas de la emigración international de peruanos e inmigración de extranjeros, 1990–2009*. Lima: INEI.
INEI, IOM, and MIGRACIONES. 2013. *Perú. Estadísticas de la emigración internacional de peruanos y inmigración de extranjeros, 1990–2012*. Lima: INEI.
Istat (Italian National Institute of Statistics). 2010. "Foreigner Citizens: Resident Population by Sex and Citizenship on 31th December 2009." http://demo.istat.it/str2009/index_e.html.

Jimenez, Miguel A. C. 2009. "Household Development in Tlapanalá: A Comparative Study between Households Receiving Remittances and Households Not Receiving Remittances." *Journal of Poverty* 13 (3): 331–49.

Johnson, Kristin. 2009. *Many Happy Returns: Remittances and Their Impact: How Money Sent Home by Migrant Workers Helps the American Economy.* Washington, DC: Immigration Policy Center.

Jones, R. C. 1998. "Remittances and Inequality: A Question of Migration Stage and Geographic Scale." *Economic Geography* 74 (1): 8–25.

Julca, Alex. 2011. "Multidimensional Re-creation of Vulnerabilities and Potential for Resilience in International Migration." *International Migration* 49 (S1): e31–e49.

Kapur, Devesh. 2008. "Remittances: The New Development Mantra?" In *Remittances: Development Impact and Future Prospects*, edited by S. M. Maimbo and D. Rathap, 332–60. Washington, DC: World Bank.

Kapur, Devesh, and John McHale. 2003. "Migration's New Payoff." *Foreign Policy* 139 (Nov.–Dec.): 48–57.

Ketkar, Suhas L., and Dilip Ratha. 2010. "Diaspora Bonds: Tapping the Diaspora during Difficult Times." *Journal of International Commerce, Economics and Policy* 1 (2): 251–63.

Kopytoff, Igor. 1986. "The Cultural Biography of Things: Commoditization as Process." In *The Social Life of Things: Commodities in Cultural Perspective*, edited by A. Appadurai, 64–94. Cambridge: Cambridge University Press.

Krögel, Alison. 2010. "Quechua Sheepherders on the Mountain Plains of Wyoming: The (In)hospitality of U.S. Guest Worker Programs." *Journal of Latin American and Caribbean Anthropology* 15 (2): 261–88.

Kyle, David. 2000. *Transnational Peasants: Migration, Networks and Ethnicity in Ecuador.* Baltimore: Johns Hopkins University Press.

La República (Lima). 1996. August 16, 11.

———. 2007. March 23, 21.

Lacroix, Thomas. 2013. "Collective Remittances and Integration: North African and North Indian Comparative Perspectives." *Journal of Ethnic and Migration Studies* 39 (6): 1019–35.

Le Espiritu, Yen. 2005. "Gender, Migration and Work: Filipina Health Care Professionals to the United States." *Revue Européenne des Migrations Internationals* 21 (1): 55–75.

Leeves, Gareth. 2009. "Migration Plans and Received Remittances: Evidence from Fiji and Tonga." *International Migration Review* 43 (1): 160–77.

León, Pericles. 2001. "Peruvian Sheepherders in the Western United States." *Nevada Historical Society Quarterly* 44 (2): 147–65.

Levitt, Peggy. 2001. *The Transnational Villagers.* Berkeley: University of California Press.

Levitt, Peggy, and Deepak Lamba-Nieves. 2011. "Social Remittances Revisited." *Journal of Ethnic and Migration Studies* 37 (1): 1–22.

Lianos, Theodore, and Jennifer Cavounidis. 2008. "Immigrant Remittances, Stability of Employment and Relative Deprivation." *International Migration* 48 (5): 119–41.

Lindley, Anna. 2009. "The Early-Morning Phonecall: Remittances from a Refugee Diaspora Perspective." *Journal of Ethnic and Migration Studies* 35 (8): 1315–34.

López-Córdova, Andrea Tokman, and Eric Verhoogen. 2005. "Globalization, Migration and Development: The Role of Mexican Migrant Remittances." *Economía* 6 (1): 217–56.

Mahler, Sarah. 1995. *American Dreaming: Immigrant Life on the Margins*. Princeton, NJ: Princeton University Press.

Maimbo, Samuel Minzele, and Dilip Ratha, eds. 2005. *Remittances: Development Impact and Future Prospects*. Washington, DC: World Bank.

Maisonave Cortés, Almudena. 2011. "The Transnational Governance of Ecuadorian Migration through Co-Development." *International Migration* 49 (3): 31–51.

Mallon, Florencia. 1983. *The Defense of Community in Peru's Central Highlands: Peasant Struggle and Capitalist Transition, 1860–1940*. Princeton, NJ: Princeton University Press.

Manners, Robert. 1965. "Remittances and the Unit of Analysis in Anthropological Research." *South Western Journal of Anthropology* 21: 179–95.

Manrique, Nelson. 1987. *Mercado interno y región. La sierra central 1820–1930*. Lima: DESCO (Centro de Estudios y Promoción de Desarrollo).

Mansour, Wael, Jad Chaaban, and Julie Litchfield. 2011. "The Impact of Migrant Remittances on School Attendance and Education Attainment: Evidence from Jordan." *International Migration Review* 45 (4): 812–51.

Massey, Douglas, Joaquin Arango, Graeme Hugo, Ali Kouaouci, Adela Pellegrina, and J. Edward Taylor. 1998. *Worlds in Motion: Understanding International Migration at the End of the Millennium*. Oxford: Clarendon Press.

Mauss, Marcel. 1966. *The Gift*. London: Routledge & Kegan Paul.

Mazzucato, Valentina, Bart van den Boom, and N. N. N. Nsowah-Nuamah. 2008. "Remittances in Ghana: Origin, Destination and Issues of Measurement." *International Migration* 46 (1): 103–22.

Mazzucato, Valentina, and Mirjan Kabki. 2009. "Small Is Beautiful: The Micro-politics of Transnational Relationships between Ghanaian Hometown Associations and Communities Back Home." *Global Networks* 9 (2): 227–51.

McKenzie, Sean, and Cecilia Menjívar. 2011. "The Meanings of Migration, Remittances and Gifts: Views of Honduran Women Who Stay." *Global Networks* 11 (1): 1470–2266.

Meisch, Lynn. 2002. *Andean Entrepreneurs, Otavalo Merchants and Musicians in the Global Arena*. Austin: University of Texas Press.

Menjivar, Cecilia. 2000. *Fragmented Ties: Salvadoran Immigrant Networks in America*. Berkeley: University of California Press.

Mercer, Claire, Ben Page, and Martin Evans. 2009. "Unsettling Connections: Transnational Networks, Development and African Home Associations." *Global Networks* 9 (2): 141–61.

Merino Hernando, María Asunción. 2004. "Politics of Identity and Identity Policies in Europe: The Case of Peruvian Immigrants in Spain." *Identities: Global Studies in Culture and Power* 11: 241–64.

Miles, Ann. 2004. *From Cuenca to Queens: An Anthropological Story of Transnational Migration*. Austin: University of Texas Press.

Monopatra, Sanket, Dilip Ratha, and Ani Silwal. 2011. "Outlook for Remittance Flows 2012–2014." *Migrant and Development Brief*. Washington, DC: World Bank.

Mooney, Margarita. 2004. "Migrants' Social Capital and Investing Remittances in Mexico." In *Crossing the Border: Research from the Mexican Migration Project*, edited by J. Durand and D. S. Massey, 45–62. New York: Russell Sage Foundation.

MPI. 2014. *Migration Information Source*. Washington, DC: Migration Policy Institute. http://www.migrationinformation.org/usfocus/display.cfm?ID=935.

Mutersbaugh, Tad. 2002. "Migration, Common Property, and Communal Labor: Cultural Politics and Agency in a Mexican Village." *Political Geography* 21: 473–94.

Naik, Asmita, Jobst Koehler, and Frank Laczko. 2008. *Migration and Development: Achieving Policy Coherence*. Geneva: IOM.

Nielsen, Kristine. 2003. "Back to Trujillo: The Use of Local and Transnational Networks in Peru." Master's thesis, University of Copenhagen.

Nuijten, Monique, and David Lorenzo. 2009. "Ruling by Record: The Meaning of Rights, Rules and Registration in an Andean *Comunidad*." *Development and Change* 40 (1): 81–103.

Nuñez Carrasco, Lorena. 2008. "Living on the Margins: Illness and Healthcare among Peruvian Migrants in Chile." Ph.D. diss., Vjije Universiteit, Amsterdam.

Ochs, Elinor, and Lisa Copps. 1996. "Narrating the Self." *Annual Review of Anthropology* 25: 19–43.

OECD (Organisation for Economic Co-operation and Development). 2009. *International Migration Outlook*. Amsterdam: SOPEMI (Continuous Reporting System on Migration).

O'Neil, Kevin. 2004. *Labor Export as Government Policy: The Case of the Philippines*. Washington, DC: Migration Information Source.

Orozco, Manuel. 2002. "Globalization and Migration: The Impact of Family Remittances in Latin America." *Latin American Politics and Society* 44 (2): 41–66.

Orozco, Manuel, and Katherine Well. 2005. "Hometown Associations and Development: Ownership, Correspondence, Sustainability, and Replicability." In *New Patterns for Mexico: Observations on Remittances, Philanthropic Giving and Equitable Development*, edited by B. Merz, 157–81. Cambridge, MA: Harvard University Press.

Østergaard-Nielsen, Eva. 2011. "Codevelopment and Citizenship: The Nexus between Policies on Local Migrant Incorporation and Migrant Transnational Practices in Spain." *Ethnic and Racial Studies* 34 (1): 20–39.

Paerregaard, Karsten. 1987. *Nuevas Organizaciones en comunidades campesinas. El caso de Usibamba y Chaquicocha*. Lima: Pontificia Universidad Católica del Perú.

———. 1997. *Linking Separate Worlds: Urban Migrants and Rural Lives in Peru*. Oxford: Berg Publisher.

———. 2002a. "The Vicissitudes of Politics and the Resilience of the Peasantry: Contesting and Reconfiguring of the Political Space in the Peruvian Andes." In *In the Name of the Poor: Contesting Political Space for Poverty Reduction*, edited by L. Engberg-Pedersen and N. Webster, 52–77. London: Zed Press.

———. 2002b. "Business as Usual: Livelihood Strategies and Migration Practices in the Peruvian Diaspora." In *Life and Work in a Global World*, edited by K. F. Olwig and N. N. Soerensen, 126–44. London: Routledge.

———. 2005. "Inside the Hispanic Melting Pot: Negotiating National and Multicultural Identities among Peruvians in the United States." *Journal of Latino Studies* 3 (2): 76–96.

———. 2007. "La migración femenina. Estrategias y redes sociales entre migrantes peruanos en España y Argentina." *Antropológica* (Lima) 25: 61–82.

———. 2008a. *Peruvians Dispersed: A Global Ethnography of Migration*. Lanham, MD: Lexington Books.

———. 2008b. "In the Footsteps of the Lord of the Miracles: The Expatriation of Religious Symbols in the Peruvian Diaspora." *Journal of Ethnic and Migration Studies* 34 (7): 1073–89.

———. 2010a. "Globalizing Andean Society: Migration and Change in Peru's Peasant Communities." In *Vicos Experience: New Perspectives on Rural Development in Peru*, edited by T. Greaves and R. Bolton, 15–213. San Francisco: AltaMira Press.

———. 2010b. "The Show Must Go On: The Role of Fiestas in Andean Transnational Migration." *Latin American Perspectives* 37 (5): 50–66.

———. 2010c. "Interrogating Diaspora: Power and Conflict in Peruvian Migration." In *Diaspora and Transnationalism: Concepts, Theories and Methods*, edited by R. Bauböck and T. Faist, 54–77. Amsterdam: IMESCOE.

———. 2011a. "Transnational Crossfire: Local, National and Global Conflicts in Peruvian Migration." In *Local Battles, Global Stakes: The Globalization of Local Conflicts and the Localization of Global Interests*, edited by T. Salman and H. de Theije, 155–74. Amsterdam: VU University Press.

———. 2011b. "Bands of Brothers: Spiritual Kinship and Religious Organization in Peruvian Migration." In *Mobile Bodies, Mobile Souls: Global Families and Religious Practices*, edited by K. F. Olwig and M. Rytter, 181–99. Aarhus: Aarhus University Press.

———. 2012a. "The Wrath of Grass: US Labour Migration and Organizing Practices among Peruvian Sheepherders." In *The Byways of the Poor: Organizing Practices and Economic Control in the Developing World*, edited by K. Paerregaard and N. Webster, 227–50. Copenhagen: Museum Tusculanum Press.

———. 2012b. "Commodifying Intimacy: Women, Work, and Care in Peruvian Migration." *Journal of Latin American and Caribbean Anthropology* 17 (3): 493–511.

———. 2013. "Movements, Moments and Moods. Generation as Unity and Strife in Peruvian Migration." *Ethnic and Racial Studies* DOI:10.1080/01419870.2013.809132.

Paerregaard, Karsten, and Ulla D. Berg. 2005. Introduction to *El Quinto Suyo. Transnacionalidad y formaciones diaspóricas en la migración peruana*, edited by U. Berg and K. Paerregaard, 11–34. Lima: IEP.

Paerregaard, Karsten, Ayumi Takenaka, and Ulla D. Berg. 2010. Introduction to "Peruvian Migration." Special issue, *Latin American Perspectives* 37 (5): 1–11.

Parella, Sónia, and Sónia Cavalcanti. 2006. "Una aproximación cualitativa a las remesas de los inmigrantes peruanos y ecuatorianos en España y a su impacto en los hogares transnacionales." *REIS* (Revista Española de investigaciones Sociológicas) 116: 241–57.

Pfau, Wade Donald, and Long Thanh Giang. 2009. "Determinants and Impacts of International Remittances on Household Welfare in Vietnam." *International Social Science Journal* 60 (197–98): 431–43.

Philpott, Stuart. 1968. "Remittance Obligations, Social Networks and Choice among Montserratian Migrants in Britain." *Man* 3 (3): 465–76.

Pickert, Kate, and Feilding Cage. "The Flow of Money: Mapping World Remittances." 2006. *Time*. http://content.time.com/time/interactive/0,31813,1737566,00.html.

Portes, Alejandro. 1998. "Social Capital: Its Origin and Applications in Modern Sociology." *Annual Review of Sociology* 24: 1–24.

———. 2008. "Migration and Development: A Conceptual Review of the Evidence." In *Migration and Development: Perspectives from the South*, edited by S. Castles and R. Delgado Wise, 19–41. Geneva: IOM.

———. 2009. "Migration and Development: Reconciling Opposite Views." *Ethnic and Racial Studies* 32 (1): 5–22.

Pribilsky, Jason. 2004. "*Aprendemos a convivir*: Conjugal Relations, Co-parenting, and Family Life among Ecuadorian Transnational Migrants in New York City." *Global Networks* 4 (3): 313–34.

———. 2007. *La Chulla Vida: Gender, Migration, and the Family in Andean Ecuador and New York City*. Syracuse, NY: Syracuse University Press.

Ratha, Dilip. 2005. "Workers' Remittances: An Important and Stable Source of External Development Finance." In *Remittances: Development Impact and Future Prospects*, edited by S. M. Maimbo and D. Ratha, 19–52. Washington, DC: World Bank.

———. 2007. *Leveraging Remittances for Development*. Washington, DC: Migration Policy Institute.

Reichert, Joshua. 1981. "The Migrant Syndrome: Seasonal U.S. Wage Labor and Rural Development in Central Mexico." *Human Organization* 40 (1): 56–66.

Rhoades, Robert. 1978. "Intra-European Return Migration and Rural Development: Lessons from the Spanish Case." *Human Organization* 37 (2): 136–47.

Roberts, Bryan, and Carlos Samaniego. 1978. "The Evolution of Pastoral Villages and the Significance of Agrarian Reform in the Highlands of Central Peru." In *Peasant Cooperation and Capitalist Expansion in Central Peru*, edited by N. Long and B. Roberts, 241–64. Austin: University of Texas Press.

Rose, Susan, and Robert Shaw. 2008. "The Gamble: Circular Mexican Migration and the Return of Remittances." *Mexican Studies/Estudios Mexicanos* 24 (1): 79–111.

Rosenblum, Marc, and Kate Brick. 2011. *US Immigration Policy and Mexican/Central American Migration Flows: Then and Now*. Washington, DC: Woodrow Wilson International Center for Scholars and Migration Policy Institute.

Sana, Mariano, and Douglas. S. Massey. 2005. "Household Composition, Family Migration, and Community Context: Migrant Remittances in Four Countries." *Social Science Quarterly* 86 (2): 509–28.

Scott, James. 2009. *The Art of NOT Being Governed: An Anarchist History of Upland Southeast Asia*. New Haven, CT: Yale University Press.

Semyonov, Moshe, and Anastasia Gorodzeisky. 2005. "Labor Migration, Remittances and Household Income: A Comparison between Filipino and Filipina Overseas Workers." *International Migration Review* 39 (1): 45–68.

Service, Robert. 2009. *The Spell of the Yukon*. Riverdale Electronic Books, Inc. Nook edition.

Smith, Gavin. 1989. *Livelihood and Resistance: Peasants and Politics of Land in Peru*. Berkeley: University of California Press.

Soruco, Ximena, Giogina Piani, and Máximo Rossi. 2008. "What Emigration Leaves Behind: The Situation of Emigrants and Their Families in Ecuador." Working Paper R-542, Inter-American Development Bank and Latin American Research Network, Cuenca, Fundación Sur, Ecuador.

Soto Priante, Sergio, and Marco Antonio Velázques Holguín. 2006. "El proceso de institucionalización del Programe 3x1 para Migrantes." In *El programa 3x1 para migrantes. Primera Política Transnacional en México?* 5–6. México, DF: ITAM/UAZ/Porrúa.

Stark, Oded. 1991. *The Migration of Labour.* Cambridge: Basil Blackwell.
Stoller, Paul. 2002. *Money Has No Smell: The Africanization of New York City.* Chicago: University of Chicago Press.
Tamagno, Carla. 2003. "Entre Acá y allá. Vidas transnacionales y desarrollo. Peruanos entre Italia y Perú." Ph.D. diss., Wageningen University, the Netherlands.
Taylor, Matthew, Michelle Moran-Taylor, and Debra Rodman Ruiz. 2006. "Land, Ethnic, and Gender Change: Transnational Migration and Its Effect on Guatemalan Lives and Landscapes." *Geoforum* 37: 41–61.
Terry, Donald. 2005. "Remittances as a Development Tool." In *Beyond Small Change: Making Migrant Remittances Count*, edited by D. Terry and S. R. Wilson, 3–20. Washington, DC: Inter-American Development Bank.
Thieme, Susan, and Simone Wyss. 2005. "Migration Patterns and Remittances Transfer in Nepal: A Case Study of Sainik Basti in Western Nepal." *International Migration* 43 (5): 60–98.
Travick, Paul. 2003. *The Struggle for Water in Peru: Comedy and Tragedy in the Andean Commons.* Palo Alto, CA: Stanford University Press.
UN Data (database). United Nations, New York, http://data.un.org/.
UNDP (United Nations Development Programme). 2009. *Human Development Report 2009: Overcoming Barriers: Human Mobility and Development.* New York: UNDP.
van Hear, Nicholas. 2002. "Sustaining Societies under Stain: Remittances as a Form of Transnational Exchange in Sri Lanka and Ghana." In *New Approaches to Migration? Transnational Communities and the Transformation of Home*, edited by N. Al-Ali and K. Koser, 202–23. London: Routledge.
VanWey, Leah, Catherine Tucker, and Eileen Diaz McConnell. 2005. "Community Organization, Migration, and Remittances in Oaxaca." *Latin American Research Review* 40 (1): 83–107.
Vásquez-Alvarado, Irene Barboza-Carrasco, and J. Arturo Matus-Gardea. 2008. "Multiplying Effect of Remittances on the Mexican Economy." *Agrociencia* 4 (2): 939–47.
Vela Borda, Joel Manuel. 2006. "Impacto de las remesas de los peruanos residentes en Japón." *Cuadro Difusión* 11 (20): 133–51.
Vilcapoma, José Carlos. 1984. *Movimientos campesinos en el centro. Perú 1920–1950.* Huancayo: Nuevo Mundo.
Vogel, Ann, and Kim Korinek. 2012. "Passing by the Girls? Remittance Allocation for Educational Expenditures and Social Inequality in Nepal's Households 2003–2004." *International Migration Review* 46 (1): 61–100.
Wagle, Udaya. 2012. "Socioeconomic Implications of the Increasing Foreign Remittance to Nepal: Evidence from the Nepal Living Standard Survey." *International Migration* 50 (4): 186–207.
Waldinger, Roger, Eric Popkin, and Hector Aquiles. 2008. "Conflict and Contestation in the Cross-Border Community: Hometown Associations Reassessed." *Ethnic and Racial Studies* 31 (5): 843–70.
Wanda: Órgano cultural y informativo de la Sociedad Representativa del Distrito de Bolognesi. 1960. Año 1, No. 1. Lima, Peru.
WDI (World Development Indicators) (database). 2013. World Bank, Washington, DC, http://data.worldbank.org/data-catalog/world-development-indicators.
"Weaving the World Together." *Economist.* 2011. November 19, 72–74.
World Bank. 2011. *Migration and Remittances Factbook.* 2nd ed. Washington, DC: World Bank.

World Bank. 2013a. *Migration and Development Brief* 21. Migration and Remittances Team, Development Prospects Group, World Bank, Washington, DC.

World Bank. 2013b. *Remittances Data/Migration Data*. Washington, DC: World Bank. http://econ.worldbank.org/WBSITE/EXTERNAL/EXTDEC/EXTDECPROSPECTS/0,,contentMDK:22759429~pagePK:64165401~piPK:64165026~theSitePK:476883,00.html#Migration.

Zárate-Hoyos, German. 2004. "Consumption and Remittances in Migrant Households: Toward a Productive Use of Remittances." *Contemporary Economic Policy* 22 (4): 555–65.

———. 2008. "International Labor Migration as a Strategy of Economic Stabilization at the Household Level in Mexico and Central America." *Papeles de Población* 56: 19–36.

Zhou, Min. 2004. "Revisiting Ethnic Entrepreneurship: Convergences, Controversies, and Conceptual Advancements." *International Migration Review* 38 (3): 1040–74.

Index

Page numbers in **boldface** refer to figures and tables.

Abdih, Yaser, 16
Acosta, Pablo, 10, 18
Adams, Richard, 10
age
   accountability about use of remittances and, 204
   of case study participants, 67
   migrant organizations and, 141
   of migrant populations, **47**–48, 200, 201
   of remittance recipients, 58–**59**
agriculture
   cofinancing for, 182
   economic importance of, 116
   investments in, 123, 125, 163–64, 165, 172, 173
   land restructuring and, 117
   low status of work in, 50
   migrant work in, 166–67
Airola, Jim, 11
Åkesson, Lisa, 22
Alfonso (migrant), 189–90, 192
altruism, 3, 112–13
Ambrosetti, Elena, 12
American Popular Revolutionary Alliance (APRA), 137, 189
amnesty programs, 39, 97
Ancash region, Peru, 37, **62**, 139n20, 141
   See also Bolognesi, Peru

APRA. *See* American Popular
 Revolutionary Alliance
Arequipa, Peru, **62**, 128, 133, 134,
 146, 147, 187
Argentina
 amnesty program in, 39
 case studies of migrants to, 84–89,
  158–60
 as destination, 37, 38–40, 45, 52,
  198
 economic crisis in, 205
 gendered migration to, 45–46,
  166–3
 percentage of migrants received by,
  43–44
 remittances from, 27, **55**–56
Arroyo Alejandre, Jesús, 17
art, 183–85, 186
Asociación Cultural Deportiva de
 Peruanos, 189, 190
Aurora (migrant), 84–89

Bada, Xochitl, 24–25
Bangladesh, **7**, 53, **54**
Barcelona, Spain
 case studies of migrants to, 69–70,
  96–99, 169–70, 182–83,
  189–90
 percentage of Peruvians in, **44**
Basques, 118, 121, 121n8, 121n9
Batnitzsky, Adina, 20
Belgium, **7**
Bernardo (migrant), 105–6, 172
Binford, Leigh, 15
Boccagni, Paolo, 27
Bolognesi, Peru, 136–45
 annual fiesta of, 144–45, 149
 migrants from, 139–43, 145,
  147–48, 149, 150, 180–81
 migration history of, 115,
  137–39
 social status and, 146

Bracking, Sarah, 11
Bridge Academy, 187
Bridgeport, Connecticut, United
 States, 187–88
Buenos Aires, Argentina, **44**, 85,
 158–60
business management, 181, 185–86
business networks, transnational,
 176–77

Cabanaconde, Peru, 127–36
 annual fiesta of, 130, 133–35, 136,
  144–45, 149, 150
 effects of migration on, 149–50
 land conflicts in, 145–46
 migrants from, 129–33, 147–48,
  149, 166–67
 migration history of, 115, 128–29
 newcomers to, 135–36
Cabanaconde City Association (CCA),
 129–31, 147, 148, 150
Callao province, Peru, 52–**53**, 61–**62**,
 201
Canada, **44**–45
Canales, Alejandro, 17
Caracas, Venezuela, **44**
Carling, Jørgen, 21–22, 26n7
Carmen Irma (migrant), 75–79
Castles, Stephen, 14, 16
cattle, investment of savings in, 123,
 124, 163, 164, 172, 173, 207
Cavaco, Carminda, 9
Cavalcanti, Leonardo, 22
Cavounidis, Jennifer, 3n2
CCA. *See* Cabanaconde City
 Association
Cecilia (migrant), 69–71
Cela, Eralba, 12
Cerro de Pasco mining corporation,
 116, 118
Chaaban, Jad, 12
Chami, Ralph, 16

Chaquicocha, Peru
  effects of migration on, 147–49
  history of, 115–19
  land conflicts in, 145–46
  land reform in, 117
  migration restrictions in, 123–27, 149
charisma, 186–93, 194
Chavica (migrant), 182–83, 185, 186
Chicago, Illinois, United States, 37, 70–71
Chile
  amnesty program in, 39
  case studies of migrants to, 75–79, 83–89, 160–61, 174–75, 179
  as destination, 38–40, 84, 198
  family reunification in, 86–88
  female migration to, 166n3
  percentage of migrants received by, **43–44**
  remittances from, 27, **55**–56
  remittances sent to, 94
Chimbote, Peru, 75–76, 138, 139, 146, 160
China, 6, **7**, 53, **54**
churches, 31, 33, 113, 115, 129n18, 131, 137, 142–43, 145, 204
class
  migrants' occupations and, 49–51
  migration waves and, 37, 39
  of Peruvian migrants, 63, 198–99, 202
  remittance men and, 5–6
  remittances and, 18, 22, 27–28
  See also middle-class migrants; working-class migrants
Claudia (remittance recipient), 91, 93–94, 95
Club Cultural de Bolognesi, 138
Club Social Bolognesi (CSB), 141–43, 148, 150
coastal region of Peru
  migrants from, 68, 72, 75–76, 84–85
  migration originating from, **51**–52
  remittances received by, **60**–61, 62–63
codevelopment programs, 182–83, 197–98
Cohen, Jeffrey, 19–20
collective remittances
  vs. individual remittances, 66, 107, 111–12
  matching of by governments, 24–26, 197–98
  uses of, 31, 33, 204, 206–7
  See also voluntad (community commitment)
Colombia, 7, 54, 63–64
communal companies, 117
communitarian approach, 13
community commitments.
  See voluntad (community commitment)
compromiso (family commitment), 4, 65–109
  defined, 30, 65–66
  discussion of case studies of, 32, 66–68, 107–9
  endings of, 96–106, 107
  as force behind remittances, 20
  by multiple family members, 83–95, 107
  reasons for, 65–66
  second *compromiso* (extramarital partnership), 66, 88n14
  by solo migrants, 68–83, 107
computer center, construction of, 33, 113, 142–43
comuneros (members of peasant communities), 117–18, 123–25, 163–64
comunidad campesinas (peasant communities), 117

conflicts
　about land, 116–18, 145–46
　about remittances, 21, 72–75, 98–99, 203
　between migrant and local Cabaneños, 134–35
　between migrants and locals in Spain, 190
Connecticut, United States
　Bolognesinos in, 139–43, 145, 148, 149, 150
　case studies of migrants to, 139–40, 180–81, 187–88
　percentage of Peruvians in, **44**
contract labor
　absence fees and, 124
　case studies of shepherds, 105–6, 163–64, 165–66, 168, 190–91
　from highlands districts, 115
　networks for, 121–22, 124, 126, 148–49
　by shepherds, 118–23
convivientes (unmarried partners), 48, 66, 198
cooperatives, 116–18, 119n4
Córdoba, Argentina, **44**
Cornellá, Spain, 189–90
Corpacancha, Peru, 105
Corvera Valenzuela, Isabel, 17
Cox-Edwards, Alejandra, 18
creativity, 185–86, 194
CSB. *See* Club Social Bolognesi
Cubans, 23
cultural capital, 27, 156, 179, 194

de Haas, Hein, 11, 16, 19, 196n1
dentistry, 177–79
development
　in Bolognesi, 137–38
　codevelopment policy, 182–83, 197–98
　communal land system and, 125–26
　investments' contribution to, 162–63
　migrants as agents of, 146–47, 150–52
　remittances as problem for, 14–16
　remittances as resource for, 13–14, 22–23, 63
development organizations, 2, 13–14, 151
development policies, remittance-driven, 33–34, 196–98, 206, 207
devotos (sponsors of village fiesta), 133–35, 144, 145, 149
Dias Garay, Alejandro, 17
DIGEMEN. *See* Dirección General de Migraciones y Naturalización
Dirección General de Migraciones y Naturalización (DIGEMIN), 35
　data from, **41**, **45**, **46**, **47**, **48**, **49**, **53**
divorce, 71–75
domestic work
　in Argentina, 38–39, 45–46, 85, 159, 205
　in Chile, 38–39, 46, 77–78, 86, 88, 160–61
　in Italy, 38, 45
　in Philippines, 7
　post–World War II migration for, 37
　self-employment and, 174
　in Spain, 38, 45, 97
　in United States, 100, 103, 138–39
Dominican Republic, 22, 54
donations
　as symbolic, 151–52
　types of, 33
　uses of by migrant organizations, 141–42, 206
　voluntad as, 30–31, 112–13, 115
DREAM Act (2001), 188, 192
Dyer, Sarah, 20

earthquake relief, 141
Eckstein, Susan, 23
economic capital, 155–56, 179, 194
Ecuador, 7, 18, 21, 22, 27, 43, 54
education
   attendance of, 12
   of case study participants, 67
   for immigrants, 187–88, 192
   migrants' occupations and, 49, 50
   remittances' effect on, 18
   remittances used for, **62**–63, 74, 92, 205
Egypt, **7**, 53, **54**, 63
Elena (migrant), 90–95
Ellerman, David, 15
Emilio (migrant), 100–102
employee compensation, 16–17
entrepreneurship, 104, 153, 154–56, 174–80, 181, 194
environment, the, 182–83
Escobar Latapí, Agustín, 17
Eugenio (migrant), 165–66, 172, 173
Evans, Martin, 23
Ever (migrant), 170–72, 173
extramarital affairs, 66, 88n14

factory work
   in Japan, 38, 69, 81, 94, 109, 176
   in Spain, 97
   in United States, 103, 139
family commitment. See *compromiso* (family commitment)
family relations
   divorce and, 71–75
   during long absences, 81–82
   remittance flows and, 83–95
   remittances and, 28
family reunification
   age distributions and, 47–48
   citizenship and, 74
   high cost of, 87–88
   locations of, 71
   as part of *compromiso*, 99
   remittances and, 75, 205
   in Spain, 97–99
   in United States, 100–101, 104, 139–40, 149, 171
family roles, 19–22
fees, 124–26, 149, 207
Felipe (migrant), 187–88, 192
fiestas, religious, 130, 132, 133–36, 138, 144–45, 149, 150, 151–52, 204
Fiji, 11
fishing industry, 50, 75–76, 160
Fokkema, Tineke, 12
folk art, 183–85, 186
Fox, Jonathan, 24–25
France
   codevelopment programs in, 197
   hometown associations in, 26
   percentage of Peruvian migrants in, 43
   remittances received by, 6, **7**, 17
Fujimori government (1990–2001), 37, 41

García government (1985–1990), 37, 159, 177
Gastón (migrant), 80–83
GDP. *See* gross domestic product
Gelles, Paul, 127, 133–34
GEN. *See* Global Entrepreneurship Network
gender
   accountability about use of remittances and, 95, 107–8, 204
   of case study participants, 67, 155
   economic dependence and, 74–75
   labor migration and, 21, 38–39
   of migrant populations, 166n3, 198, 200, 201

gender *(continued)*
　of remittance recipients, **58**, 63, 108, 199
　remittances and, 20–21, 28, 83
　waves of migration and, 45–**47**
Germany, 6, **7**, 17, 43, 80
Ghana, 18, 26
Giang, Long Thanh, 12
gifts, 3–4, 28, 112–13, 206
Global Entrepreneurship Network (GEN), 181
globalization, 114, 146–47
Goldring, Luin, 17, 25–26
Goya (migrant), 91, 92–93
Goza, Franklin, 20
Granovetter, Mark, 179
green cards, 139, 171
gross domestic product (GDP), 7, 10, 41, 54, **55**, 199, **201**
Guarnizo, Luis, 19
Guatemala, 18, 54
Guyana, **55**

H-2A visas, 119, 119n2, 119n6, 120, 191
haciendas, 116–17, 126, 145
Haiti, 7, 18, **55**
Hansen, Peter, 23
Hartford, Connecticut, United States
　Bolognesinos in, 139–43, 145, 148, 149, 150
　case studies of migrants to, 139–40, 180–81
　percentage of Peruvians in, **44**–45
highlands region of Peru
　case studies of migrants from, 105–6, 163–67, 168–70, 180–81, 183–85, 190–92
　changes in, 114–15
　economy of, 116–17
　labor migration from, 118–23
　land reform in, 116–18

　migration originating from, 36, **51**
　remittances received by, **60**–61
　rural-urban migration from, 28, 36, 115, 128, 146, 148
　See also Bolognesi, Peru; Cabanaconde, Peru
Hilmer (migrant), 180–81, 185–86
hometown associations (HTAs). *See* migrant organizations
household planning, 20–21
household spending, **62**–63
housing
　remittances used for, **62**–63, 86, 205–6
　savings used for, 123, 153, 164
Huancayo, Peru
　case studies of migrants from, 168–69, 169–70, 173
　investment in, 164, 165
　rural-urban migration to, 146
　transport to, 106, 123
human capital, 156, 194
Human Development Report 2009 (United Nations), 21
humanitarian commitments, 4

IMF. *See* International Monetary Fund
immigration policies, 38, 119n2, 131–32, 171, 199
Immigration Reform and Control Act (1986), 37–38
income groups
　of case study participants, 67, 83–84
　of migrants, **50**–51
　of remittance recipients, 59–**60**, 63, 199
India, 3, 6, **7**, 26, 53, **54**, 93n16
individual commitments. See *superación* (personal commitment)

individual remittances, 66, 107, 111–12
INEI. *See* Instituto Nacional de Estadistica e Información
inequalities
　in access to migration networks, 124, 126, 135, 136, 139, 147, 148–49
　in highland villages, 117–18, 124, 150
　migration's effect on, 150
　remittances increasing, 14, 17, 56–61, 63, 206–7
　remittances reducing, 11–12, 18
innovation, 154, 180–86
Instituto Nacional de Estadistica e Información (INEI), 31, 35–36
　data from, **41**, **42**, **43**, **44**, **45**, **46**, **47**, **48**, **49**, **50**, **51**, **52**, **53**, **55**, **57**, **58**, **59**, **60**, **61**, **62**
Inter-American Development Bank, 2, 13, 196n1, 198
international migration, 28, 36, 52n4, 115, 148–49
International Monetary Fund (IMF), 2
International Organization for Migration (IOM), 2, 13, 35, 198
　data from, **41**, **42**, **43**, **44**, **45**, **46**, **47**, **48**, **49**, **50**, **51**, **52**, **53**, **55**, **57**, **58**, **59**, **60**, **61**, **62**
internet cafes, 171–72
investments, 162–74
　contribution to development, 162–63
　discussion of case studies of, 172–74
　in rural areas, 123, 124–26, 163–67, 207
　savings used for, 153, 154, 194
　in urban areas, 167–72
　use of economic capital in, 155–56
　uses of, 207
IOM. *See* International Organization for Migration
Iquique, Chile, **44**–45
Italy
　as destination, 40, 198
　immigrant population in, 39n2
　immigration laws in, 38
　percentage of migrants received by, **43**–**44**
　remittances from, 27–28, **55**–56

Japan
　case studies of migrants to, 69, 80–83, 91, 175–77, 179
　as destination, 40, 71, 198
　immigration laws in, 38, 70
　percentage of migrants received by, **43**
　Peruvians' dispersal in, 45
　remittances from, 27, **55**–56
Jimenez, Miguel, 11
Jones, R. C., 17
Jordan, 12
Juan (migrant), 84–89
Juan José (migrant), 91, 94
Juan Pablo (migrant), 166–67, 172, 173
Juárez Gutiérrez, María, 17
Julca, Alex, 23
Julia (migrant), 160–61, 161–62
Julio (migrant), 71–75
jungle region of Peru, **51**, **60**–61
Junín region, Peru, 37, **62**–63, 119n4

Kabki, Mirjan, 26
Kapur, Devesh, 13, 24
Koehler, Jobst, 21
Korinek, Kim, 21, 93n16

Kosovo, **55**
Kyrgyz Republic, 7, 54, **55**

labor, loss of, 7
labor migration, 20
  effects of on development, 12–16
  fees on, 124–26
  gender and, 21, 38–39
  from highlands districts, 115–16, 118–23
  labor rights and, 190–91
  in Mexican communities, 124n16
  in Philippines, 197
  rural investments and, 162–67
  urban investments and, 167–74
labor rights, 191–92, 193
Lacroix, Thomas, 26
Laczko, Frank, 21
land reform, 116–19, 123–26, 145–46, 164
La Plata, Argentina, **44**
Latin America
  development in, 13, 18
  gender bias in, 20
  immigration and, 38–39
  remittances in, 18–19, 22
  See also specific countries
Lazio, Italy, **44**
Lebanon, 53, **54**
Leeves, Gareth, 11
legal migration
  amnesty programs and, 39
  case studies involving, 70, 79, 87, 89, 91, 97, 106, 115, 139, 147–48, 171
  voluntad and, 33
legislators, 188
Lesotho, 7, 54, **55**
Levitt, Peggy, 28
Lianos, Theodore, 3n2
Liberia, **55**
Lily (migrant), 88

Lima, Peru
  case studies of migrants from, 72–74, 90–95, 100–102, 102–5, 157–59
  as epicenter of migration, 52–**53**
  migrant organizations in, 137–38, 143, 145, 147
  remittances received by, **60**–61, 61–**62**, **201**, 202
  retirement in, 158, 159–60
  rural-urban migration to, 128–29, 138, 146, 157
  transnational business network in, 176–77
Litchfield, Julie, 12
Livio (migrant), 157–58, 161–62
loans
  entrepreneurship and, 181
  migration decisions and, 77
  remittances requested for, 96, 98, 205
  for travel expenses, 85, 87, 89
Los Angeles, California, United States
  case studies of migrants in, 102–5, 178–79
  percentage of Peruvians in, **44**
Luzvila (migrant), 140

McDowell, Linda, 20
McHale, John, 13
McKenzie, Sean, 21
macroeconomic models, 10
Madrid, Spain, **44**
Magda (remittance recipient), 80–83
Maimbo, Samuel Minzele, 14
Majes canal project, 127, 146
Manners, Robert, 9
Mansour, Wael, 12
manufacturing. *See* factory work
Marco (migrant), 175–77, 179–80

Mario (migrant), 139–40, 180–81
marital status, **48**, 53, 66, 198
Maritza (migrant), 158–60, 161–62
Maryland, United States, **44**
Massey, Douglas, 12, 13n4, 15, 22
Mauss, Marcel, 3–4
Mazzucato, Valentina, 18, 26
Melvin (migrant), 169–70, 173
Memo (remittance recipient), 91, 92–93, 94
men
  patterns of migration of, 45–**47**
  as providers, 75, 83
  See also gender
Mendoza, Peru, 182–83, 186
Menjívar, Cecilia, 21
"Men That Don't Fit In, The" (Service), 6
Mercer, Claire, 23
Mexico
  absence fees in, 124n16
  compared with Peru, 199–202
  development in, 11, 207
  fiesta sponsorship in, 134–35n19
  remittances in, 6, **7**, 17–18, 22, 53, **54**, 199, 200–202
  3x1 program in, 24–26, 197
Mexico City, Mexico, **201**, 202
Miami, Florida, United States, 37, **44**, 45, 139, 157–58, 161, 171, 178, 184
middle-class migrants
  case studies of, 67, 72, 80–83, 90–95, 169–72
  early waves of, 37
  labor migration by, 167–68
  numbers of, 49–50, 63
  remittances and, 8, 109
  social mobility of, 42
MIGRACIONES. *See* Superintendencia nacional Perú

migrant organizations
  Bolognesino, 137–38, 141–43, 148, 150
  Cabaneño, 129–31, 147, 148, 150
  Mexican, 24–26, 197, 200
  Peruvian, 27
  projects undertaken by, 151–52, 204
  in Spain, 182, 189, 190
migrants
  adult children of, 101–2
  images of, 193, 195–96
  role of in world economy, 2
  talents of, 4, 193–94, 207–8
migrants' transfers, 16–17
migration
  as exit strategy, 24
  value of, 193–94
  waves of, 37–39, 45–47
migration-remittance balances, 56, 57, 59, 61, 199
migration studies, 9–10
Milan, Italy, **44**
military government of Peru (1968–1980), 116
mining industry, 116, 118, 126
Ministry of Education, Peruvian, 142
Modesta (migrant), 139–40, 180–81
Moldova, 7, 54, **55**
Montreal, Quebec, Canada, **44**–45
Mooney, Margarita, 11
Moran-Taylor, Michelle, 18
Morocco, 8, 11, 12, 13, 63
multiple remittances, 92–94

Naik, Asmita, 21
National Council of La Raza, 188
Nena (migrant), 91, 93
Nepal, 7, 11–12, 21, 54, **55**, 93n16
networks
  Cabaneño, 129–33
  emptying out sending areas, 13, 15–16

networks *(continued)*
　entrepreneurship and, 156, 174, 176–77, 179–80
　fiestas and, 134–35, 136, 144–45, 149
　importance of, 12–13
　inequalities in access to, 124, 126, 135, 136, 139, 147, 148–49
　Mexican, 200
　for shepherding contracts in US, 121–22, 124, 126, 148–49
new economics of labor migration, 12, 13n4, 15–16
New Jersey, United States, 28, 37, **44**, 45, 139
New York, New York, United States, 37, **44**, 45, 139
NGOs. *See* nongovernmental organizations
Nicario (migrant), 183–85, 186
Nigeria, **7**, 53, **54**
Nilo (migrant), 80–83
nongovernmental organizations (NGOs), 22–23, 113, 148, 182–83, 186
Nsowah-Nuamah, N. N. N., 18

OECD. *See* Organisation for Economic Co-operation and Development
occupations, distribution of, 48–50
Organisation for Economic Co-operation and Development (OECD), 2, 12, 198
Orozco, Manuel, 24
Oscar (migrant), 177–79

Page, Ben, 23
Page, John, 10
Pakistan, 53, **54**, 63
Parella, Sónia, 22
Patria Grande amnesty program, 39
peasant communities, 116–17, 117–18, 123–25, 127
Peru
　economy of, 41
　government of, 145–46, 150–51
　HTAs and, 27
　population of, 200
　regional imbalance in, 109
　remittance economy in, 7–8
　remittances received by, 53–**54**, **55**
　See also specific cities or regions
Perú de los 90 (newspaper), 191
Peruvian migration
　compared with Mexican migration, 198–202
　data on, 35–36
　diversity of, 45–51, 53, 198
　growth/dispersal of, 40–45, 52–53, 198
　history of, 36–40
　origins of, 51–52, 53
Pfau, Wade, 12
Philippines
　gender biases in, 20, 63
　new development paradigm in, 13
　remittance policy in, 197, 207
　remittances received by, 6, **7**, 53, **54**
Philpott, Stuart, 9
Piani, Giogina, 18
political empowerment, 24–26
politics, engagement with, 154, 181, 188, 189–90, 194
Portes, Alejandro, 13, 15–16
poverty, 10–12, 17, 18, 108–9
　See also middle-class migrants; working-class migrants
President's Service Award, 188
Pribilsky, Jason, 21
priostes (sponsors of village fiesta), 144–45, 149
professional skills, 180–86, 194
professions, distribution of, 48–50

PSOE. *See* Spanish Socialist Workers' Party

Ratha, Dilip, 3, 14
reestructuración de tierras (restructuring of land), 117, 123–25
Reichert, Joshua, 14–15
religious organizations. *See* churches; fiestas, religious
Remigio (migrant), 163–64, 172, 173
remittance flows
   circulation of, 92–93, 108, 203
   family involvement in, 83–95
   management of, 21, 93–94, 108, 204
remittance men, 6, 195, 196, 206
remittance policies, 24–26, 196–98, 202, 207
remittance recipients
   age of, 58–**59**
   case studies of, 80–83, 91–95
   gender of, **58**, 63, 108, 199
   by income group, 59–**60**
   migrants as, 92–93, 203, 206
remittances
   accountability around use of, 93–95, 107–8, 203, 204
   analytical approaches to, 27–30
   areas of Peru receiving, **60**–**62**, **201**, 206–7
   countries receiving, 6–7, 17, 53–**54**, **55**
   defined, 5
   distribution of, 56–62, **201**
   ending of, 96–106, 203, 205
   as gifts, 3–4, 28, 206
   individual *vs*. collective, 66, 107, 111–12
   inequality of, 53–56, 198–99
   multiple, 92–94
   reasons for, 2–3

   sacrifices made for, 108
   as source of conflict, 21, 72–75, 98–99, 203
   statistics on, 16–17, 35–36, 200–**201**
   uses of, 11, 17–18, **62**–63, 68, 199, 203, 205–6
   value of, 9–19, 22–27, 204
   See also collective remittances
restaurant business, 169–70, 174–75
retablos (traditional art), 183–85, 186
retirement
   ending of remittances and, 101–2
   return migration and, 128, 140, 161–62
   savings for, 153, 154, 155, 157–62, 194
return migration
   among shepherds, 122, 123–25
   economy and, 205
   low rate of, 42
   retirement and, 128, 140, 161–62
   studies of, 9
   use of savings and, 148, 149, 164
   See also contract labor
reunification. *See* family reunification
reverse remittances, 93–94
Rhoades, Robert, 9
"Rhyme of the Remittance Man, The" (Service), ix, 6
Richard (migrant), 86–89
Rocío (migrant), 86, 87–88
Rodríguez-Oreggia, Eduardo, 18
Rómulo (migrant), 102–5
rondas campesinas (peasant militias), 118
Rose, Susan, 19
Rossi, Máximo, 18
Ruiz, Debra, 18
rural areas of Peru
   changes in, 114–15
   economy of, 116–17

rural areas of Peru *(continued)*
  fieldwork in, 113–14
  investments in, 163–67
  land reform in, 116–19, 123–26, 145–46
  migration originating from, 51–52
  remittances received by, **61**, **201**, 206–7
  See also highlands region of Peru; rural-urban migration
rural-urban migration, 102
  from highlands, 28, 36, 115, 128, 146, 148
  investment and, 173
  as origin of international migrants, 36, 52n4
  reestructuración de tierras and, 123–24
Ryabov, Igor, 20

Sachikonye, Lloyd, 11
SAIS. *See* Sociedad agrícola de interés social
Samoa, 7, **55**
Sana, Mariano, 13n4, 22
San Antonio de Padua fiesta, 144–45, 149
San Francisco, California, United States, **44**
Santiago, Chile
  case studies of migrants in, 77–79, 85–89, 160–61, 174–75
  percentage of Peruvians in, **44**
Sara (migrant), 88
savings
  percentage of remittances used for, **62**–63
  for retirement, 153, 154, 155, 157–62, 194
  from shepherding contracts, 106, 123, 124
  superación and, 154, 155, 156–62

uses of, 148–49, 150, 156–57, 164
Scott, James, 24
See the Government in Action program, 187
Segundo (migrant), 174–75, 179
segundo compromiso (extramarital partnerships among migrants), 66, 88n14
Service, Robert W., 6, 195, ix–x
Shaw, Robert, 19
sheep-ranching industry, 118–23
  contract work for, 105–6, 168, 190–91
  difficulty of work in, 120–21
  in highlands region, 116
  labor rights and, 191, 193
  recruitment of migrants by, 118–19, 121–22, 125, 148–49
shepherds, 118–23
  case studies of, 105–6, 163–64, 165–66, 168, 190–91
  labor rights and, 191, 193
  recruitment of, 118–19, 121–22
  treatment of, 120–21
Shining Path, 118
Silvia (migrant), 178
soccer, 129–30, 141, 189–90
social capital, 27, 156, 179, 194
social justice, 153, 186–93
social mobility, 40, 42
  See also superación (personal commitment)
social status, 146, 149, 151–52, 153, 204
Sociedad agrícola de interés social (SAIS), 116–17, 119n4
Sociedad Representativa del Pueblo de Bolognesi, 137–38
Solidaridad con la Amazonía, 182–83
solo migrants
  Carmen Irma, 75–79

Cecilia, 69–71
compromiso and, 32, 68–83
Julio, 71–75
Nilo, 80–83
Soruco, Ximena, 18
Soto Priante, Sergio, 25
Spain
  amnesty program in, 39
  case studies of migrants to, 69–70, 96–99, 166–67, 169–70, 182–83, 189–90
  codevelopment program in, 182, 198
  as destination, 37, 40, 71, 198
  immigration laws in, 38
  percentage of migrants received by, **43–44**
  remittances from, 27–28, **55**–56
Spanish Socialist Workers' Party (PSOE), 189
sponsorship of fiestas, 133–35, 144–45, 149
step migration, 36, 138–39
stockbreeding, 116, 125
  See also sheep-ranching industry
Stoller, Paul, 203
Student Adjustment Act (2001), 188
superación (personal commitment), 153–94
  creativity/innovation and, 185–86
  defined, 31, 153–54
  discussion of case studies of, 33, 155, 193–94
  entrepreneurship as, 174–80
  importance of, 22
  innovation and, 180–86
  investment as, 162–74
  retirement savings as, 156–62
  social justice and, 186–93
Superintendencia nacional Perú (MIGRACIONES), 35
  data from, **41**, **42**, **43**, **44**

Tajikistan, 7, 54, **55**
Taylor, Matthew, 18
Telmo (migrant), 96–99
temporary stay permits, 72, 77, 171
Teógenes (migrant), 168–69, 172, 173
Terry, Donald, 1, 14, 23
Thieme, Susan, 11
3x1 program, 24–26, 197
thrift, 155, 161–62, 174, 185, 194
Toledo, Alejandro, 138, 139n20
Tonga, 11
tourist industry, 128, 135
tourist visas, 40, 169
  overstaying, 39, 69, 70, 81, 91, 97, 157, 177–78, 189
tractors, investments in, 123, 124, 125, 165, 166, 167, 172, 173
transportation business, 76–77, 106, 123, 125, 157, 172
travel expenses, 85, 87, 89, 92, 123
Trujillo, Peru
  case studies of migrants from, 69–71, 80–83, 84–89, 97–99, 170–72
Turin, Italy, **44**
Turkey, 12

unauthorized immigrants, case studies of, 69, 70, 77, 80, 81, 85, 91, 106, 157, 158, 178, 191
undocumented immigrants
  amnesties granted to, 38, 39
  from Cabanaconde, 115, 131–32, 147–48
  case studies of, 97, 161
  in Hartford area, 139
  legislation and, 37, 188, 192
  shepherds as, 119n6, 125
Unión de Pastores Ovejeros, 191
United Nations Development Programme, 21

United States
  case studies of migrants to, 69–70, 71–75, 84, 90–95, 100–102, 102–5, 105–6, 139–40, 157–58, 165–66, 170–72, 179, 180–81, 183–85, 187–88, 190–92
  as destination, 40, 71, 198
  economy of, 12, 205
  history of migration to, 37, 115, 138–40, 199–200
  immigration control by, 37–38, 119n2, 131–32, 171, 199
  percentage of migrants received by, **43–44**
  Peruvians' dispersal in, 45
  remittances from, 27–28, **55**–56
  sheep-ranching industry in, 118–23
  See also specific cities or states
urban areas of Peru
  investments in, 167–72
  migration from, 51–52, 198, 202
  remittances received by, **61**, **201**
  See also rural-urban migration
Usibamba, Peru
  case studies of migrants from, 163–64
  effects of migration on, 148–49
  experiences of migrants from, 147, 148
  history of, 115–19
  labor migration from, 121–22
  land conflicts in, 145–46
  land reform in, 117
  migration restrictions in, 123–26, 149

van den Boom, Bart, 18
Vanesa (migrant), 96–99
van Hear, Nicholas, 20
Velázques Holguín, Marco, 25

Venezuela, **43**, **44**
Victor (migrant), 190–92, 192–93
videotape rentals, 176–77
Vietnam, 12, **54**
Virginia, United States, **44**
Virgin of Carmen fiesta, 130, 133–36, 144–45, 149, 150
Vogel, Ann, 21, 93n16
voluntad (community commitment), 4, 111–52
  in Bolognesi, 136–45
  in Cabanaconde, 127–36
  defined, 30–31, 111–13
  discussion of case studies of, 33, 113–14, 146–52
  as donation, 113, 115
  as fee, 113, 115, 124–26
  globalization and, 146–47
  rural communities and, 113–15
  as sponsorship, 113, 115, 133–35
  in Usibamba/Chaquicocha, 115–26
volunteerism, 187–88

Wagle, Udava, 11–12
Washington, D.C., United States
  Cabaneño community in, 129–34, 147, 149
  case studies of migrants to, 100–102
  percentage of Peruvians in, **44**
water rights, 127
Well, Katherine, 24
Western Range Association (WRA), 105, 106, 119, 121, 123
Wise, Raúl, 14, 16
women
  as caregivers, 89
  as remittance recipients, 58, 108, 199, 201
  role of in migration, 109
  sacrifices by, 71

waves of migration and, 38–39, 45–**47**
  See also gender
workers' remittances, 16–17
working-class migrants
  case studies of, 67, 84–89
  early waves of, 37
  numbers of, 50
  remittances and, 8
  social mobility of, 42

World Bank, 1n1, 2, 3, 13, 196n1, 198
  data from, **7**, **54**, **55**, **200**, **201**
WRA. *See* Western Range Association
Wyss, Simone, 11

Yugoslavia, 12

Zárate-Hoyos, German, 11, 17
Zimbabwe, 11